BILINGUALISM, EDUCATION AND IDENTITY

Jac L. Williams (1918–1977)

BILINGUALISM, EDUCATION AND IDENTITY

Essays in honour of
JAC L. WILLIAMS

Edited by

BOB MORRIS JONES

and

PAUL A. SINGH GHUMAN

CARDIFF
UNIVERSITY OF WALES PRESS
1995

© The contributors, 1995

All rights reserved. No part of this book may be reproduced stored in a retrieval system, or transmitted, in any form or by any means, electronic, mechanical, photocopying, recording or otherwise, without clearance from the University of Wales Press, 6 Gwennyth Street, Cardiff, CF2 4YD.

A catalogue record for this book is available from the British Library.

ISBN 0-7083-1288-8

Typeset by Action Typesetting Limited, Gloucester.
Printed in Wales by Dinefwr Press, Llandybïe.

CONTENTS

List of figures, graphs and tables   vii

List of contributors   xi

Foreword   xiii

Introduction
  Bob Morris Jones and Paul A. Singh Ghuman   1

I   JAC L. WILLIAMS: MAN AND SCHOLAR
1   Jac L. Williams – Ysgogwr Addysg Gymraeg:
    Portread Personol   13
    Jac L. Williams – The Catalyst of Welsh Education:
    A Personal Portrait
    D. Gareth Edwards   24

2   Jac L. Williams and Bilingualism
    J. E. Caerwyn Williams   26

II   BILINGUALISM IN WALES
3   Questions Concerning the Development of Bilingual
    Wales
    Colin H. Williams   47

4   Schools and Speech Communities in a Bilingual Setting
    Bob Morris Jones   79

5   The Effects of Second-language Education on
    First/Second-language Development
    C. J. Dodson   108

6   Bilingual Education and Assessment
    Colin Baker   130

7	Psychology and Bilingual Education: Intelligence Tests and the Influence of Pedagogy WYNFORD BELLIN	159
III	BILINGUALISM IN OTHER COUNTRIES	
8	Aspects of Bilingual Education in Australia J. A. W. CALDWELL and M. J. BERTHOLD	189
9	Acculturation, Ethnic Identity and Community Languages: A Study of Indo-Canadian Adolescents PAUL A. SINGH GHUMAN	213
10	Aspects of Bilingual Education in Nigeria ADEBISI AFOLAYAN	237
	Jac L. Williams: A Selected Bibliography ELGAN DAVIES	253
	Index	261

FIGURES, GRAPHS AND TABLES

Chapter 3 Questions Concerning the Development of Bilingual Wales

Table 1	Proportion of population speaking Welsh, by county, 1921–1981	52
Table 2	Welsh-speakers, 3–15 years	53
Table 3	County-level variations in Welsh fluency and Welsh born	54
Table 4	Welsh language capacities, 1991	55
Table 5	Welsh by age, 1992	57
Table 6a	Percentages of Welsh-speakers by county, 1992	58
Table 6b	Frequencies of Welsh-speakers by county, 1992	59
Table 7	Welsh-speakers' current use of Welsh, 1992	61

Chapter 4 Schools and Speech Communities in a Bilingual Setting

Table 1	Numbers of pupils in Welsh-medium education in maintained schools 1991–92	80
Graph 1	The use of Welsh in the immediate family	84
Graph 2	The use of Welsh in the immediate family (conflated into groups)	85
Graph 3	Welsh- and English-speakers' use of Welsh with grandparents	86
Graph 4	Welsh- and English-speakers' language choices with school friends	87
Graph 5	Welsh- and English-speakers' language choices with friends at home	88
Graph 6	Welsh- and English-speakers' language choices with neighbours	89
Graph 7	Welsh- and English-speakers' use of Welsh in shops	89

Graph 8	Welsh- and English-speakers' use of Welsh in community domains outside the family	90
Graph 9	Welsh- and English-speakers' use of Welsh in all community domains except the family	91
Graph 10	Welsh- and English-speakers' use of Welsh in reading books and magazines	91
Graph 11	Welsh- and English-speakers' use of Welsh watching TV programmes	92
Graph 12	The use of Welsh on the curriculum	93
Graph 13	Welsh- and English-speakers' use of Welsh on the curriculum	94
Figure 1	The organization of teacher-centred classroom discourse	101
Figure 2	The teacher's control over initiation in teacher-centred classroom discourse	101
Figure 3	The teacher's overall control over the direction and content of classroom discourse	102

Chapter 6 Bilingual Education and Assessment

Table 1	Teacher assessment, and standardized test and task assessment	139
Graph 1	Oral attainment in Welsh at Key Stage 3 by first- and second-language Welsh children	143
Graph 2	Reading attainment in Welsh at Key Stage 3 by first- and second-language Welsh children	144
Graph 3	Writing attainment in Welsh at Key Stage 3 by first- and second-language Welsh children	145
Graph 4	Overall subject attainment in Welsh at Key Stage 3 by first- and second-language Welsh children	146
Table 2	Home language Welsh (as a first-language) attainment	147
Graph 5	Key Stage 1 Mathematics: attainment of fluent and non-fluent Welsh children	149
Graph 6	Key Stage 1 Science: attainment of fluent and non-fluent Welsh children	150
Graph 7	Key Stage 1 Mathematics: the attainment of children in Welsh-medium and English-medium education	151

FIGURES, GRAPHS AND TABLES ix

Graph 8   Key Stage 1 Science: the attainment of children in Welsh-medium and English-medium education   152

Chapter 6 Psychology and Bilingual Education: Intelligence Tests and the Influence of Pedagogy

Figure 1	Relationships between bilingualism and intelligence as envisaged between the wars and until the 1960s	164
Figure 2	Views of 'intelligence' which reject the equation with 'educability'	172
Figure 3	Relations between social position and intelligence test performance according to McClelland's 'competencies' point of view	174
Figure 4	Modification to the McClelland system description to include higher level factors with a second-order linkage as well as the first-order linkages with feedback	178
Figure 5	Changes in relations between bilingualism and intelligence test performance in Welsh studies	179

Chapter 9 Acculturation, Ethnic Identity and Community Languages: A study of Indo-Canadian Adolescents

Table 1	Mean and S.D. of the sample's scores on the scale	218
Table 2	Factor structure with girls' sample	219
Table 3	Factor structure with boys' sample	220
Table 4	Items on which differences appeared between the boys and girls	222
Table 5	Response pattern on equality of treatment of boys and girls at home	228
Table 6	Cultural activities – Asian music and videos	229

THE CONTRIBUTORS

Professor Adebisi Afolayan was the founding Professor of the Department of English Language in the Obafemi Awolowo University, Ife-Ife, Nigeria, and has been Dean of the Faculty of Arts there. He is an applied linguist who specializes in Language in Education, and served as consultant on the Six-Year Primary (Yoruba–English Bilingual Education) Project of the Institute of Education at Obafemi Awolowo University. Professor Afolayan is the founder of the Centre for Language in Education and Development, Ife-Ife, which he now serves as Chief Consultant.

Professor Colin Baker is Professor of Education in the School of Education, University of Wales at Bangor, and Director of the College's Research Centre Wales. He is Wales's foremost authority on the organization of bilingual education, and has published extensively on bilingualism, both in journals and books.

Dr Wynford Bellin is a Lecturer in the Education Department of the University of Wales at Cardiff, and previously held a lecturing post in the Psychology Department of the University of Reading. His main research interest is in the psychological aspects of bilingualism, and he has published several studies in this field.

Michael J. Berthold is a Lecturer in the Centre for Language Learning and Teaching at the University of Southern Queensland. He is the initiator of the first partial immersion programme through French on the secondary level in Australia. As an experienced practitioner and observer of language teaching at all levels, he serves as a consultant in areas of second-language education, especially bilingual education.

Associate Professor J. A. W. Caldwell is Deputy Dean of Education at the University of Newcastle, NSW, Australia. His research interests are in the areas of bilingual education, language teaching methodology and language planning, and he has published studies of educational management and classroom practice in several countries.

ELGAN DAVIES is Librarian-in-charge, Old College, University of Wales at Aberystwyth, and has collected a bibliography of Jac L. Williams's publications. He was a student of Professor Williams and, like him, has written stories and novels in Welsh.

PROFESSOR C. J. DODSON was a member of Professor Williams's staff at the Department of Education at Aberystwyth. He is well-known for his views on language teaching methodology. His approach to second-language teaching has been influential, and is relevant to the study of the acquisition of bilingualism.

DR GARETH EDWARDS was the founding Director of the Welsh Language Education Development Committee (also known by its Welsh acronym PDAG), and is currently Dean of the Faculty of Arts at Aberystwyth. He is an experienced educator, particularly interested in language curriculum planning and assessment. He was a member of the Department of Education at Aberystwyth while Professor Jac L. Williams was Head.

DR PAUL A. SINGH GHUMAN, Senior Lecturer in Education in the University of Wales at Aberystwyth, is another contributor who served under Professor Williams. He is an experienced researcher whose interests are two-fold: cross-cultural psychology and multi-culturalism. He has published widely in both fields.

BOB MORRIS JONES is Senior Research Associate in the Department of Education of the University of Wales at Aberystwyth. He researches the Welsh language from both linguistic and socio-linguistic standpoints, and specializes in studies of the Welsh of young children.

PROFESSOR J.E. CAERWYN WILLIAMS is a former Professor of Irish in the University of Wales at Aberystwyth, and former Director of the Centre of Advanced Celtic Studies also at Aberystwyth. He is a distinguished Celticist whose scholarship is much respected in Europe and North America.

PROFESSOR COLIN WILLIAMS is Professor of Sociolinguistics of Welsh in the Department of Welsh, University of Wales at Cardiff. He is a productive and well-known researcher into multilingual societies from the point of view of the Social Sciences and Human Geography, and an experienced worker on Welsh bilingualism.

FOREWORD

Language, along with religion, is one of the most significant manifestations, as well as one of the great symbols, of culture. As the anthropologist Mary Douglas argued, to speak a language is to partake in a ritual and that ritual affirms basic social relations and asserts common values. It is a marker of identity, which is a synonym for those roots which shape and give meaning to living. But the world is not divided into discrete monolingual cultures contained within well-defined geographical areas. Indeed, it is the interaction of cultures, represented by language and religion, which has become a defining element of the post-modern world. Postmodernism in this sense is marked by the decline of the great monolithic empires which dominated the modern world. As that has happened the bivalence of individual living has come to the fore. There is a constant tension between the ideals of harmony in multicultural polities on the one hand, and of a universal humanity on the other. It is not without significance that Judeo-Christianity presents languages as derived from the Tower of Babel and representing a sinful departure from the universality which was the way of God. As Steiner writes, 'Babel was a second fall'.

Though the Biblical interpretation might indicate one source, in practice bilingualism, or multilingualism, is the product of a variety of sources. It is classically brought about in a colonial situation where an indigenous language is submerged in a process of occupation, engendering a lesser-used or minority language over against a world language. Without the colonial overtones, it can be the product of population migrations, such as those which are turning California into an Hispanic as much as an English-speaking state, or which in earlier times brought both English- and French-speakers to Canada. Or again, there are the migrations from former colonial territories into contemporary European cities. It can be the consequence of border locations between states and the shifting of frontiers. And, of course, it can be the consequence of a simple desire to break out of a monolingual limitation and to experience the contrasts and riches of other cultures and ways of living. Bilingualism, therefore, is not the product of a simple and single process.

Whatever the process, however, it is a crucial characteristic of the contemporary world. Students of urbanism refer to the concept of the non-place urban realm. It argues that the dominance of a single homogeneous place within which life is lived has disappeared. People conduct their lives in a series of realms which are not necessarily connected. Thus the business man will work in a city which constitutes one realm. He will make phone calls, maybe partaking in discussions linked by television with colleagues in another part of the world, a different realm. He will return home in the evening to a local realm, possible attending a meeting at the local parish level. But not only are these different realms, it is possible that different languages will be used for each of them, that they form different domains of language use.

All this emphasizes the importance of understanding bilingualism, both in its general cultural context, and especially in its educational needs. How does education cope with what is now a universal condition of meeting demands from bilingual communities? How does the desideratum of cultural identity respond to the overwhelming need to be fluent in one of the world's major languages? How do migrants into new lands preserve their culture and its prime vehicle, their language? These are crucial problems which this book sets out to explore. It is entirely proper that it does so to honour the memory of the late Professor Jac L. Williams. He was a man totally committed to the creation of a bilingual Wales, not in any way in an anti-English sense for he fully appreciated the need for total competence in English. But he was also acutely aware of the relationship between language and cultural identity. It is right therefore that the volume examines bilingualism, even multilingualism, not in a narrow or limited way, but in its broadest world context. It is an appropriate commemoration of Jac L.'s vision. Indeed, because of the provenance of many of the authors, it is a part of it.

Emeritus Professor HAROLD CARTER

INTRODUCTION

Bob Morris Jones and Paul A. Singh Ghuman

This volume is in honour of the late Professor Jac L. Williams, who was deeply committed to bilingualism in general and to its promotion in Wales in particular. His writings on the subject are prolific and varied, as is indicated by the list of his publications which is given in this work. Through these and his teaching, he has influenced generations of students interested in the theoretical and the applied aspects of bilingualism. We feel sure that he would have been pleased with the increasing development and popularity of this field, reflected in the steady emergence of standard works on the subject (for example, Baker 1985, 1988, 1993; Baetens Beardsmore 1986; Cummins and Swain 1986; Hamers and Blanc 1989; Romaine 1989; Hoffman 1991; and Paulston 1994). We should like to think that this volume, as a contribution to the study of several aspects of bilingualism, is a fitting way to honour Jac L.'s extensive interest in the subject in many contexts.

Bilingualism is a multidisciplinary subject *par excellence*. It touches upon so many aspects of human behaviour: it is a fruitful area for the study of language contact; it is intriguing for the way that it relates to the human mind; it reflects social behaviour and the organization of society; and it can shape educational systems. It is not surprising therefore that linguists, sociolinguists, psychologists, sociologists, human geographers, and educationalists all contribute to the field. The chapters in this volume reflect many of these aspects of bilingualism. As might be expected, however – given Jac L.'s background as a professor of Education – pedagogical aspects of bilingualism are strongly represented in this collection. This is an important field which involves the design of the curriculum and classroom methodology, and the contributions by Bob Morris Jones, Carl Dodson, Colin Baker, John Caldwell and Michael Berthold, and Adebisi Afolayan variously explore specific aspects of the use of education to promote bilingualism.

Jac L. Williams: Man and Scholar

Jac L. Williams was one of the most charismatic personalities amongst the Welsh academics of his time. He was beloved by his students, and all who experienced his teaching can affectionately recall his memory. In a volume which is largely devoted to the study of aspects of bilingualism, it would be unfortunate if Jac L., the man, was hidden by academic content. As editors we were very pleased when Dr Gareth Edwards willingly accepted the task of presenting a personal portrait of the many facets of Jac L. Dr Edwards became a member of Jac L.'s staff at an early age, and is uniquely suited to recalling private and public qualities. His account indicates the impressive range of Jac L.'s abilities and interests.

The second chapter is written by J. E. Caerwyn Williams, a distinguished Celtic scholar and contemporary of Jac L. Williams, who is able to provide both personal and professional recollections. His contribution explores many themes which were characteristic of Jac L.'s views on bilingualism. Caerwyn Williams gives a poignant account of his own early monolingual schooling in English which provides a perspective to the importance that Jac L. attached to bilingualism. He examines some of the attitudes which accounted for the rejection of Welsh as a medium of instruction, and underlines the notion of linguistic equality of all languages. Caerwyn William's contribution emphasizes the predominance of bilingual speech communities throughout the world, and speculates on whether language contact produces a form of bilingualism even within predominantly monolingual settings. His chapter deals at length with ways of developing the vocabularies of minority languages in order for their speakers to be able to address modern concepts. Jac L. was anxious to promote the lexical resources of Welsh, and Caerwyn Williams provides both the historical background to Welsh lexicography and an account of the contemporary work in which Jac L. was so closely involved.

Bilingualism in Wales

There are two broad circumstances in which societal bilingualism can occur: there are indigenous groups which are relatively well-established in an area; and there are immigrants who bring with them their own languages and cultures to add to those of the country of their adoption. Both possibilities are discussed in this volume.

Where we have a minority and a majority language, as is the case in Wales, a frequent concern is the extent to which the minority language can maintain its status. One obvious support of status is a geographical one, whereby the minority language can be identified with a particular area. In Wales, Welsh in the twentieth century is identified mainly with western regions, sometimes referred to as *Y Fro Gymraeg* (The Welsh Region). There are a number of problems which are associated with the geographical identity of a language. One is that if this identity is pressed too hard, the status of the minority language becomes weakened outside this region. Another one is that demographic changes can radically alter the linguistic character of regions. Such changes have been seen in recent decades in Wales where in-migration has introduced greater numbers of mainly English-speakers and out-migration has depleted the numbers of Welsh-speakers.

The dispersal of Welsh-speakers and the status of the language is the concern of Colin Williams's contribution. His perspective is essentially a socio-historical one. He provides empirical data from census returns and statistical surveys which facilitate discussion of a Welsh heartland – the geographical identity of the language. But his chapter probes beyond statistical surveys to explore an array of social agencies influencing language use which throw light upon the allegiance of the Welsh to their historical language. This contribution provides a wide-ranging and perceptive discussion of the links between language, geography and social institutions. His discussion of institutional bilingualism and several 'unresolved questions' relating to Welsh has world-wide relevance. For instance, his critical question as to whether the 'internationalization of English' will threaten a minority language like Welsh has significance for other linguistic communities across the world. Adebisi Afolayan in this volume shows that English as an international language is a prominent competitor with Nigerian languages. Colin Williams's examination of the role of organized religion in maintaining and sustaining a minority language and culture will also have a universal appeal. Another critical issue which he examines is whether a 'nationalist' base to bilingualism and biculturalism can obscure shared values, and lead to the seizure of the language issue by small interest groups. This line of thought leads us to consider related matters such as the overall role of language in maintaining distinctive ethnic identities, and whether an excessively linguistic approach can obscure other factors in ethnic survival.

A critical issue in bilingual education is the relationship between the language(s) of the pupils and the language(s) used as the medium of teaching. It is possible for bilingual children to be educated either through their first or second langauge. The crucial question relates to the relative control over the two languages. A particular problem occurs with incipient bilinguals when a child is educated in the second language which he or she has not fully mastered. There are two types of incipient bilingualism which are relevant to this point. One is where the child's bilingualism is reinforced by societal bilingualism. The other is where the child's bilingualism is mainly or wholly dependent upon the school. Take the possibilities in Wales, for example. Welsh-speaking children acquire English as their second language in the wider society. English-speaking children acquire Welsh as their second language mainly through the school: they are taught in the language that they are also learning. This raises two critical questions: can second language acquisition and first language development effectively take place in this way, and are the subjects on the school curriculum effectively taught? Both these questions are discussed in contributions to this volume.

Bob Morris Jones's contribution takes a fairly critical look at language teaching. He specifically examines the use of the curriculum as the main, if not sole, means of exposure to the second language. His concern is that the curriculum cannot offer a child a sufficient variety of linguistic experiences to promote the effective acquisition and development of the second language. He discusses both empirical data and models of language use and discourse to show that for many pupils the domain of the use of Welsh is too narrow. He concludes his analysis by discussing activities which extend the use of Welsh beyond the curriculum, in particular the recent development of enterprises (*mentrau*) to promote Welsh in the wider society.

Carl Dodson is particularly concerned with the respective roles of the first and second languages in bilingual education and language teaching, and compares the bilingual approach and the immersion approach. He is critical of the immersion approach where children are taught solely in their second language, arguing that it has three weaknesses: it does not effectively encourage the acquisition of the latter; consequently, the children do not fully understand the subject teaching; and the exclusion of the children's first language means that its development is not promoted. He is especially concerned with the emergence of errors in the second language which, if they are not remedied, will lead to their permanent establishment in a variety of language which he terms 'fossilized interlanguage' (FI). He advocates the use of the first language and the second language in bilingual education. He holds that the acquisition of the second language should not be left for the child to *learn*, on the assumption that he or she will acquire it in the same way that the first language was acquired. Carl Dodson urges that the second language should also be *taught*, using a language teaching methodology which involves systematic classroom techniques and the use of the first language to introduce the second language.

It is very difficult to generalize about these issues. In the case of ethnic minorities for whom the second language is a majority language, the bilingual approach has obvious merits: it maintains the home language and introduces the majority language. But where the second language is itself a minority language which is under pressure from a majority language, and where the children's home language is the majority one, immersion can also be seen not exclusively as a teaching methodology but also as an agency which establishes a domain of use which promotes the minority language. These circumstances are found in Wales in the use of the minority language, Welsh, as a medium of instruction for children whose home language is the majority language, English. The chapter by Bob Morris Jones highlights the problem of domains of use for minority languages in education. In a different way, this problem also affects modern language teaching where the taught language can only be experienced in a language lesson. Immersion has proved to be attractive to some who see it as a way of establishing a more concentrated use of the target language. In this same volume, the chapter by Jack Caldwell and Michael Berthold describes the use of immersion to teach French in Australia, and argue that it has produced good results. The role of the mother tongue in language teaching in general has been controversial since the advocacy of the direct method. It seems likely that the debate about the role of the first language in language teaching will continue.

Colin Baker looks at the performance of children from different linguistic backgrounds on the National Curriculum (of Wales and England) in schools in Wales. His concern is not simply with the results of testing but also with the goals and methods of assessment. His discussion looks at assessment within the context of a curriculum and testing schedule determined by central government. Colin Baker is particularly concerned with the way in which assessment can be applied to pupils who are experiencing bilingual education within the requirements of a curriculum which is determined by national government. Tension can frequently occur between those who emphasize the role of the school as an agency to promote bilingualism and those who see the essential purpose of the school as being to equip their pupils with the necessary skills for social and professional advancement. If one of the languages in the bilingual setting is a minority language − as is frequently the case − then the amount of support for bilingualism will be affected, on the one hand, by the perceived utilitarian advantages of the majority language and, on the other hand, by the more non-material values of the minority language which are based on identity and tradition. A system of assessment which could monitor the progress of pupils experiencing bilingual education would contribute substantially to this debate. Colin Baker's detailed analysis of young children's attainment in maths and science leads him to assert a positive role for a bilingualism. Colin Baker examines the results of the testing of both linguistic and subject attainment, and links his discussion with international findings and analyses. He refers to the low achievement of Pakistani and Bangladeshi children on attainment tasks in English and Mathematics and to the attribution of this to their different home languages − this provides an instance of the subtractive aspects of bilingualism which are discussed in the chapter by Bellin.

It is tempting to think that at the close of this century we have achieved a general acceptance of bilingualism. But as this volume was being put together the BBC Welsh News reported on a proposal for road signs to be monolingual, based on the language of the area, rather than bilingual. The reported reason for this was that bilingual signs involve having to read them twice. It is difficult to quantify the extent of this inconvenience on the basis of a news report. But, in the case of road signs, we are only likely to gain a few seconds but lose visible reinforcement of the dual linguistic identity of Wales. The rationale behind this retreat to monolingualism is characteristic of several objections which have been made against bilingualism over the years. This latter-day case seeks out inconvenience as an objection. But in the past, rejection of bilingualism has been based on the notion that bilingualism is harmful. Central to this complaint is the relationship between bilingualism and intelligence.

The chapter by Wynford Bellin traces the history of the debate on this relationship and, indeed, presents views about the notion of intelligence itself. It is particularly fitting that Dr Bellin describes Jac L.'s contribution to this debate in Wales. This debate is of contemporary significance. Both editors can testify anecdotally to being asked (often by undergraduates, for instance) whether learning two languages somehow 'mixes you up', particularly for young children experiencing schooling as well. Some parents have been wrongly led to believe, as Bellin indicates, that bilingualism may cause mental confusion and retardation. Colin Baker, too, refers to these fears. Wynford Bellin discusses the psychological theories of mental development and testing which underpinned the debate on bilingualism in Wales and elsewhere until the beginning of the 1960s. After an era which saw the use of psychometric testing, new ideas and concepts from cognitive psychologists, particularly those from Vygotsky, began to have a benign influence on the policy and practice of bilingualism. Bellin writes critically of theories of intelligence which lead to the widespread testing of mental abilities and excessive reliance on quantitative data. He is particularly scathing of an over simplistic view of the relationship between bilingualism and performances on mental tests. Bellin shows how such a simple approach led to the belief that the learning capacity of young children was curtailed by having two languages, and that bilingual children were likely to underachieve because they were being asked to put too much effort into learning another language. Bellin draws extensively on the writings of Vygotsky to argue that any assessment of bilingual children must acknowledge wider considerations, particularly teaching methods and the social context in which bilingualism is practised.

Bilingualism in other countries

The relationship of language and geography has meant that there is a fairly old tradition which studies bilingualism in terms of well-established indigenous peoples. Wales is one obvious example among many. But recent decades have seen a growing interest in newly founded communities which arise through immigration. Most western countries in Europe and north America have immigrant communities which introduce new languages and cultures into the adopted country. Indigenous bilingual groups generally have cultural differences within a broader set of similar traditions. But immigrants can bring with them quite different cultural traditions and religious beliefs. As a result, multiculturalism is now a field of study in its own right. One aspect of this field is the study of the comparison of the home values of the immigrant families with the values of the wider society of the adopted country. The children of immigrant families experience both sets of values via parental influence on the one hand and school influence on the other hand.

Paul A. Singh Ghuman's contribution is an empirical study of the attitudes of adolescents from Asian families to western values and traditional family values. He presents a picture of young people picking their way through two societies, balancing and modifying those things which they find acceptable in two traditions. Paul Ghuman's contribution takes a very close look at ethnic identities through examining the nature and extent of acculturation in second-generation Canadian adolescents of Indian origin — and also making many interesting comparisons with the values of ethnic adolescents in the UK. The study which he describes found that most young people are bilingual on an informal spoken level, and that they shape their identity as Indo-Canadians — thus holding on to their origins and embracing their contemporary context. Exploring parental attitudes to bilingualism, he found that there is support for maintaining the home languages, but there is uncertainty as to the best way to organize teaching. Currently, the school system is minimally involved and it falls to the communities to make their own arrangements. It is interesting to compare these views with the development of community and state provisions for ethnic groups in Australia described in the chapter by John Caldwell and Michael Berthold.

Many countries have both linguistic and cultural diversity from both indigenous and immigrant groups. Jack Caldwell and Michael Berthold give an account of the diversity which arises in Australia where the Aboriginal peoples, and then European settlers, and latterly non-English-speaking immigrants created that country's multilingual and multicultural character. This one study brings together several crucial issues relating to language and culture. The authors explore attitudes towards, and provisions for, the linguistic and cultural identities of such different groups as those of Greek origin, those of Asian origin, and, belatedly, the indigenous Aboriginal peoples. The informative historical account in this chapter, supported by case studies of specific Australian programmes, epitomizes so many facets of bilingual and bicultural education, and will be of universal interest. The development of policies on bilingual education shows a shift from individual and group responsibility to national responsibility – a development which will interest many ethnic communities who currently maintain the home language outside the education system. The authors outline the development of the goals of bilingualism and biculturalism, including language maintenance for minorities, cognitive and linguistic development for all, and economic advantages. This paper is a good example of how policies and practices of bilingualism are shaped by *Zeitgeist*, and underlines how bilingualism needs to be considered within socio-historical contexts. The influence of prevailing political and economic ideologies cannot be underestimated.

If monolingual speakers find bilingualism a strange animal, bilingual speakers in their turn find it difficult to comprehend extensive multilingualism. There are countries where there are numerous languages (which may be counted in hundreds – although there is the old problem of deciding where dialectological differences end and language differences begin): there are local indigenous languages, official and national indigenous languages, and in some instances a remaining colonial language. This is the case in Nigeria, and the scale of the challenge facing language planners and educationalists is described by Adebisi Afolayan in his account of that country. The organization of the school curriculum in such countries is extremely challenging. A multitude of questions arise. Which language should be used as the medium of instruction when a young child begins his or her education? How many other languages should a child be expected to acquire – an official national language (if the child does not have one), a local language (if the child does not have one), and the old colonial language (which in the case of English is an international language). Adebisi Afolayan describes Nigera's reaction to its multilingual identity in the field of education. He outlines existing national provisions and gives a critical assessment of their objectives and implementation. He urges sensitivity to language needs in three respects: local community languages; national and major Nigerian languages; and English as an international language. He recommends the introduction and use of these language types at different levels in the educational system. Multiple economic and political issues add to the linguistic complexities facing many multilingual countries, and Adebisi Afolayan emphasizes the importance of political will and parental support gained through promoting public awareness of the additive aspects of bilingualism and multilingualism. The Nigerian multilingual situation is not untypical – it is found in other African countries and also in India. This account will be relevant to educationalists in other countries which possess an extensive diversity of languages and groupings of people.

References

Baetens Beardsmore, Hugo (1986). *Bilingualism: Basic Principles*, 2nd ed. (Clevedon, Multilingual Matters Ltd.).
Baker, C. (1985). *Aspects of Bilingualism in Wales* (Clevedon, Multilingual Matters Ltd.).
Baker, C. (1988). *Key Issues in Bilingualism and Bilingual Education* (Clevedon, Multilingual Matters Ltd.).
Baker, C. (1993). *Foundations of Bilingual Education and Bilingualism* (Clevedon, Multilingual Matters Ltd.).
Cummins, Jim and Swain, Merrill (1986). *Bilingualism in Education* (London, Longman).
Hamers, Josiane F. and Blanc, Michel H. A. (1989). *Bilinguality and Bilingualism* (Cambridge, Cambridge University Press).
Hoffman, Charlotte (1991). *An Introduction to Bilingualism* (Harlow, Longman).
Paulston, Christina B. (1994). *Language Maintenance and Language Shift* (Amsterdam, John Benjamin).
Romaine, Suzanne (1989). *Bilingualism* (Oxford, Basil Blackwell).

I

Jac L. Williams: Man and Scholar

1
JAC L. WILLIAMS – YSGOGWR ADDYSG GYMRAEG: PORTREAD PERSONOL

D. Gareth Edwards

Yn sicr, nid ystrydeb yw honni fy mod i'n cofio'n glir ble roeddwn a beth roeddwn yn ei wneud pan glywais y newyddion ysgytwol am farwolaeth gynamersol yr Athro Jac L. Williams, un noswaith braf yn gynnar yn haf 1977, wrth iddo ddisgwyl y trên ar orsaf Casnewydd ar ei ffordd i gyfarfod yn Llundain. Fore trannoeth pallodd fy amynedd pwyllgoraidd ar ôl rhyw awr a rhuthrais yn ôl i Aberystwyth o Gaerdydd i rannu gyda'm cyd-weithwyr y gwacter a'r ing o golli pennaeth a oedd hefyd yn gyfaill, arweinydd a oedd hefyd yn ysbrydolwr, athrylith a oedd hefyd yn ddynol agos-atoch; brysio'n ôl i gydalaru â chymdeithas y coleg a Chymry'r dref o glywed am golli un o wir gewri ein cenedl. Canys mawr fu'r galar drwy Gymru gyfan.

Jac L. – pennaeth

Mawr fu'r galar yn arbennig yma yn ei Geredigion annwyl hoff, ac nid lleiaf ymhlith ei fyfyrwyr yn y Coleg ger y Lli, oherwydd gorchwyl trist i nifer ohonynt yn yr Adran Addysg, drannoeth marwolaeth eu hathro, oedd ateb y papur arholiad a osodwyd ganddo ar Astudiaethau Dwyieithog, sef y cwrs y bu'n ei ddysgu'n ffyddlon ddi-fwlch ers blynyddoedd er yr holl alwadau arno. Gwyddent mai mud bellach y llais a draddodai iddynt yn wythnosol-reolaidd, a dall y llygaid pefriog dan aeliau duon a ddylai fod yn darllen eu cynigion. Eithr, braint yr un mor drist i mi fu marcio'r sgriptiau ychydig ddyddiau'n ddiweddarach, a darllen sawl cyfeiriad a sylw mwy personol ac angerddol nag a ddisgwylid mewn papur arholiad, a amlygai barch dwfn ac anwyldeb tyner at eu hen athro.

Er iddo fwynhau ymrafael mewn ymgyrchoedd dros achosion cenedlaethol a oedd yn agos at ei galon, ac er iddo gyfrannu'n helaeth i bwyllgorau addysgol ac eglwysig, nid anghofiodd fyth mai ei briod waith oedd addysgu myfyrwyr ac arwain ei staff. Arloesodd ddatblygiadau academaidd cynhyrfus oddi mewn i'w adran ac y mae llawer sy'n greiddiol i'w gweithgarwch heddiw wedi'u hadeiladu ar y seiliau a osododd ef. Mynnodd mai drwy agor y drysau ac arddangos Cymru a'r Gymraeg i'r byd a datgelu'r byd i'w gyd-Gymry y byddai gwerthoedd gorau ein gwareiddiad yn ffynnu; roedd hyn yn unol â'i gred ddiysgog o blaid darlledu rhaglenni Cymraeg ar bob sianel deledu er mwyn sicrhau bod yr iaith yn cael mynediad i bob cartref drwy'r wlad yn lle ei chyfyngu 'i gwtsh dan staer y bedwaredd sianel'.[1] O ganlyniad i'w erthyglau ysgolheigaidd, ei ddarlithoedd ar hyd a lled Ewrop – yn enwedig mewn nifer o'r gwledydd comiwnyddol lle y siaredid nifer o ieithoedd ar y cyd – ac i'r bri a roddwyd ar ei waith gan y Cyngor Prydeinig, gwelwyd yn ystod y pum mlynedd cyn ei farw gynnydd syfrdanol yn nifer y myfyrwyr tramor yn yr Adran Addysg, a'r mwyafrif ohonynt yma ar berwyl – onid pererindod – ieithyddol. Ar sail y bri a enillodd i'w adran, parhawn i groesawu ymwelwyr o'r pum cyfandir i drafod addysg iaith a dwyieithrwydd ac y mae nifer o'r darlithwyr presennol, yn eu tro, wedi creu cysylltiadau â phrifysgolion ledled y byd gan ymestyn y rhwydwaith a greodd yr Athro ar ei rawd. Ond, rywsut, dydi pethau ddim yr un fath!

Jac L. – y cymdeithasegydd iaith

Roedd gwybodaeth yr Athro am sefyllfaoedd gwahanol ieithoedd[2] – llawer ohonynt yn fwy cymhleth o bell ffordd na Chymru – yn peri iddo osod dwyieithrwydd, ac yn arbennig materion yn ymwneud â statws y Gymraeg ym mywyd beunyddiol ein gwlad ni, mewn persbectif sydd bellach yn gwbl gyfoes a pherthnasol. Roedd yr hyn a grybwyllodd[3], ar hyd ei yrfa, ynglŷn â chreu'r amodau cymdeithasol i gynnal yr iaith y tu allan i furiau'r ysgol yn y gymuned leol, yn paratoi'r ffordd ar gyfer sefydlu corff cynllunio iaith, digon tebyg i Fwrdd yr Iaith Gymraeg a sefydlwyd yn ddiweddar. Pe bai'n fyw heddiw, byddai ei gyfraniad i waith y Bwrdd yn amhrisiadwy.

Ymhellach, ar sail ei ddealltwriaeth o brif egwyddorion y broses addysgol, gwerthfawrogai'n llawn holl arwyddocâd seicoieithyddol iaith – ei nerth i ystwytho ac ymestyn y meddwl, ei hegni i ddatblygu cysyniadau, a'i grym i gyfoethogi cronfa profiadau'r unigolyn. Dyna oedd yn cyfrif am ei frwdfrydedd dros iaith fel rhywbeth oedd yn llawer mwy na chyfrwng cyfathrebu; roedd iaith yn greiddiol i holl hunaniaeth person ar y naill law, ac ar y llall yn costrelu gwareiddiad cenedl a theithi ei meddwl. A'i obaith oedd trosglwyddo'r etifeddiaeth, o safbwynt yr unigolyn a'r genedl, i'r dyfodol. Gorau oll pe câi ei gyd-Gymry brofi'r cyfoeth o edrych ar y byd drwy ffenestri dwy neu ragor o ieithoedd.

Er mai gwrthun oedd ei gwleidyddiaeth iddo, hoffai gyfeirio at ddwyieithrwydd gweriniaeth De Affrig lle y sefydlwyd Afrikaans yn iaith i adlewyrchu hunaniaeth y genedl yn lle'r Saesneg drefedigaethol; edmygai hefyd bolisïau iaith nifer o'r cenhedloedd comiwnyddol am iddynt bwysleisio pwysigrwydd eu hieithoedd unigryw yn ogystal â Rwsieg fel *lingua franca* i uno pob un o'r gweriniaethau'n gymuned organig.[4] Ond ei fodel oedd Israel lle'r oedd y frwydr i atgyfodi iaith a'i hadfer ar dafodau ac ym meddyliau ei dinasyddion wedi ei hennill yn llachar-ogoneddus. Iddo ef, roedd cenedligrwydd ac iaith genedlaethol yn annatod.

Jac L. – yr addysgwr

Roedd ganddo ryw chwilfrydedd di-ball, a allai ymylu ar fod yn ffobia ar adegau, i ddysgu am bob math o sefyllfaoedd lle y deuai dwy neu ragor o ieithoedd i gyswllt â'i gilydd. Os clywai fod gan rywun rywbeth diddorol i'w ddweud ni fyddai fawr o dro yn dod i'w adnabod. Ac nid adnabod i gymryd mantais mohono; byddai'n meithrin y berthynas drwy gydol y cwrs coleg, gan wneud i'r person hwnnw deimlo'n rhywun go arbennig. Byddai wrth ei fodd yn dysgu myfyrwyr tramor ag iddynt gefndir neu brofiadau anghyffredin, megis yr athro hwnnw o Awstralia a fu wrthi'n dysgu Saesneg i lwythau brodorol peithdiroedd y Northern Territory, neu'r gŵr o'r Congo a ddysgai iaith i'w fyfyrwyr dan gysgod coeden enfawr, neu'r darlithydd a gafodd ei erlid gan y Comiwynddion o'i brifysgol yn Kampuchea. Wrth ymgomio â hwy ar ddiwedd darlith neu ar ei aelwyd, ac yn aml yn eu croesholi'n ddyfal, hefyd wrth osod iddynt draethodau ymchwilgar, llwyddodd i loffa ystôr digyffelyb o wybodaeth nad yw ar gael mewn unrhyw lyfr. Nid oedd pall ar ei frwdfrydedd i ddysgu oddi wrth brofiadau eraill, a chyfrannai yntau yn fawrfrydig o hael yn ei dro o'i wybodaeth a'i ddoethineb er eu lles.

Y traethawd Ph.D. diwethaf a arolygodd oedd un yn ymdrin ag agweddau ar ddysgu iaith yn Nigeria, gwlad ag iddi o leiaf 400 o ieithoedd cofrestredig. Ond nid ar chwarae bach yr ymdaflodd i'r gwaith hwn.

Er yr holl alwadau ar ei amser, a'r holl egni corfforol a meddyliol a dreuliai i gyflawni ei lu orchwylion beunyddiol, amlygodd drylwyredd ac amynedd oedd yn ddigon i ddychryn neb. Canys tywysodd yr Athro ei fyfyriwr, digon bratiog ei Saesneg, drwy ddrysni'r holl lenyddiaeth gefndirol, drwy gymhlethdodau arbrofion ystadegol, nes cyflawni yn y diwedd draethawd gyda damcaniaethau arbennig o ddiddorol. Trylwyredd a manylrwydd ochr yn ochr â gallu'r Athro i gadw mewn golwg y cyffredinol a'r eang, y delfrydol ochr yn ochr â'r perthnasol a'r ymarferol, a sicrhaodd iddo ei statws fel un o ysgolheigion ieithyddiaeth gymhwysol a chymdeithasegol amlycaf y byd.

Yn ogystal â'r cynnydd croesawus hwn mewn myfyrwyr tramor, gwelwyd dan ei arweiniad gynnydd yr un mor syfrdanol yng nghyfanswm y Cymry Cymraeg yn yr adran nes iddynt, y flwyddyn y bu farw, fod yn draean o gyfangorff y myfyrwyr. A deuai i'w hadnabod bob un. O gofio am ei ddiddordeb personol ynddynt ac o ddeall bod dros hanner darlithwyr yr Adran yn dysgu trwy gyfrwng y Gymraeg, doedd dim rhyfedd bod y myfyrwyr Cymraeg mor gartrefol dan adain eu pennaeth. Byddai Jac L. wrth ei fodd o glywed i nifer y myfyrwyr graddedig, Cymraeg eu hiaith, ar gyrsiau hyfforddiant dysgu'r Adran Addysg godi'n sylweddol dros y blynyddoedd, a bod 105 yn siarad Cymraeg o blith 270 o fyfyrwyr erbyn 1993. Mae'r cynnydd hwn, er nad yn ddigonol, yn cyfrannu'n sylweddol at y galw am athrawon i gyflenwi'r twf mewn addysg gyfrwng Cymraeg ac i'w dysgu fel ail iaith yn sgil y Cwricwlwm Cenedlaethol.

Jac L. a Chymru'r bröydd

Mewn teyrnged a luniais ar gyfer rhifyn coffa *Barn* am yr Athro Jac L. Williams cyfeiriais, gyda manylder, at nifer o ddigwyddiadau rwy'n falch yn awr i mi eu crybwyll, gan eu bod yn ailgynnau dwyster a thristwch yr achlysur. Er enghraifft, yn ei fag ar y daith olaf honno yng Ngwent yr oedd pecyn o draethodau myfyrwyr yr oedd newydd eu marcio. Arolwg ieithyddol o'u bröydd oeddynt – Peniel, Porth-y-rhyd, Cilcain, Cwm lfor, Pontrhydfendigaid, Henllan Amgoed a'r Tymbl – tasg a roddai'n flynyddol i'w ddosbarth. Ar ben y pecyn, ar gefn dogfennau'r pwyllgor y bu'n ei gadeirio'r diwrnod cynt, yn ei lawysgrifen-feiro-du roedd crynodeb o gynnwys pob un o'r traethodau, yn cynnwys sylwadau ar y Gymraeg yn ennill neu'n colli tir ac yna restri o fân ystedegau a gododd yn sgil holiaduron manwl y myfyrwyr. Ailadroddaf y ffaith hon er mwyn ei phwysleisio. Yr oedd tynged Henllan Amgoed a thynged pob cwm arall yng Nghymru o'r pwysigrwydd mwyaf iddo yn ei frwydr ddi-ildio yn erbyn y llif Seisnigrwydd a gyrhaeddodd ei benllanw yn Nyfed, yn eironig, yn ystod y degawd ar ôl ei farw. Casgliad o fröydd lle yr oedd yn dyngedfennol cynnal neu adfer yr iaith oedd Cymru iddo. Ymboenai i'r byw am bob bro, ac yn arbennig am y Fro Gymraeg lle roedd yr iaith ar dafodleferydd ei thrigolion a'i phlant, ac yr oedd ei adnabyddiaeth ohoni'n drylwyrach na neb. Credaf y byddai wedi ymgyrchu hyd yr eithaf o blaid y polisïau iaith a luniodd awdurdodau addysg Gwynedd a Dyfed yn ystod y blynyddoedd diwethaf hyn i ymateb i'r newidiadau dramatig ym mhroffil ieithyddol eu hysgolion. Gellid dadlau i'r polisïau hyn gael eu seilio ar lawer o'r egwyddorion y bu Jac L. yn ddyfal yn cenhadu drostynt ar hyd ei yrfa. Ynddynt gwireddwyd a gweithredwyd ar eiriau'r proffwyd.

Jac L. – yr ymgyrchydd cenedlaethol

Pan fyddai angen brwydro ni cheid ei well,[5] oherwydd amddiffynnai ei egwyddorion drwy ymosod ar ei wrthwynebwyr ar y ffrynt ehangaf bosibl. Byddai unrhyw berson neu fudiad a feiddiai wrthsefyll polisïau democrataidd y Gymru Gymraeg, fel a welwyd yn Nyfed yn ddiweddar, wedi gorfod derbyn holl angerdd ei gerydd, a hynny mewn tôn o lais a fyddai'n ddeifiol ac yn rhesymegolgwrtais yr un pryd. Ac ni fyddai byth yn dal dig.

Ni wn am neb a lwyddodd i ddefnyddio'i lais, ei lygaid, ystumiau ei wyneb a symudiadau ei gorff, yn arbennig ei ddwylo, mor ddramatig effeithiol i bwysleisio ei safbwynt nag ef. Fel y gwelsom sawl gwaith ar y teledu, ac mewn ambell gyfarfod cyhoeddus, er bod ganddo'r holl ddoniau i swyno'i gynulleidfa, pan gâi ei gythruddo defnyddiai drydan ei bersonoliaeth i'w fflangellu. Wrth ei wylio, fe gawn i, beth bynnag, f'atgoffa o Laurence Olivier yn actio. Roedd Jac L. yn actor a feistrolodd ei sgript a'i lwyfan i'r dim. Yn wahanol i'w gyfaill a'i gydymgyrchydd dros y Gymraeg, Alwyn D. Rees, yr oedd yn mwynhau brwydro. Meddai Bobi Jones am y ddau, 'Yr oedd Alwyn yn poeni'n gorfforol am bethau; ond gyda Jac, ar y cyfan, fe welai'r ymdrech mewn cyd-destun tawel na tharfai mo'i gwsg ac na ddrysai'i ymroddiad achlysurol i bethau eraill'. Yr oedd gan Jac y ddawn i weithredu ar sawl ffrynt ac ar sawl lefel yr un pryd, heb adael i un broblem effeithio ar un arall.

Talodd Vincent Kane, a fu'n amlwg wrth ei fodd yn ei groesholi, deyrnged arbennig o drawiadol iddo,

In a dozen years of news and current affairs about the Welsh language I have introduced to listeners and viewers hundreds of persons and points of view; sadly all too many of them aflame with passion and hostility to the other side of the argument. So much prejudice, and so much ignorance and fear, too. In this context Jac L. was formidable: no prejudice, no ignorance and no fear. On the contrary, an understanding of the other point of view, a great wealth of evidence and research, a steadfast optimism that his vision of a bilingual Wales could, and would be, achieved.

Jac L. a'r chwyldro yng Ngwent

Roedd amseriad a lleoliad ei huno dirybudd — platfform rheilffordd yng Nghasnewydd ar ei daith i'w gyfarfod nesaf — rywsut yn briodol, er mor alaethus y digwyddiad. Casnewydd yng Ngwent — y dref a'r sir y tyngai y byddai'n rhaid eu hennill drosodd i'r Gymraeg pe bai'r iaith am oroesi. Byddai'n gorfoleddu heddiw wrth weld yr adfywiad yno. Yn ystod y degawd ers ei farw cynyddodd cyfanswm yr unedau cynradd Cymraeg yng Ngwent, gan dyfu'n fwy na'r fam ysgol mewn sawl achos. Yn dilyn eu llwyddiant ac i ateb y gofyn gan rieni am addysg uwchradd Gymraeg yn y sir, agorwyd Ysgol Gyfun Uwchradd Gymraeg Gwynllyw yn 1988. Mae hithau wedi tyfu'n fwy na'r adeiladau gwreiddiol yng Nghwmcarn a bellach mae ar gampws helaeth ym Mhont-y-pŵl a'i disgyblion cyntaf yn y chweched dosbarth yn dechrau ar eu cyrsiau ym 1993. Yn yr un flwyddyn gwelwyd agor ysgol gynradd Cymraeg gyntaf Gwent yng Nghasnewydd mewn adeiladau newydd sbon sydd gyda'r mwyaf ysblennydd yng Nghymru. Mae'n debyg yr agorir ysgolion cynradd Cymraeg eraill yn eu tro i gartrefu'r unedau sy'n cyflym ddatblygu drwy'r sir.

Câi Jac L. ei blesio'n arw hefyd o wybod bod y Gymraeg ail iaith i'w chyflwyno ym mhob ysgol gynradd ac uwchradd yng Ngwent (a Chymru gyfan) yn sgil Deddf Addysg 1988 a'r Cwricwlwm Cenedlaethol. Yn un o gyfarfodydd cyntaf Pwyllgor Datblygu Addysg Gymraeg un o'r cwestiynau mwyaf pryfoclyd y bu'n rhaid i mi ei wynebu oedd hwnnw a holwyd gan brifathro ysgol uwchradd mewn ardal lle roedd y mewnlifiad yn amlwg yn trawsnewid iaith ei ysgol, sef 'Pa bolisi iaith mae PDAG yn ei argymell a fyddai'n sicrhau fod y Cymry'n parhau i astudio'r Gymraeg, a bod yr hwyrddyfodiaid yn ei dysgu?' Yr awgrym y tu ôl i'w gwestiwn oedd, os nad oedd gan PDAG yr awdurdod i osod polisi iaith perthnasol ar ysgolion, yna mai gwastraff amser fyddai ei holl waith. Yn ddistaw bach, ni allwn anghytuno â'r ergyd. Ond drwy ryw ryfedd wyrth, yr un wythnos, clywsom fod dogfen ynglŷn â mesur addysg newydd ar fin cael ei chyhoeddi a fyddai'n sirchau lle i'r Gymraeg o fewn cwricwlwm ysgol gyfan. Ni fu raid i PDAG lunio polisi, fel y cyfryw, ond ymateb i gynlluniau'r llywodraeth drwy sicrhau fod statws y Gymraeg, yn iaith gyntaf ac yn ail iaith, cyn gryfed â phosibl, a sicrhau hefyd bod y diffiniad o ysgol Gymraeg yn realistig a chefnogol.

Jac L. – y diplomydd a'r pwyllgorddyn

Soniais am ddyrchafu statws y Gymraeg yn y cwricwlwm newydd gan fy mod yn gwbl argyhoeddedig fod y tir ar gyfer y datblygiadau breision hyn wedi ei fraenaru, i raddau helaeth iawn, gan ymdrechion diplomataidd yr Athro Jac L. Williams ar hyd y blynyddoedd.[6] Drwy ei gyfraniad i wahanol bwyllgorau, yn arbennig Cyd-bwyllgor Addysg Cymru, lle câi glust rhai cynghorwyr a gweinyddwyr mwy sgeptig na'i gilydd o'r siroedd Seisnigedig, cenhadai'n dawel-adeiladol dros y Gymraeg gan ddangos y manteision a ddeuai yn ei sgil. I raddau helaeth, roedd blynyddoedd o gael ei gyflyru ganddo wedi paratoi'r sefydliad addysgol i dderbyn safle llawer cryfach i'r iaith mewn unrhyw gynllun cwricwlaidd newydd. Llwyddasai i wneud y Gymraeg yn destun i'w ystyried o ddifrif ym mhrofiadau addysgol unrhyw blentyn o Gymro – o Wynedd i Went.

Ymfalchïai ei fod yn bwyllgorddyn prysur. Bu sôn ei fod yn aelod o ryw hanner cant adeg ei farwolaeth. Hawdd credu hynny gan iddo roi'r pwys mwyaf ar waith pwyllgor. Pwysai arnom, yn arbennig y Cymry ar ei staff, i fod ar bwyllgorau, a gorau oll os oeddynt yn penderfynu polisïau cenedlaethol ynglŷn â'r Gymraeg. Ar ei awgrym ef y deuthum yn arholwr Cymraeg i'r Cyd-bwyllgor gan wasanaethu, yn y man, ar wahanol bwyllgorau yn ymwneud â dysgu'r iaith. Rhoddwyd dimensiwn newydd i'm gwaith gan y profiadau hyn na fyddwn, efallai, wedi manteisio arnynt heb ei gyngor. Wrth edrych yn ôl, cytunaf yn llwyr â'i safbwynt bod gwasanaethu ar y pwyllgorau iawn yn allweddol i sicrhau'r polisïau cywir o safbwynt ffyniant yr iaith ym myd addysg. Cysylltaf Jac ac L. yn arbennig â dau bwyllgor oedd, mi gredaf, yn adlewyrchu ei gefnogaeth ymarferol i'r iaith. Bu, am flynyddoedd, yn gadeirydd pwyllgor llyfrau Cymraeg y Cydbwyllgor Addysg a fu'n gyfrifol am gyhoeddi 700 o lyfrau yn ystod ei gyfnod. Ac nid ystadegyn ar bapur oedd hyd yn oed y llyfryn symlaf iddo; bodiai ef, archwiliai ansawdd yr iaith, edrychai ar ei ddiwyg, sylwai ar y lliwiau a maint y print. Bu hefyd yn aelod, am gyfnod hwy nag y gallai neb ei gofio, o bwyllgor llywio Ysgol Feithrin Aberystwyth — yr unig ddyn yng nghanol twr o wragedd ifainc.[7] Ni fyddai byth yn colli cyfarfod. Ni fyddai byth ychwaith yn colli bore coffi Dydd Gŵyl Dewi yr Ysgol Gymraeg, na chyngerdd ysgol, na drama. Roedd Jac L. yn gefnogwr heb ei ail.

Jac L. — y golygydd

Yn ystod ei gyfnod yn bennaeth, llwyddodd yr Athro Jac L. Williams i drawsnewid ei adran yn un lle roedd y Gymraeg ac addysg Gymraeg yn cael eu cymryd o ddifrif. Sicrhaodd ddelwedd gwbl unigryw i'w adran, ac fe'i creodd hi'n bwerdy pob math o ddatblygiadau cyffrous ym maes addysg Gymraeg. Golygodd chwech o gyfrolau swmpus yn y gyfres *Ysgrifau ar Addysg*.[8] Ynddynt trafodir ystod eang o feysydd i'r sawl sydd am wybodaeth ehangach a dealltwriaeth amgenach o rai o brif egwyddorion addysg fel pwnc academaidd, megis seicoleg y plentyn, addysg trwy lygaid athronwyr, natur cymdeithas, hanes addysg a chyfeiriadur cynhwysfawr ar ddysgu iaith. I ddisgyblion safon uwch trefnodd gyfres werthfawr o ddarlithoedd dydd Sadwrn ar amryfal bynciau llenyddol perthnasol i'w cwrs Cymraeg a'u cyhoeddi dan y teitl *Cyfres Pamffledi Llenyddol Cyfadran Addysg Aberystwyth*.[8] Comisiynodd hefyd nifer o gyfrolau Saesneg am addysg yng Nghymru yn y gyfres *Welsh Studies in Education*[8] a bron ugain o astudiaethau academaidd gan arbenigwyr, y mwyafrif yn Saesneg, yn y gyfres *Pamffledi Cyfadran Addysg Aberystwyth*.[8]

Rhan yn unig, o'i fydysawd eang ac amryliw, oedd y byd academaidd. Roedd hefyd yn addysgwr cwbl ymarferol ei anian — *entrepreneur* fyddai'r gair gorau i'w ddisgrifio efallai. Canfyddai'r bylchau yn y ddarpariaeth, yn arbennig o safbwynt adnoddau, a brysiai i'w llenwi. Er enghraifft, i ddilyn cyfrolau arloesol Bobi Jones ar gyfer dysgwyr aeddfed, sef *Cymraeg i Oedolion* a gyhoeddwyd gan Wasg Prifysgol Cymru, 1965–6, sicrhaodd Jac L. gyllid i gyhoeddi nifer o lyfrau (detholiadau llenyddol a geiriadur yn eu plith) a fyddai'n cyfoethogi eu Cymraeg dan yr enw *Cyfres y Dysgwyr*.[8] Ond un o'i gyfraniadau mwyaf gwerthfawr oedd recordio lleisiau rhyw bymtheg o brif lenorion y dydd yn darllen detholiad o'u gwaith, sef *Cyfres yr Ysgol a'r Aelwyd*.[8]

Byddai'r Athro wrth ei fodd yn gweld y cynnyrch swmpus a gyhoeddwyd yn y Ganolfan Astudiaethau Addysg yn ystod y degawd ers ei sefydlu. Unwaith eto Jac L. a fraenarodd y tir ar gyfer lleoli uned gynhyrchu adnoddau addysgol yn yr Adran Addysg. Erbyn hyn, gyda chymorth ariannol blynyddol gan y Swyddfa Gymreig a PDAG mae'r Ganolfan ymhlith prif gyhoeddwyr deunyddiau yn y Gymraeg, gyda chyfanswm y llyfrau'n cael ei gyfrif fesul cannoedd.

Jac L. – bathwr termau

Mae'n fwriad gan y corff addysg newydd, Awdurdod Cwricwlwm ac Asesu Cymru, gomisiynu asiantaeth i resymoli a chyflenwi bylchau ym maes termau arbenigol addysg a meysydd y cwricwlwm. Canlyniad yw hyn i'r cynnydd syfrdanol mewn defnyddiau dysgu yn y Gymraeg dros y blynyddoedd diwethaf, a'r rheidrwydd i gael cysondeb mewn termau a ddefnyddir gan yr awdurdod wrth ymdrin â materion y meysydd llafur ac asesu. Un gyfrol y bydd yr asiantaeth honno'n debyg o bwyso'n drwm arni yw *Geiriadur Termau*[8] a olygwyd dan gyfarwyddyd yr Athro Jac L. Williams ugain mlynedd yn ôl. Mae hanes hir a diddorol i'r ymdrechion a roes fod i gannoedd o'r termau sydd bellach yn britho gwersi mathemateg, gwyddoniaeth, daearyddiaeth ac ati ein plant. Oddi wrth Jac L. y deuai'r ysgogiad cyntaf i lunio termau ar gyfer maes arbennig, a hynny mewn gweithgorau rheolaidd yn ei adran. Ef hefyd a gynigiai y rhan helaethaf o'r termau ar sail ei wybodaeth gyffredinol eang, ei ddeallwriaeth o wahanol feysydd a'i adnabyddiaeth o deithi'r Gymraeg a'r ieithoedd clasurol. Câi rhestr ddrafft gyntaf ei thrafod yn fanylach wedyn gan weithgor y Brifysgol dan gadeiryddiaeth yr Athro Caerwyn Williams – fel arfer mewn sesiynau penwythnos mewn gwesty yn Nolgellau. Casgliad cynhwysfawr o'r holl restri pynciol yw *Geiriadur Termau* a fu'n gaffaeliad gwerthfawr ar hyd y blynyddoedd. Ond bellach mae angen ei ddiweddaru yn sgil cyflwyno pynciau newydd ac yn dilyn datblygiadau cyffredinol yn y byd addysgol. Pa bynnag restr newydd a gyhoeddir yn y man, bydd addysgwyr y dyfodol yn ddyledus i Jac L. am lawer iawn o'r termau a fydd yn llithro'n rhwydd o'u genau.

Wrth fwrw trem yn ôl ar yrfa'r Athro Jac L. Williams ac wrth ystyried, yr un pryd, weithgarwch yr adran yn ystod y cyfnod ar ôl ei farw, canfyddir maint aruthrol ei ddylanwad arnom. Er nad oedd y dulliau cyfoes o ddatblygu ac arfarnu staff ar gael yn ei ddyddiau ef, cyflawnai hynny'n reddfol gan fod ei ddiddordeb personol ynom yn gyson gefnogol, a'i fryd ar sicrhau ein bod yn gwneud yn fawr o'n doniau a'n cyfle. Cefnogai bob dim a wnaem yn gyhoeddus ac roedd ei eiriau o glod, pan ddeuent, yn haeddiannol ac yn ysbrydoliaeth ar gyfer y dasg nesaf. Disgwyliai i ni ymroi'n gyfan gwbl, fel y gwnaeth yntau, i'n swydd fel addysgwr mewn prifysgol, drwy gwblhau ymchwil am raddau uwch, cyhoeddi a gweithredu ar bwyllgorau; yn ychwanegol at hyn disgwyliai i'r Cymry yn ein plith wasanaethu fel arholwyr safon O neu A ac ymddiddori'n gyffredinol yn addysg ac yn niwylliant ein gwlad. Pwysai arnom i gadw cydbwysedd rhwng agweddau ymarferol hyfforddi athrawon a'r theori a berthynai i faes astudiaeth arbenigol (megis seicoleg, ieithyddiaeth ac ati). Dyna'r fantais fawr o berthyn i adran a gyflwynai amrywiaeth o gyrsiau, megis gradd anrhydedd mewn addysg, ymchwil am raddau uwch yn ogystal â hyfforddiant athrawon. Yn ffodus, mae'r cynnydd diweddar yn nifer y myfyrwyr ar ein cyrsiau gradd yn sicrhau bod addysg yn debyg o barhau'n bwnc academaidd yn Aberystwyth, ond tanseiliwyd elfennau damcaniaethol amlwg ym maes hyfforddi athrawon gan bolisïau diweddar y llywodraeth, a'u pwyslais ar yr ymarferol.

Er yr holl alwadau arno, ymddiddorai Jac L. ynom fel pobl a holai hynt a helynt ein teuluoedd yn gyson. Caem groeso cynnes ar aelwyd Gwyneth ac yntau, weithiau sawl gwaith mewn blwyddyn pan fyddai ymwelwyr diddorol yn yr adran. Caem ein trin fel cyfeillion agos a theimlem yn hollol gartrefol yng nghwmni'r ddau. Treuliais rai o'r oriau mwyaf dedwydd yn Quebec, Llanbadarn, yn trafod hyd oriau hwyr y nos amryfal bynciau llosg. Collodd Cymru gawr o Gymro, ac addysg Gymraeg ladmerydd proffwydol pan fu farw'r Athro Jac L. Williams. Mae'r golled, hyd yn oed heddiw, yn ingol.

Nodiadau

1 Amlygir cryfder teimladau yr Athro Williams ynglŷn â'r mater hwn yn ei gyhoeddiadau 1973e,f,g, 1976f ac 1977g (yn y bennod hon, cyfeirir at weithiau sy'n cael eu rhestru yn y llyfryddiaeth o'i ysgrifau a roddir yn y gyfrol hon).
2 Gweler, er enghraifft, 1971b.
3 Er enghraifft, gweler 1953 (traethawd doethuriaeth), 1957a, 1958d, 1959c, 1961a, 1965a ac 1968a.
4 Gweler adolygiad yr Athro Williams, 1974b, o waith Glyn Lewis ar y pwnc hwn.
5 Fel y dengys rhestr cyhoeddiadau yr Athro Williams, rhoddodd ei ysgrifau mewn cyhoeddiadau a oedd ar gael i'r cyhoedd yn gyffredinol, yn enwedig *Y Faner* a *Barn*.
6 Mae'r cyhoeddiadau 1962a, 1968a ac 1972a yn tystio i'w ymdrechion i ddylanwadu ar fywyd cyhoeddus.
7 Mae cyhoeddiadau yr Athro Williams yn y cylchgrawn *Meithrin* 1972b, 1972d, 1972j, 1973b ac 1974, yn dangos ei ddiddordeb mewn addysg feithrin.
8 Rhydd y llyfryddiaeth o'i ysgrifau fanylion am y gweithiau a olygwyd ganddo.

JAC L. WILLIAMS – THE CATALYST OF WELSH EDUCATION: A PERSONAL PORTRAIT

D. Gareth Edwards

Though he enjoyed campaigning for national causes close to his heart, and though he contributed extensively to educational and ecclesiastical affairs, Professor Jac L. Williams never forgot that his true calling was to teach students and guide his staff. He pioneered exciting developments within his department at Aberystwyth and much of its present activity is based on the foundations he established during his tenure of the chair of education. He insisted that it was by opening doors and exhibiting Wales and the Welsh to the wider world, as well as interpreting that world to his compatriots, that the finest values of our civilization could properly flourish – this was in harmony with his staunch belief in broadcasting Welsh-language programmes on every television channel so that the language would penetrate every home in the land rather than isolating it as a mainly optional frequency on the fourth channel.

On the basis of his perception of the educational process, he fully appreciated the profound psycho-linguistic significance of language – its power to expand the mind and endow it with flexibility, its energy to develop concepts and to enrich the reservoir of personal experience. This explained his enthusiasm for language as a means of communication; language was vital to the whole aspect of a person's identity on the one hand, and on the other it conserved a nation's culture and its intellectual traits. And this glorious inheritance – both personal and national – should be handed on to future generations. All the better if his fellow Welshmen could experience the wealth of looking through the windows of two or more languages. Israel was his model for cultural planning; a small nation, where the struggle to revive the language and restore it on the tongues and in the minds of its citizens, provided a realistic ambition. To Jac L. nationhood and national language were inseparable.

No one matched him as a campaigner. He used his crisp yet beautifully modulated voice, his sparkling dark eyes beneath bushy eyebrows, his frown, smile and body language, and especially his hands, with dramatic effect to emphasize his viewpoint. His slight stoop added a compelling attractiveness to his vibrant personality and, I suspect, engendered a hidden sympathy. Despite the dire sadness of his death – on the platform at Newport Station on the way to another of his endless rounds of meetings – the timing and location of his cruel and untimely collapse was in some ways appropriate. Newport in Gwent – the town and county which he swore would have to be won over to Welsh if the language was to survive. He would be rejoicing today on seeing the steady revival there.

Taking a retrospective view of Professor Jac L. Williams's career, and considering at the same time departmental activities in the period after his death, one perceives his enormous influence on us. Though the recent methods of developing and assessing staff were not so prominent during his time, he accomplished these aims instinctively because of his personal interest in his colleagues whom he continuously supported. He supported all our public activities, and his words of encouragement and praise, wherever given, were always positive and gave inspiration for further work. He encouraged us to keep a balance between the practical aspects of training teachers and the theory related to a specific field, such as psychology or linguistics. This was the great advantage of belonging to an establishment that offered a variety of courses such as an honours degree in education, research for higher degrees as well as training teachers.

He succeeded in transforming his department into one where Welsh and Welsh education were taken seriously. He secured for it a unique image, moulding it into a power house of exciting developments. He edited academic volumes, inspired course compilers, arranged conferences on a national and international scale as well as providing journals and magazines with an endless flow of stimulating articles. He could best be described perhaps as an educational entrepreneur.

Sadly, Wales lost a remarkable national figure and Welsh education a fearless and prophetic advocate when Professor Jac L. Williams died. The loss, even today, is agonizing.

2
JAC L. WILLIAMS AND BILINGUALISM
J. E. Caerwyn Williams

Introduction

I do not remember when I first met the late Professor Jac L. Williams but we seem to have established a close rapport and firm friendship from the beginning. It was characteristic of our relationship that one of our earliest conversations revolved round the question of which of us had the most thoroughly Welsh background. He was the son of a farming family in the district of Aber-arth in mid-west Wales. I was the son of a coalminer who had come from the village of Groeslon a few miles west of Caernarfon in north-west Wales to find work in south Wales, to marry a girl from Cwmllynfell, and to settle in Gwaun Cae Gurwen where I was born. Most of the people there were Welsh-speaking although many were not monoglot Welsh. I still remember my bewilderment when I first went to school to find as my teacher a relative of my mother's who would not allow me to speak Welsh to her although previously we had never spoken anything but Welsh to each other. One of the arguments I put forward in support of my greater Welshness was that I had been brought up as a Calvinistic Methodist whereas JLW had been brought up as a member of the Church in Wales! On the Waun, as we used say, for a Welshman to be attached to the Church in Wales had to mean a degree of Anglicization. Of course, JLW would have none of this, and I have to admit he was Welsh through and through; his *cynefin*, his home-background, was much more part and parcel of him than mine ever was. I believe that even had he tried to separate the language he spoke from the scenes of his childhood and his memory of them, he could not have succeeded. It is significant that one of his early articles was on 'Rhai o eiriau'r clos a'r buarth' (Williams 1948–50), and it is this inextricable bond between his language and his home-background which provides the key to his success as a short-story writer. It will be remembered that he himself published two volumes of short stories, *Straeon y Meirw* (1947) and *Trioedd* (1973) and that a third, *Straeon Jac L.* (1981), was published after his death. Indeed, his interest in Welsh literature was so deep that he edited a series of pamphlets entitled 'Cyfres Pamffledi Llenyddol Cyfadran Addysg Aberystwyth' ('The Literary Pamphlets Series of the Faculty of Education, University College of Wales, Aberystwyth').

Our argument regarding the comparative degrees of our Welshness was not incidental. It sprang from the importance we both attached to language and to our native language in particular. I have had occasion to quote the words of Leonard Bloomfield and Whitney before, and I would not be surprised to learn that I had quoted their gist in conversation with JLW. I am sure that, like myself, he would have subscribed to them wholeheartedly. Here are Bloomfield's words (1935): 'Each community is formed by the activity of language: speech utterances give us the most direct insight and play a part in everything that is done. In order to observe a group, we must understand its language.' These are Whitney's: 'Every single language has ... its own peculiar framework of established distinctions, its (own) shapes and forms of thought, into which, for the human being who learns the language as his "mother tongue" is cast the content and product of his own mind, his store of impressions, however acquired, his experience and knowledge of the world.' Had we been called to express these thoughts in our own words, we would in all probability have framed them in words more like those of Wilhelm von Humboldt to the effect that the language of a people is its soul, and its soul its language – that is, in more romantic terms. I do not know whether JLW would have become a disciple of J. L. Weisgerber in such books as *Von den Kräften der deutschen Sprache*, Bd. 1 *Grundzüge der inhaltsbezogenen Grammatik* (Düsseldorf, 1962). I must confess that I have found Weisgerber's thesis very attractive.

I need not expatiate further on the point that JLW and I shared to a very considerable extent the view that language is most important in all sorts of ways, but I have to add that what made him a remarkable professor of education in my eyes was the fact that he was the only professor of education of my acquaintance who attached such importance to language, and was in consequence convinced of the supreme value of the Welsh language to the Welsh people. What is still more remarkable, perhaps, is that JLW had an unshakeable faith in the ability of the educational process not only to halt the decline of the Welsh language but also to promote it so as to help it to regain some of the ground it had lost.

Parenthetically, I may perhaps be allowed to observe that JLW and I had tremendous faith in education, and that in this we were children of our time. I have a feeling that in spite of all the talking and writing about education these days, we are not discussing the education we used to discuss years ago. The emphasis nowadays is on vocational skills, on adapting to the needs of the new age, whereas it used to be on preparation for life, for a life of better quality. No doubt we were naïve. Our belief in the power of education was probably coloured by the equally naïve belief, then current, in the inevitability of progress and the perfectability of human nature.

Bilingualism and monolingualism

The other feature in JLW as professor of education which attracted me and many of my contemporaries to him was his profound interest in bilingualism, an interest so profound and practical that he came to be regarded as an international expert on the subject. A glance at his bibliography which is listed in this volume will show the extent of his interest. It was he more than any one else who promoted the publication of the two volumes *Llyfryddiaeth dwyieitheg / Bilingualism: a bibliography with special reference to Wales* and *Bilingualism / Dwyieitheg: a bibliography of 1000 references with special reference to Wales*. It was he who appointed Dr R. M. Jones as a member of his staff, and unless I am mistaken he had more than a little to do with the fact that Dr Jones spent a sabbatical year studying bilingualism and more general linguistics at Québec. One of the founders of the linguistic centre there, William F. Mackey, produced the *Bibliographie internationale sur le bilingualisme / International Bibliography on bilingualism* (1972).

Bilingualism is difficult to define but it would not be wrong to say that in our youth most people in Wales thought of bilingualism in terms of the familiar 'bilingual Welshman' who had learnt English but had retained his mother tongue to use at home, in chapel and on certain cultural occasions such as the local or national eisteddfod. In other words, the 'bilingual Welshman' was, generally speaking, the

Welshman who had learnt English but had not lost his Welsh. Bilingualism is, of course, a much more complex phenomenon. When is a person truly bilingual? When he or she has achieved a facility in the use of a second language equal with that in the first? There are people who are bilingual in that sense and in the sense that they are accepted as one of their own by both groups who use one or other of the two languages. But that is an ideal bilingualism. Most bilinguals have a preferred language. Some understand a second language but never use it; others use it occasionally or in certain circumstances or when forced to do so. Many have been bilingual at one stage of their lives but have forgotten one of their two languages. We know that the first language learned by a child is not necessarily that of the mother but quite often that of the servants or other persons who are in close contact with it.

Bilingualism should be studied side by side with monolingualism. Who are the true monoglots? According to André Martinet (1964, 159), they are the 'people who in all their linguistic communications never bring into play more than one set of [linguistic] habits, who always use the same phonological structure, the same morphology, the same syntax and even the same vocabulary'. In Wales there are people who speak the Welsh of south Wales but insist that they cannot understand the Welsh of north Walians. Is the person who can switch from north-Welsh to south-Welsh, monoglot or bilingual? No single person can be said to have mastered his or her own language to perfection. No two people speak the same language in exactly the same way. There are differences of pronunciation, of syntax and vocabulary. There are professional differences: we speak in Wales of *Cymraeg y pulpud* (pulpit or preacher's Welsh). There are group variations: the Welsh of the pupils in the so-called Welsh schools differs from that of their parents and when they enter college the same pupils find that their Welsh drops certain characteristics and picks up others. In other words, there is a degree of bilingualism even within monolingualism, and it can be said that most people are bilingual if not multilingual in some sense and to a certain extent.

Bilingual Welsh people did not need to be persuaded that it was possible to learn two languages, and several advocated in the nineteenth century the possibility and the desirability of developing a bilingual Wales. One name springs immediately to mind, Daniel Isaac Davies, the author of a series of articles which appeared first in

Y Faner and were then reprinted under the title *Tair Miliwn o Gymry Dwy-ieithawg* ('Three Million Bilingual Welshmen') (1885, 1886). Davies had been an assistant inspector of schools in England and had returned to work in the same capacity in Wales. He played a prominent part in the establishment of Y Gymdeithas i Ddefnyddio'r Gymraeg, afterwards Cymdeithas yr Iaith Gymraeg (The Welsh Language Society). He and his fellow enthusiasts had probably derived great encouragement from the fact that in 1886 Welsh was first accepted as a subject to be taught in the schools of Wales and, like other officially recognized subjects, to qualify for government financial support. However, there was strong opposition to the policy advocated by Davies and others, an opposition which was probably stronger because it was based on prejudice against bilingualism on the one hand and against the Welsh language on the other.

We would need to go back as far as the time of Henry VIII to trace the origins of this prejudice, but it will suffice to say that the report completed in 1847 by the commission appointed to 'enquire into the state of education in the Principality of Wales, especially into the means afforded to the labouring classes of acquiring a knowledge of the English language' – the report better known as 'Brad y Llyfrau Gleision' (The Treachery of the Blue Books) – was symptomatic of this prejudice and contributed in no small measure to its strength. Much has been written on this report and on the public reaction to it in Wales. I need only say that it was written with the assumption that ignorance of English was synonymous with illiteracy and that most of the evils from which Welsh society suffered – and, according to the commissioners, there were many – were derived from its adherence to the Welsh language. In other words, bilingualism, especially the bilingualism of English and Welsh, should not be encouraged or even tolerated. Implicit in all this was the belief that English was superior to Welsh as a language, and for every school inspector who, like D. I. Davies, pressed the claims of Welsh to be taught, there was at least one, probably more, who, like the Revd Shadrach Pryce, HMI, preached the superiority of English, if not as the language of literature, at least as the language of science and commerce.

A great deal could be said on this point, much of which will be made explicit later. At this juncture it seems enough to quote David Crystal (1987, 7):

A belief that some languages are intrinsically superior to others is widespread, but it has no basis in linguistic fact. Some languages are of course more useful or prestigious than others, but this is due to the pre-eminence of the speakers at that time, and not to any inherent linguistic characteristics.

I would add, however, E. H. Sturtevant's remark (1961, 160):

> It is not even certain that a language tends to improve in all respects with the advancing civilisation of its speakers. In two directions, however, a progressive improvement may be observed; languages tend to become more adequate and convenient tools for the expression of thought.

As we shall see, the Welsh in modern times have been acutely aware of the paucity of their Welsh vocabulary and it is probable that as bilinguals, at least recently, they have availed themselves of the resources of English rather than develop the resources of their mother tongue. They have been sensitive to the charge that in earlier times they needed fewer words because they had fewer ideas, although it can be argued that an unusually large vocabulary does not necessarily indicate a correspondingly great number of ideas. The English dictionary is crammed with synonyms, many of which are unfamiliar to a large part of the speakers of the language. It should be pointed out that, if a link is to be made between words and ideas, the fact that the Eskimo has a number of different words for various kinds of snow, and the Arab has different words for various kinds of camel, and that both lack words for philosophical concepts, the logical deduction is not that Eskimo and Arab have fewer ideas than the Englishman and German but that their ideas are more immediately concerned with their environment and less immediately, if at all, concerned with philosophy.

As I have said, JLW was not the first Welsh educationalist to be convinced that a bilingual Wales was a practical objective. However, in his case the realization that it was practical was reinforced by the cumulative evidence that community bilingualism was more of a world phenomenon than had ever been supposed in Britain, and that the efforts to achieve or to retain bilingualism in Wales had parallels all over the world. The general opinion in Britain and western Europe until fairly recently was that community bilingualism was exceptional and this opinion was and is being fostered by governments all over the world. There are apparently between 4,000 and 5,000 languages in the world (based on discussion in Crystal 1987, 284−5) whereas there are only about 200 countries. Less than a quarter of the world's nations give official recognition to two languages and only about six recognize three or more. There must be a great deal of contact between languages and wherever there are such contacts, there is a degree of bilingualism. Apparently there are now about a hundred languages current among groups of nationals in Great Britain. In Italy there are some eleven language minorities. Under Franco the Spanish government recognized only one language, but since his death there have been calls for regional autonomy and for the recognition of the regional languages, Catalonian, Castilian and Basque.

In 1789 the French National Constituent Assembly asked l'Abbé Gregoire to prepare a report on the linguistic situation in France. He distributed a questionnaire and, on the basis of the replies received, he reported in 1794 the astonishing fact that the majority of French people especially in the countryside either understood no word of French or were unable to carry on a conversation in the language. They spoke rather German, Flemish, Breton, Basque, Provençal, Catalonian, Corsican, etc... 'trente patois différents', 'une diversité d'idiomes grossiers'. Only a minority spoke French, the 'Language of Freedom'! This diversity of languages continues to characterize France. The population of the south of France, a third of the country, does not speak official French, the language descended from the *langue d'oïl*, but rather the French descended from the *langue d'oc*, and Occitan (Provençal) poetry experienced a revival, a renaissance, in the nineteenth century. Frédéric Mistral, called the 'Homer of Provence', was awarded the Nobel Prize in 1905 for his much acclaimed narrative poem *Mirèio*.

Like English, German has borrowed extensively from other languages and it still does to the extent that dictionaries containing only loan words are published even today, such as *Knaurs Fremdwörter Lexikon*. Like English, it has borrowed many words from French. Goethe, who next to Luther has exercised most influence on the German language, described in *Dichtung und Wahrheit* (XI) how French was like a second mother tongue to him: '*Sie war mir ohne Grammatik und Unterricht, durch Umgang und Übung wie eine zweite Muttersprache zu eigen geworden.*' (I acquired it like a second mother tongue through using and practising it without grammar and instruction.) And like French, German has borrowed many words from English. But there seems no need to quote examples to prove that English, French and German are as much plurilanguages as languages. One can quote any number of words from German, such as *Phantasie, Melancholie, Poesie, Lyrik, Drama, Theater, Orchester, Musik, Rhythmus*, and ask whether they are really German, French or English words, only to find that they are all common to the three languages and are ultimately derived from Greek.

Canada's linguistic history illustrates many of the problems of community bilingualism. Since 1969 the country has had two official languages, English and French; but the latter is not *français français* any more than the former is English or British English. Actually, as Irenè de Buisseret's book (1975) shows, six European languages confront each other in Canada: British English, Canadian English, US English, Canadian French, *le français universel* and *le néo-français*. French Canadians fight, as do the French of France, desperately against the numerous Anglicisms which have found a place in their language, and one can understand why René Etiemble (1964, 1973) is afraid that the French of Voltaire and Rousseau is in danger of becoming a hybrid *franglais*, a *babélien*, a *sabir atlantique*.

English has developed into one of the great languages if not *the* great language of the world: 'English is used as an official or semi-official language in over 60 countries, and has a prominent place in a further 20. It is either dominant or well established in all six continents. It is the main language of books, newspapers, airports and air-traffic control, international business and academic conferences, science, technology, medicine, diplomacy, sports, international competitions, pop music and advertising. Over two-thirds of the world's scientists write in English. Three quarters of the world's mail is written in English' (David Crystal 1987, 358). There are, of course, more speakers of Chinese than of English but, if it is true that whereas some decades ago the book which ordinary Chinese people would carry in their pockets would be *The Thoughts of Chairman Mao*, nowadays it would be a book on elementary English. It seems likely that soon the number of English-speakers will surpass even that of Chinese-speakers! However, in expanding English has had to pay a certain price. The English spoken in the USA, Canada, Australia, New Zealand and India is not the same as British English and there is every indication the languages spoken in these countries will differ more and more from their origin. On the other hand, it does not seem likely that the 'dialects' of English will ever differ as much from each other as the dialects of Indo-European. If there are centrifugal influences these are countered by centripetal influences.

If British English has invaded the USA, Americanisms have staged a counter-invasion. And if Anglicisms are to be found in French, German, Italian and Russian, it is no less true that Gallicisms, Germanisms, etc., are to be found in English. Towards the end of the last century, E. Windisch (1897) proposed a theory concerning mixed or hybrid languages which was later endorsed by Otto Jespersen (1922, ch.ix). It turns on this formula: it is not the foreign language a nation learns that changes into a mixed language, but its own language becomes mixed under the influence of the foreign language. When we try to learn a foreign language, we are at pains not to intermix it with words taken from our own. We speak the foreign language as purely as possible. We avoid using words taken from our first language in the language we are learning. What we avoid in speaking the foreign language, we are prone to do in speaking our own. Frederick the Great prided himself on the purity of his French and never spoke a German word when speaking it. However, he was prepared to intersperse his spoken and written German with French words and phrases.

One understands why the people who learn English do their best to speak it purely and correctly, and that they have no hesitation in using English words in their native language. Indeed, some do so with panache, and if a substantial number of them do so, they reduce the status of their own language. The other day I heard a husband saying that his wife had learned Welsh well, except that she had not learned when to use English words instead of the Welsh words in conversation! However, when a Welsh person uses a great number of English words in Welsh he or she realizes that this is not good Welsh and, rather than speak 'bad' or 'poor' Welsh, will be tempted to abandon it altogether.

The theory proposed by Windisch and Jespersen was not designed to explain the rise of English to the status of a world language and it is clearly inadequate for that purpose, for far more factors are involved than in the process of learning English; but perhaps at the risk of oversimplification and of missing other motives of importance, we can note two factors in the creation of mixed languages, the 'prestige motive' and the 'need-filling motive'. When speakers of two different languages live together in one region, usually one of the languages is spoken by those in power and comes to be regarded as the upper or dominant language while the other is regarded as the lower or subservient language. In this state of affairs, the prestige factor will lead to extensive borrowing from the dominant into the subservient language. The other obvious motive is the need to fill a gap in the borrowing language. When speakers of a certain language are confronted with an object or a phenomenon they have never seen before they will tend to accept its name from those to whom it is familiar and is already known by that name. Note the way English-speakers have borrowed such words as *sputnik* from Russian and *typhoon* from Chinese.

Even before it became a world language English was a hybrid language. Bradley (1904) was prepared to call it 'mixed' in comparison with the comparatively 'pure' German language, although the latter is far from pure, and we can understand his reason. Both are Teutonic languages but English has borrowed so extensively French words and either directly or indirectly through French so many Latin words, that it has almost become a Romance language. The close relationship between English and French is particularly noteworthy. Under the Norman and Angevin kings there was a considerable influx of French people into England. French became the language of the court and the nobility, and all those who aspired to high social status had to learn French. It would seem that in the thirteenth century many of the population must have been bilingual, and, during the thirteenth, fourteenth and fifteenth centuries, there was a large accession of French words, some of which can be traced to the northern dialect, the speech of Normandy and Picardy, others to the speech of central France. Many of the learned words borrowed from French had been taken from Latin, and these served as a pattern after which Latin words could be Anglicized directly from Latin, especially during the period of the Renaissance. During the more recent past English has tended to borrow French words in their French form, and notably in those areas of life where the French are admired or deemed to be more advanced, such as gastronomy: *cuisine, chef, maître d'hôtel, hors-d'œuvre, entrée*; fashion: *toilette, couture, haute couture, mannequin, chic*; games, entertainment, art and literature: *roulette, baccara, parterre, parquet, logo, foyer, aquarelle, gouache, chef d'orchestre, bâton, nom de plume, monologue interieur*; society: *le beau monde, homme du monde*, etc. In the same way, French has taken many words from English and American English in the field of social institutions: *le jury, le verdict, le vote;* sports: *la boxe, le ring, le round, le punch, le hockey*; leisure activities: *le meeting, caravaning, camping, le music-hall, le festival, le fox-trot*, etc.

The development of Welsh vocabulary

Living side by side with English-speakers it is no wonder that Welsh-speakers at a very early stage in their history became aware of the fact that their language lacked the rich vocabulary of their near neighbours' language. This section will consider the development in past centuries of new words in the Welsh language through its historical association with the English language and, particularly, through the production of Welsh–English dictionaries. I will then proceed to discuss the response to the challenges of the twentieth century by the development of a new technical vocabulary.

The early Welsh humanist William Salesbury in his *Oll Synnwyr Pen Kembero Ygyd* (1547) urged his fellow Welshmen to demand that the new learning should be accessible to them in the Welsh language unless they wished to become animals without the gift of understanding given to man. Gruffydd Robert, author of *Dosparth Byrr ar y rhann gyntaf i ramadeg Cymraeg* (1567), realized that the new learning could not find expression in the Welsh language without a considerable expansion in its vocabulary. He urged Welsh writers to follow the example of authors in other countries and to borrow words from other languages, in the first instance from Latin if it was possible to give them a Welsh form without trouble, but, if this was difficult, to borrow from Italian, French and Spanish, and not to neglect English words if they had already found a place in the Welsh language.

Gruffydd Robert's words were addressed primarily to Welsh prose writers. He was rather dismissive of the Welsh poets and one can imagine that they would not have welcomed his words for they had no quarrel with the Welsh language as it was. Indeed, Morris Kyffin in his address to the reader in his *Deffiniad Ffydd Eglwys Loegr* (1593) refers to that class of vacuous people who inspect a few words here and there and say immediately that these are English and Latin words corrupting the Welsh. He adds that such people know little, they have seen less, and it is useless to talk of teaching them. The *Cywyddau* exchanged in the contention between Wiliam Cynwal and Edmwnd Prys illustrate the ideological clash between the protagonists of the old and the new learning. Cynwal is content with the traditional culture of the Welsh bards. He has mastered it and can rightly claim to be a poet. Despite his mastery of the new learning, Prys, according to Cynwal, is not a poet at all. Prys, on the other hand, argues that Cynwal, like every other Welsh poet, needs to embrace the new learning.

The translation of the Bible into Welsh and other achievements in Welsh prose, Welsh grammar and lexicography, are monuments to the success of the humanists in one field, but they had very little influence on Welsh poetry, and as Thomas Parry (1955, 216–17) has said, 'that is the great disaster of our literature in the seventeenth and eighteenth centuries'.

During those centuries any criticism of the Welsh language was taken as criticism of themselves by the Welsh people, and they devoted much effort to demonstrating its copiousness and to proving its superiority in at least one respect over English, its purity. Whereas English had borrowed and was borrowing extensively from other languages, Welsh was making use of its wealth of prefixes and suffixes to coin the new words it needed. All this can be traced in the Welsh dictionaries which were compiled. The title of one of them is indicative, *Y Gymraeg yn ei Disgleirdeb* (1688), 'Welsh in its glory'. However, the lexicographers were aware that the Welsh people were not exploiting the resources of its languages as they should. Recommending Dr John Davies's *Dictionarium Duplex* to the printer John Beale in 1629, Bishop Lewis Bayly said that it was a work 'which all our Welsh preachers so much want . . . it is work that hath long been desired'. And Lewis Morris was acutely aware that Welsh was lagging behind English and that the process of coining words should be expedited at all costs. Writing to his brother William in 1755 (J. H. Davies 1907, 347), he tells him:

> You must make your *cregyn* (shells) Welsh names if they have none. You may give them names in Welsh. I'll send you a catalogue of ye English names of some sales here . . . and it is an easy matter to invent new names, and I warrant you they will be as well received as Latin and Greek names. Tell them they are old Celtic names, that is enough. They'll sound as well as German or Indian names and better . . .

In his 'Dissertation on the Welsh Language, etc.' first published in 1771 and then attached to his *An English and Welsh Dictionary* (1770–1794), the Revd John Walters says (p. 9) that 'nothing can be more derogatory to a language than a paucity of words, and a scantiness of expressions'; he observes (p. 9):

> The English language indeed, as it appears in it's modern garb, discovers nothing of it's orginal meanness and pristine nakedness; so far from this, that it exhibits at present a very specious figure; but it hath learned the art to make itself thus fine with the spoils of other languages, i.e. of the *Greek, Latin, Italian, French*, etc...

On the other hand (p. 10),

> In respect of synonymous primitives the *Cambro-British language* is rivaled by few, but excelled by none except it be the *Arabic* ...

and (p. 11),

> The *Cambro-British* compounds and decompounds have always been, and ever will be, the admiration of all that are acquainted with the language: for here we may observe *two, three, four, five* and sometimes *six* words coalesce so naturally, through the change of initials, as to produce harmoniousness of sound, as well as expressiveness of sense.

It is no wonder that Walters rebuts in his 'Preface' (p. xii) the charge that his dictionary 'hath a tendency to revive the WELSH Language' and proudly proclaims (p. xii):

> If the native charms and intrinsic excellence – if the *antiquity, copiousness* and *grammatical* perfection, of a Language can have weight and authority sufficient to recommend it, the *Antient-British* will long be studied, and long admired ...

He adds (p. xiii):

> that the *Work* is as well calculated for propagating and extending the *English* Language in *WALES* as for assisting the *Learned* of either Country in acquiring a critical skill in the *Welsh*.

Walters's real objective seems to have been to teach the Welsh how to translate English idioms into their own language but in the process he coined many Welsh words, several of which have been adopted into the language.

Some time was to elapse before the Revd D. Silvan Evans published *An English and Welsh Dictionary*, the first part in 1852 and the second together with the first in 1858. By this time Britain had entered on a period (1815–1914) of relative peace when her industries flourished, her empire expanded and her navy safeguarded her interests throughout the world. The English language shared the prestige of the British Empire, a prestige far greater than Welsh could ever hope for. This can be discerned in Silvan Evans's brief Preface. He shared many of his predecessors' convictions that the Welsh language 'is one of those comparatively few languages capable of furnishing from native roots a complete terminology, for all the varied branches of human learning'. However, he admits that it has not 'kept pace with one of the most copious of modern European tongues' – that is, English – for his aim is 'to represent by Welsh equivalents all the authorized words and the principal idioms of which English is composed'. To achieve this object he has had to coin many new Welsh terms 'especially those relating to science and art', and he is encouraged that not a few of those terms 'have already passed into our literature where they are likely to maintain their ground'.

Silvan Evans acknowledged his debt to the labours of the Revd John Walters and Dr William Owen-Pughe whose *A Welsh–English Dictionary* had appeared in 1803 in two parts together with a Welsh grammar; the first part had appeared in 1793. Unfortunately, Owen-Pughe was influenced, like many of his contemporaries, by the belief that the Welsh language was closely related to the original language of mankind and that the meanings of the primitive elements could be found by studying it. Moreover, he was prepared to adapt those meanings as well as to coin new words in accordance with that belief. It would have been difficult for D. Silvan Evans to escape the influence of Owen-Pughe, for that influence was widespread and provides the reason why some of his own verbal coinages were accepted for a time, but that influence was unhealthy in so far as it tended to make an artificial language far removed from the spoken language. One of the achievements of the so-called twentieth-century renaissance in Welsh literature and scholarship was the rejection of Owen-Pughe's misguided theory and its baneful influence on Welsh literature, although that renaissance itself can be criticized for its excessive purism and for its support for a literary language too conservative in idiom and too dilettante in taste. In retrospect we can see that although a number of D. Silvan Evans's coinages were accepted for a time, many failed to find a permanent home in the language.

With the new-born Welsh nationalism of the twentieth century there came greater confidence in the Welsh language and greater aggressiveness on the part of its protagonists. The most tangible signs of this were the establishment first of the so-called Welsh schools and then of the Welsh secondary schools, and a new demand that other subjects in the school curriculum should be taught through the medium of the Welsh language. For this teaching to be successful new technical terms had to be coined. Indeed, it can be said that an unprecedented number of new Welsh words have been coined during the twentieth century and that Professor Jac L. Williams played a pivotal part in the process.

As editor of *Geiriadur Termau/Dictionary of Terms* (published on behalf of the University of Wales School of Education, Cardiff, 1973), Professor Williams described in some detail how the *Geiriadur* came into existence. It is based for the most part on lists of terms, such as *Termau Addysg* (Education) and *Termau Daearyddiaeth* (Geography). These lists were prepared in the first instance by Vocabulary Committees set up by the Faculty of Education of the University of Wales, Aberystwyth, and were then revised, extended and completed by Translation Committees appointed by the University of Wales School of Education and meeting under my chairmanship. It would be pointless for me to repeat Professor Williams's description here although the part played by him as the initiator and driving force behind both the Vocabulary Committees and the Translation Committees needs to be emphasized. However, as Chairman of the Translation Committee for some twelve years, I had occasion to observe those processes whereby the new terms were coined and I believe that it will serve a useful purpose if I indicated briefly the main ones.

1. A specialized sense was given to some words rather than the generalized sense. Thus the teachers of physics in schools required three words for what they termed 'force', 'power', and 'energy', and they accepted that they could use *grym* as the Welsh equivalent of 'force', *nerth* as the equivalent of 'power', and *egni* as the equivalent of 'energy'.

2. When two English words denote the same thing for the layman but two different things for the specialist, it was agreed that two different terms could be used in Welsh and that sometimes it would

be helpful to bring back into use a word fallen into disuse; for example: *cyflymder* (velocity) and *buanedd* (speed). It was possible to develop the meanings of *cyflymder* to get *cyflymu* (to accelerate), *cyflymiad* (acceleration) and *cyflymiadur* (accelerator).

3. New words could be made by forming new compounds; for example: *ceugrwm* (concave), from *cau* and *crwm*; *amgrwm* (convex), from *am* and *crwm*; and *llorwedd* (horizontal), from *llawr* and *gwedd*.

4. New terms could be formed from the words by using one of the many prefixes found in the language, such as *am-, ad-, ar-,* etc.; for example: *amsugno* (absorb), *am + sugno*; *arsugno* (adsorb), *ar + sugno*; *hydraidd* (pervious), *hy + traidd*; *athraidd* (permeable), Brit.**ad + traidd*.

5. There was no fundamental objection to using an element not recognized as a prefix in the grammar books and dictionaries; for example: *esblygiad* (evolution), cf. *esboniad* and *esmwyth*; *endorri*, *engrafu*, cf. *en-* in *enwaedu*.

6. It was possible to use one of the many suffixes in the language to good effect; for example: *-ig in elfennig* (elemental) to distinguish between it and *elfennol* (elementary); *-us* in *bodlonus* (complacent) to distinguish between it and *bodlon* (satisfied); and *-edd* in *pwysedd* (pressure), etc.

7. It was possible to imitate the processes illustrated in Welsh borrowings from Latin; for example: *-duct-, -dwyth-* in *diddwythiad* (deduction), *anwythiad* (induction) (but why not *annwythiad*?); and *-dens-, -dwys-,* in *cyddwysedd* (condensation), *cyddwyso* (to condense).

8. Again it was possible to imitate the processes illustrated in Welsh borrowings from English; for example: *-age, -ais* in *mantais* ((ad-)vantage), *bandais* (bandage).

9. The meaning of the English word could be conveyed through compounding Welsh elements; for example: *dargludo* (conduct), *dargludiant* (conductance), *dargludiad* (conduction).

10. A Latin or Greek word could be accepted in Welsh as it had been in English: for example, *cerebrum, clitellum*. (It was objected that the 'll' would be pronounced as a Welsh 'll', but it is obvious that Latin and Greek words borrowed into English are not pronounced as the Romans and the Greeks pronounced them.)

11. English words in some cases could be borrowed:
(a) in the original form: e.g. oasis, marl;

(b) by changing the orthography: e.g. *cwadrant* (quadrant);
(c) by substituting a Welsh for an English suffix: e.g., *secwndaidd* (secondary);
(d) by substituting a Welsh for an English prefix: *annhehiscent* (indehiscent).

Most of the procedures adopted by the Vocabulary and Translation Committees, and the above are but a few, are procedures in evidence in the development of other languages and can be justified on the grounds of analogy in the development of the Welsh language itself. Moreover, notwithstanding all the talk about the 'laws' governing the development of languages, there is a large element of arbitrariness, even of capriciousness in that development. For example, Latin *ca-* became *chie-, che-, cha-*, in French: *caput* – *chief, chef*; *canis* – *chien, capra* – *chèvre*, etc. However, there are numerous instances of the retention of *ca-*; for example: *cas, case, cage, caverne*. These exceptions can, of course, be explained. German has adopted more than one suffix from French; for example: *-ieren, -ie, -ei, -lei*. *-Lei* is derived from Old French *a lei de* 'according to, in the way of' (Latin, *ea lege*), and it has been quite a productive ending: *einerlei* 'of one sort; one and the same; all the same; sameness, monotony'; cf. *allerlei, keinerlei, zweierlei, beiderlei*, etc.

Members of the two committees soon learned that their lists had only temporary value. As the syllabuses changed, so did some items in the vocabulary required. The list provided for the teachers of geography was found inadequate within a short time and a second list had to be compiled. It was also found that the Welsh equivalent of a certain English technical term used by the teachers of two disciplines, for example mathematics and physics, would find favour with the teachers of one of these disciplines and be rejected by the teachers of the other. However, there was satisfaction when some terms found favour with the general public, for example *sylwebydd* (commentator), and *sylwebu* (to comment on (a game)).

Geiriadur Termau was welcomed by teachers and many sections of the public and has been reprinted several times. However, it is hardly a *geiriadur*, a dictionary, in the proper sense of the word, and if it demonstrates anything it demonstrates that the Welsh language needs new lexicographers for each generation just as English does. Every language changes in the course of time. We all know that the speed with which the world changes has increased tremendously in our time and perhaps it is a fair deduction that the main languages of the world have to change at least lexically more speedily than they ever did before. A comparison of D. Silvan Evans's *English – Welsh Dictionary* with John Walters's *An English – Welsh Dictionary* shows great changes in the vocabulary of the English language even in the short interval between their publication dates. For the verb *communicate* D. Silvan Evans gives:

cyfranu, cyfranogi, cydgyfranu, rhanu, rhoddi; mynegu, dadguddio, amlygu, hysbysu; gwneuthur yn gyfranog; gwneuthur yn gydnabyddus; cymuno, derbyn y cymun; bod yn gyfranog o'r cymun; cyfroddi; bod yn gyfranog; bod yn cydgyfranu; cydio, ymgydio; bod yn gyssylltedig, yn cydio, yn gyfun, yn nghyd neu yn ymgyffwrdd; yn cystlynu, cyfathrachu, cyweithasu; cyffredino.

Despite the 'copiousness' of Silvan Evans's Welsh entries they lack a suitable equivalent to the modern English 'buzz' word, 'to communicate'. *Geiriadur Termau* gives simply *'cyfathrebu'* (made from *cyf-, -athr-* and *(h)ebu*), and as far as I can judge it is filling a definite need. Fortunately, it is only one of the many examples that are doing so. Happily, the process of coining new Welsh terms as the need arises, goes on, and it is well for us to remember that the late Professor Jac L. Williams did much to convince us of the need for it and to encourage us to embark on it.

References

Bloomfield, Leonard (1935). *Language* (London, George Allen and Unwin Ltd).
Bradley, H. (1904). *The Making of English* (London, Macmillan).
Buisseret, Irenè de (1975). *Deux langues, six idiomes* (Ottawa, Carlton-Green).
Crystal, David (1987). *The Cambridge Encyclopedia of Language* (Cambridge, Cambridge University Press).
Davies, J. H. (ed.) (1907). *The Letters of Lewis, Richard, William and John Morris (Morrisiaid Môn) 1728–1765*, Vol. 1 (Aberystwyth, the editor).
Etiemble, René (1964, 1973). *Parlez-vous Franglais?* (Paris, Gallimard).
Jespersen, Otto (1922). *Language, Its Nature, Development and Origin* (London, Allen and Unwin).
André Martinet (1964). *Elements of General Linguistics* (London, Faber and Faber Ltd). English translation by Elisabeth Palmer of *Éléments de linguistique Générale* (Paris, Armand Colin, 1960).
Parry, Thomas (1955). *A History of Welsh Literature*, translated from the Welsh by Idris Bell (Oxford, Clarendon).

Sturtevant, E. H. (1961). *Linguistic Change: An Introduction to the Historical Study of Language* (Chicago, Chicago University Press).
Weisgerber, J. L. (1962). *Von den Kräften der deutschen Sprache, Bd. 1 Grundzüge der inhaltsbezogenen Grammatik*, 3rd ed. (Düsseldorf, Pädagogischer Verlag Schwann).
Williams, Jac L. (1948–50). 'Rhai o eiriau'r clôs a'r buarth', *The Bulletin of the Board of Celtic Studies*, 13, 138–41.
Windisch, Ernst (1897). *Zur Theorie der Mischsprachen und Lehnwörter*. Berichte über die Verhandl. d. sächs. Gesellesch. d. Wissensch. XLIX, 101ff.

II

Bilingualism in Wales

3

QUESTIONS CONCERNING THE DEVELOPMENT OF BILINGUAL WALES

Colin H. Williams

> Cymru a wybu obaith o'i hagor
> Mewn Seisnigaidd dalaith
> Daw i fri trwy adfer iaith
> A gweini uwch gwae heniaith.
>
> W. R. Evans, 'Yr Ysgol Gymraeg', 1983.

This poem was written by my former headmaster, W. R. Evans of Ysgol Gymraeg San Ffransis, Y Barri, to celebrate the development of Welsh-medium schools in Anglicized areas. Such schools represent a major post-war development in the creation of a new generation of Welsh-speakers. But they also epitomize the fragmentation of the bilingual community, because these schools often form the only significant domain within which a predominantly Welsh-medium experience could be gained outside the heartland area. Bilingualism in such areas has been a fragile if growing phenomenon, yet now at last we are on the threshold of constructing a fully functional bilingual society for the whole of Wales. In this chapter I want to raise a series of questions about how this transition came about, and to tease out the implications of a fascinating dualism whereby a declining *heartland* and a resurgent *periphery* contribute to the *core* of contemporary Welsh cultural and social life.

This is a period of profound social change in Wales as elsewhere in Europe. New opportunities exist for the expression of both traditional and novel forms of popular and élite culture, art, literature, sport, entertainment and politics. There is an open, questioning attitude to long-established modes of behaviour, of political power, of social control and of civic authority. Nothing is sacred, all is to be negotiated and evaluated, criticized and dissected. Radical approaches to issues such as local government reform, health care delivery, educational provision and legal aid all dominate our daily discussion as the structures of the post-modern society are scrutinized yet again. The content of this civic dialogue is very reminiscent of the mid- to late sixties, but its context is vastly different. In the sixties it was the unrepresentative nature of civil society which was being challenged, because the state was deemed to be supporting an outmoded class system. By contrast, today's radicalism stems less from optimistic social engineering and more from an acute fear of losing control. Its origin is top-down rather than bottom-up, and its rationale is cost-efficiency not social emancipation. It is an élite radicalism which adopts a mechanistic view of human relations and dances to the tune of the unfettered market of global capitalism in order to cope with the exigencies of an unpredictable world order.

In many ways this recharged radicalism is a logical reaction to the demise of the Cold War and the establishment of a new world order under American hegemonic control (C. H. Williams 1993a). Its intellectual origins lie in the classic emergence of the scientific-bureaucratic élite as the guiding force in modern democracy and economic expansion. After two generations of attempting to expand the role of the state in daily life in order to achieve political and social integration, a subsection of the controlling élite is now committed to transposing the many functions of the state into semi-state or private agencies, all in the name of democratizing and empowering civil-state relations. 'Rolling back the arm of the state' so as to privatize social relations once again is the dominant paradigm. And yet in certain significant respects, the actions, as opposed to the rhetoric, of this prevailing ideology, run counter to such characterizations.

One expression of such ambiguity lies in the field of bilingualism. Unlike many other facets of society of late, it has become an increasingly centrally planned and publicly financed element of Welsh life. This essay will seek to highlight some of the implications of this new dependency.

The structure of bilingual Wales

Wales is a plural society characterized by a unilingual majority and a bilingual minority. In comparative multilingual terms, it is a very simple society with fairly stable social conditions and only moderate degrees of social tension and economic differentiation. To an outsider, Wales's principal social characteristic is the survival of a distinct culture within a specific environment. In most writings upon Wales it is the non-English aspect of the people and the land which is emphasized. Nevertheless, the dominant tendency has been to increase the similarity of social life and cultural practice between the constituent regions of the United Kingdom. For many Welsh people their daily round is hardly distinguishable from that of fellow citizens elsewhere in the kingdom. But for those who are bi- or multi-lingual there is an extra *frisson* to life which at times is enrapturing and at others downright uncomfortable.

However, over this century, both the nature and context of Welsh bilingualism has changed immensely. At the beginning of the century bilingualism was a functional necessity for the 648,919 who spoke Welsh because English was becoming pervasive and advantageous in most spheres of life. The vast majority were descendants of predominantly Welsh speakers. But some were the children of non-Welsh migrants who had been attracted to the resource-rich coalfields, and had been socialized within the multilingual *mélange* of the industrial crucible and had learned Welsh *en passant*. Bilingualism was not just a one-way process of English second-language acquisition then as now. Many more were the children of slate quarry workers in north Wales, an area which did not receive the vast immigration flows of the coalfields, and thereby inhabited a predominantly Welsh environment. In both cases different means of acquiring bilingual abilities were determined by local exigencies. By today, bilingualism represents more of a social choice for some 590,800 individuals, who switch language by domain, by interlocutor and by whim as the spirit wills. Generating hard and fast rules about the social use of language in Wales is a difficult task, but we have more than enough evidence to suggest the general parameters of language use today. Additional information is a secondary not a primary issue. Our chief problem as a society is in realizing the optimum conditions wherein a genuine free choice of languages may be exercised in all domains of social life.

Successive inter-censal decline has been the marked feature of census evidence on Welsh-speakers since 1911, when 977,400 persons were returned as able to speak Welsh, 190,300 of whom were monoglots. Since this peak of language intensity the number of

Welsh-speakers has consistently declined, to reach its present low of 590,600, hardly any of whom are adult monoglots. In proportional terms this represents a decline from 43.5 per cent of the total Welsh population in 1911 to only 18.7 per cent in 1991, a loss of 24.8 per cent. Various explanations have been advanced for both the absolute and the relative rate of decline, with particular attention having been focused on the inter-war period when stigmatization, a collapse in confidence and Depression-induced out-migration created widespread language shift. The period 1921 – 39 is often conceived as the crisis turning point for Welsh. A generation was denied the opportunity to learn Welsh, reflecting both parental rejection of the language and an unresponsive school system. This powerful combination of forces reflected the apogee of imperial British values and attitudes, and deemed that Welsh was irrelevant in a modernizing world order. Since the Second World War the rate of decline has been more moderate, reflecting the already emasculated levels of Welsh fluency (C. H. Williams 1980).

However, this apparently uneven rate of decline may be more spurious than real. The late David Sopher has suggested an alternative method of calculating trends in language decline which provides a different interpretation of the rate of language shift and loss. His method involves the logistic transformation of Welsh-speakers being plotted on a semi-logit base (for Indian examples of the method see Sopher 1974, 1980). This shows that a straight line passing through the value for Welsh-speakers in 1901 (50%), 1981 or 1991 (19%) also passes through 1951 (29%). This means that the overall rate of decline in the past four decades (1951 – 1991) is the same as that in the previous half-century (1901 – 51). Using this method, rather than the precentage decrease alone,

> we obtain a 42% decrease in Welsh-speaking in the first period (i.e. 1901 – 1951), and a 34.5% decrease in the shorter second one. Taking them as annually compounding rates, we have an annual decline of 0.0704% in the first period, rising to 1.4% in the second. But the change in English monolingualism shows a different story by the same method. Going from 50% to 71% to 81%, the respective percentage increases are 42% and 14% i.e. annual rates of .704% and .441%. Computing temporal disparity as the logit difference, we get − .389% as the 1951/1901 disparity in Welsh-speaking i.e. an annual disparity of − .008. The 1981/1951 disparity in Welsh-speaking is − .241, i.e. an annual disparity of − .008, the same as in the previous period. (Sopher 1983)

The most significant element of language decline has been the collapse of the monolingual population. Table 1 demonstrates that the monolingual reservoir of Welsh speech had all but disappeared in the period 1921–1981 (C. H. Williams, 1985). Linguistic purists would remind us that this could spell the eventual demise of the language, for without an independent pool of monolinguals no separate autonomous Welsh culture would exist. So much of popular culture is heavily tinted by fluency in, and exposure to English, that inevitably Welsh runs the risk of becoming a dependent translated mediation of global English. I do not accept this rather pessimistic position, but do recognize that the elimination of the monolingual Welsh element is a key structural factor and should not be underplayed nor forgotten.

Although it is an obvious statement, the fact that all Welsh-speakers are bilinguals does change the social-psychological context of language reproduction in Wales, for unlike many other examples of diglossic societies, individual and societal bilingualism does not vary tremendously. In that respect, the bilingual population is fairly stable, predictable and likely to grow. An optimistic reading of the 1991 census data suggests that there have been significant increases in the three to fifteen age group, a consolidation of the sixteen to forty-four age group and an expected decline in the two older age groups (see Table 2). If these trends are maintained in successive decades then clearly the demographic future of Welsh is brighter than at any other time in recent history. Much will depend upon how local districts implement current reforms and how strong will be the functional motivation of future generations to exercise their language power.

Despite this national growth there are still significant spatial variations in the degree of Welsh fluency as revealed in Table 3. We see here the effect of Gwynedd's commitment to providing a local bilingual public service which maintains its high proportion of Welsh-speakers, despite having lower proportions of Welsh-born citizens than most other Welsh counties. By contrast Mid Glamorgan has the highest proportion of Welsh-born residents but one of the lowest rates of language transmission, despite its pioneering commitment to formal bilingual education. The infrastructure and demographic mass of the industrial south are not yet conducive to the realization of bilingualism as a social norm.

If we break down language fluency by county, we see even more

Table 1: Proportion of population speaking Welsh, by county, 1921–1981

	Percentage of all persons speaking Welsh							Percentage of all persons speaking Welsh only						
	1921	1931	1951	1961	1971	1981		1921	1931	1951	1961	1971	1981
Wales	37.1	36.8	28.9	26.0	20.8	18.9		6.3	4.0	1.7	1.0	1.3	0.8
Counties													
Clwyd	41.7	41.3	30.2	27.3	21.4	18.7		5.8	3.4	1.3	0.8	1.4	0.8
Dyfed	67.8	69.1	63.3	60.1	52.5	46.3		15.3	9.6	4.1	2.4	2.4	1.6
Gwent	5.0	4.7	2.8	2.9	1.9	2.5		0.2	0.1	0.1	0.2	0.1	0.1
Gwynedd	78.7	82.5	74.2	71.4	64.7	61.2		28.1	22.1	9.1	5.2	4.9	2.6
Mid Glamorgan	38.4	37.1	22.8	18.5	10.5	8.4		2.3	0.8	0.3	0.4	0.8	0.5
Powys	35.1	34.6	29.6	27.8	23.7	20.2		6.1	3.9	1.6	0.9	1.0	0.9
S. Glamorgan	6.3	6.1	4.7	5.2	5.0	5.8		0.2	0.1	0.1	0.1	0.4	0.2
W. Glamorgan	41.3	40.5	31.6	27.5	20.3	16.4		3.6	1.3	0.5	0.5	1.0	0.8

Source: Census 1981 *Welsh Language in Wales*, table 4, p. 50.

Table 2: Welsh-speakers, 3–15 years

County	Percentage of age group able to speak Welsh 1981	1991	Numbers able to speak Welsh 1981	1991	% Change 1981–1991
Clwyd	18.6	27.9	13796	18167	31.7
Dyfed	40.3	47.7	23163	25811	11.4
Gwent	2.3	4.8	1921	3490	81.1
Gwynedd	69.3	77.6	28785	27889	−3.1
Mid Glam.	8.6	16.1	8906	14604	64.0
Powys	16.7	30.0	3284	5463	66.4
S. Glam.	7.4	11.9	5152	7690	49.3
W. Glam.	9.3	15.0	6064	8719	43.8

Source: Aitchison J. and Carter, H., 1993.

revealing variations. The ability to write in Welsh is, as might be expected, the least proficient skill in all counties. But the magnitude of the disparity between each of the three functions of speaking, reading and writing suggests the degree to which citizens have recourse and reinforcement to exercise each skill on a routine basis (Table 4). Thus whilst Gwynedd and Dyfed have predictable, small differences between the 82 per cent of its male speakers able to write in Welsh and 84 per cent of Welsh-speaking females able to write, by contrast West Glamorgan which has a less conducive socio-cultural context reveals significant disparities. Its male Welsh-speaking population is recorded as 23,302 of whom 13,873 (59.5%) claim to be able to write in Welsh. However, the figures for females reveal less of a discrepancy, with 28,966 speaking Welsh and 18,614 (64.2%) able to write Welsh. Mid Glamorgan whose industrial history is similar to West Glamorgan has higher rates of speaking – writing comparability. Of the 18,599 males, 13,742 (73%) could write Welsh; similarly of the 24,664 females, 18,979 (76%) could write Welsh. What accounts for this disparity both between males and females, and more acutely between counties with relatively similar histories? This is particularly puzzling because both regions belonged to the county of Glamorgan before being separated in the 1974. An examination of the principles and achievements of Swansea City and Merthyr Borough Education policies over time would provide a fascinating insight into the relative value attached to

Table 3: County-level variations in Welsh fluency and Welsh-born

	Total persons M	Total persons F	Either speaks, reads or writes Welsh M	Either speaks, reads or writes Welsh F	As % total Welsh-born M	As % total Welsh-born F	% of whom born in Wales M	% of whom born in Wales F
Clwyd	195985	212105	35872	41663	30.1	33.5	84.0	83.6
Dyfed	166341	177202	70823	78990	57.0	59.7	92.1	91.6
Gwent	214931	227281	5498	6408	3.1	3.4	90.7	90.7
Gwynedd	112832	122620	66676	73805	86.7	90.3	89.7	88.9
Mid Glam.	259140	274961	23205	31447	10.0	12.8	94.7	94.9
Powys	57867	59600	11688	13167	32.5	37.0	82.8	81.8
S. Glam.	188925	203855	12417	15837	8.5	9.8	87.9	88.3
W. Glam.	174083	187345	26047	33008	17.3	20.3	95.3	95.7

Source: Census 1991, HMSO, Cardiff.

Table 4: Welsh language capacities, 1991

	Total persons M F	Welsh-speakers M F	Reads Welsh M F	Writes Welsh M F	Speaks, reads Welsh M F	Either speaks, reads & writes Welsh M F	Either speaks, reads or writes Welsh M F
Clwyd	195985 212105	33263 38142	28093 33746	24377 29144	25647 30413	23149 27547	35872 41663
Dyfed	166341 177202	68754 76244	56643 65262	50240 57939	54690 62642	49212 56544	70823 78990
Gwent	214931 227281	4774 5565	3954 4719	3046 3766	3265 3916	2827 3499	5498 6408
Gwynedd	112832 122620	65762 72651	57320 64457	54449 61029	56448 63348	53858 60380	66676 73805
Mid Glam.	259140 274961	18599 24664	18633 26069	13742 18979	14190 19455	12407 16966	23205 31447
Powys	57867 59600	10831 12040	8868 10527	7507 8978	8054 9455	7076 8419	11688 13167
S Glam.	188925 203855	10838 13703	9842 12949	81841 10738	8363 10923	7600 9982	12417 15837
W Glam.	174083 187345	23302 28966	18592 24901	13873 18614	15965 21026	12931 17212	26047 33008
Total	1370104 1464969	236123 271975	201945 242630	175418 209187	186622 221178	169060 200549	252226 294325

Source: Welsh Office, Statistical Section, 1992.

formal bilingualism by previous generations of political leaders. Indeed one might go further and argue that given its demographic base and potential for influencing the shape of a strong bilingual society in the region, Swansea and district's historical ambivalence towards Welsh-medium teaching has been one of the great disappointments of Welsh education.

More recent non-census-based social survey data (Welsh Office, 1993), provides an excellent adjunct to census data. The survey, commissioned by the Welsh Office, interviewed 19,056 households between September and December 1992. Careful sampling and stratification techniques make this the most comprehensive enquiry into the use of Welsh, after the census itself; thus its findings are significant. The survey revealed that Welsh-speakers represent 21.5 per cent of the total population (see Table 5). If we disaggregate this ability factor we find that the highest incidence is in the youngest age range three to fifteen, with 32.4 per cent of the population fluent in Welsh. The proportion drops dramatically in the age range of sixteen to twenty-nine, at 17.8 per cent, and falls further to 16.7 per cent for the next age range thirty to forty-four. The figures rise to 18.7 per cent for the age range forty-five to sixty-four and reaches 24.2 per cent for the sixty-five and over range. Clearly this bodes well for the future, but in- and out-migration, marriage patterns and a host of other reasons preclude any firm prediction that this youngest cohort will necessarily maintain such reasonable levels of fluency into adulthood. We need to know far more about first- and second-language patterns and in this respect the survey has anticipated this need by identifying 55.7 per cent of Welsh-speakers who considered Welsh to be their mother tongue. They represent 12 per cent of the national population. The school factor is evident here for only 27 per cent of the three to fifteen age range considered Welsh to be their mother tongue, and, as Table 5 reveals, each successive age cohort recorded higher proportions of mother-tongue speakers, reaching a peak of 79.3 per cent for the sixty-five and over group. This raises difficult questions of interpretation, for it may be that the quality of Welsh spoken by the youngest group is in general superior to that of the eldest group, but their language loyalty/affiliation may not prove to be as resolute in the future because Welsh represents their second language.

Further evidence on self-assessed language ability is provided by Tables 6a and 6b which indicate that 368,000 (13.4 per cent) are

Table 5: Welsh by age, 1992 (thousands)

Age category	Sample size	Population base (aged 3 and over)	No. of Welsh-speakers	Welsh-speakers as percentage of population	Mother-tongue speakers as percentage of all Welsh-speakers	Welsh-speakers as percentage of population, 1991 Census
3–15	5094	486.2	157.4	32.4	27.0	24.3
16–29	4809	517.0	91.8	17.8	48.9	15.9
30–44	5741	585.2	97.5	16.7	60.8	14.8
45–65	6674	664.4	123.7	18.7	70.7	17.4
65+	5335	498.0	120.4	24.2	79.3	22.6
Total	27653	2750.7	590.8	21.5	55.7	18.7

Source: Welsh Social Survey, 1992, Welsh Office, HMSO, Cardiff.

fluent in Welsh. A further 94,900 (3.5 per cent) described themselves as able to speak quite a lot of Welsh, and 467,300 (17.0%) described themselves as speaking only a small amount of Welsh. Thus, a total of 930,200 (33.9%) were able to speak some Welsh to varying degrees, of whom 462,900 (16.9%) were either fluent or were capable of speaking quite a lot of Welsh. These figures are far higher than the normally cited Welsh-speaking population of some 590,800 people and should prove useful as a rough guide to the potential Welsh-speaking mass for government services or consumer/audience affairs. The same caution applies to this survey as to the decennial census in that it is a self-ascribed language ability that is being reported here. Of those who claimed to be fluent, 80.5 per cent came from families where both parents spoke Welsh, 7.2 per cent from where the mother was fluent, 4.6 per cent from where the father was fluent and 7.7 per cent from families where neither parent was fluent.

When Welsh-speakers were asked to describe one statement which best represented their current use of Welsh (see Table 7), interesting county variations were revealed. Gwynedd and Dyfed, as might be expected, recorded the highest usage of Welsh at 79 per cent and 71.1 per cent respectively. Lower proportions are recorded for Powys and Clwyd at 51.5 per cent and 40.9 per cent, while West

Table 6a: Percentages of Welsh-speakers by county, 1992

Assessment	Wales	Clwyd	Dyfed	Gwent	Gwynedd	Mid Glam.	Powys	South Glam.	West Glam.
No Welsh	66.1	64.3	39.9	90.4	22.8	73.6	65.1	76.3	70.0
Little Welsh	17.0	21.3	19.8	7.7	14.2	18.9	18.7	18.5	17.9
Much Welsh	3.5	3.7	7.1	1.1	6.1	2.9	5.4	1.9	2.8
Fluent Welsh	13.4	10.7	33.2	0.8	56.8	4.7	10.8	3.3	9.4
Total	100	100	100	100	100	100	100	100	100
Sub-total									
Some Welsh	33.9	35.7	60.1	9.6	77.2	26.4	34.9	23.7	30.0
Good Welsh	16.9	14.4	40.3	1.9	6.3	7.5	16.2	5.2	12.2

Source: Welsh Social Survey, 1992, Welsh Office, HMSO, Cardiff.

Table 6b: Frequencies of Welsh-speakers by county, 1992 (in thousands)

Assessment	Wales	Clwyd	Dyfed	Gwent	Gwynedd	Mid Glam.	Powys	South Glam.	West Glam.
No Welsh	1814.0	249.2	130.0	381.7	53.3	374.6	73.9	299.0	252.3
Little Welsh	467.3	82.6	64.5	32.7	33.1	96.3	21.2	72.4	64.4
Much Welsh	94.9	14.4	23.2	4.8	14.3	14.6	6.1	7.6	10.0
Fluent Welsh	368.0	41.3	108.3	3.2	132.6	23.7	12.3	12.8	33.9
No answer	6.5	0.8	0.1	1.6	0.4	2.0	0.0	0.6	0.8
Total	2,750.7	388.3	326.1	424.0	233.7	511.2	113.7	392.4	361.4
Sub-total									
Some Welsh	930.2	138.3	196.0	40.7	180.0	134.6	39.6	92.8	108.3
Good Welsh	462.9	55.7	131.5	8.0	146.9	38.3	18.4	20.4	43.9

Source: Welsh Social Survey 1992, Welsh Office, HMSO, Cardiff.

Glamorgan and the amalgamated category of the three counties of the south-east record 32.8 per cent and 33.1 per cent respectively. Interestingly, whilst only 6.9 per cent of fluent Welsh-speakers in West Glmorgan would claim that they rarely use the language as many as 15.3 per cent in the industrial south-east found little reason/opportunity to use Welsh (Table 7).

Such surveys are important for they take us beyond the aggregate census data and probe into language usage by geographical context, age, gender and family linguistic type. It is much to be hoped that under the new regime of the Welsh Language Board more regular and detailed social surveys of Welsh, English and other languages will be commissioned, for such information is vital in the process of informing language policy in all spheres of the local state and private commercial practice.

The data suggests that context, family language transmission and exposure to formal bilingual education are key factors in language reproduction. But questions have been raised as to the 'naturalness' of some language acquisition patterns, especially if after leaving the school system many apparently fluent Welsh youngsters choose not to use Welsh to any significant degree. I believe that the 'why' question is intimately related to the 'where' question and thus wish to explore the status of the heartland as a resource base for language reproduction. Clearly by 1991 one pillar of Welsh culture, the monolingual reservoir, had disappeared. There is current concern that the second pillar, the western heartland, will also fragment irretrievably.

The heartland

The key issue is whether or not a viable Welsh culture can survive without its own autochthonous heartland as a resource-base. The dominant theme in the socio-linguistics of Welsh has been the collapse of the territorial frame of the north and west. Each change in a parish's linguistic status or threat to local cultural dominance has been lovingly charted by three generations geographers from the time of Southall (1892) to the currents specialist within the universities and colleges of Wales.

In Europe the relationship between an autochthonous language group and its territorial base is often described as being natural or primordial. However, in contemporary cases such as Wales,

Table 7: Welsh-speakers' current use of Welsh, 1992 (figures are percentages)

Welsh ability	Wales	Clwyd	Dyfed	Gwynedd	Powys	West Glam.	Gwent, Mid & South Glam.
Rarely speak Welsh	4.5	8.9	1.9	1.3	5.7	6.9	15.3
Occasionally	12.0	21.7	7.4	5.5	17.9	26.8	21.8
Half & half	21.2	28.5	19.6	14.3	25.3	33.6	29.7
Most or all the time	62.3	40.9	71.1	79.0	51.1	32.8	33.1

Source: Welsh Social Survey, 1992, Welsh Office, HMSO Cardiff.

Euskadi, Friuli and Brittany there is a real fear that the core area which sustained and nurtured these distinctive cultural communities is atrophying, with dire consequences for the cultural reproduction and maintenance of group identity. Changes in the New World Order and the globalization of economic organization threaten to increase the pressure for uniformity and render small-scale language communities even more vulnerable and marginal to the interests of global culture. Clearly one would be naïve to deny the rapid advancements made in technologically-induced cultural change. The whole premise of an integrated Europe depends in large part on the technical ability to realize a European Union without internal borders and trade barriers. However, globalization is not merely the sum of its parts, it is not just a mechanical aggregation of constituent units. There is a simultaneity inherent in the process which derives from two countervailing processes which operate to challenge any neat categorization of land and language and any tendency to reify socio-linguistic behaviour.

The first, centrifugal, process is the decentralist challenge of the 'ethnic revival' which has characterized the past generation. The ethnic intelligentsia in many of the lesser-used language regions of Europe have stressed the organic authenticity of language. Their focus on the inviolability of the ethnic homeland has given a literal interpretation to the search for roots in the soil, community and landscape of one's *own* people. In Wales concepts derived from *cydymdreiddiad tir ac iaith* (the interpenetration of land and language) have been given practical shape in planning policies aimed to bolster indigenous Welsh-speaking communities through environmental improvement and rural-economic diversification (J. R. Jones, 1966). The language movement has rediscovered its 'ecological' heritage, and has repackaged what were deemed to be rural community issues in the twenties and thirties as issues of 'cultural species' survival and as a local response to globalization (Williams 1994). The gift of Wales, so to speak, to the diversity of the world is the preservation and conservation of its unique cultural heritage.

The second, centripetal, process is the internationalization of language, described by Mackey (1988) as the 'definitive liberation of language from its traditional bounds of time and space . . . when language is no longer inevitably attached to spatial boundaries as it was in the past, when its speakers had to be limited to one or a few areas of the globe'. Telecommunication changes and mass migrations have empowered world languages such as English and French to perform critical inter-communicative roles which are historically predicated upon the economic power of Western capitalism. But they also derive immense power from the extension of digital technology, mini-satellite TV, and interactive computing systems to the farthest reaches of this globe. Technology further empowers such languages as essential means of communication and endows them with a cumulative relative advantage *vis-à-vis* all other languages.

The key question then becomes whether smaller languages such as Welsh and Breton can benefit from the same liberation from time and space? Whether they too can be technologically empowered so as to compensate for the loss of territorial dominance? Further, we need to know whether there is a relationship between decentralist localism and globalization? If there is, how do both processes at either end of the continuum mediate what happens in mainstream society? Is the former process a primordial reaction to cope with the new threats and demands of the latter? Put in its most fundamental form, does the increased internationalization of English inevitably threaten the ability of Welsh to compete and survive well into the next century? These are critical issues, for if the answer to the latter three questions is a resounding YES, then we are deluding ourselves in the struggle for Welsh and wasting a tremendous amount of limited energy and resources in opposing the inevitable. If, however, the answer is less certain or more probably a resounding NO, then the real issue becomes one of establishing an infrastructure whereby the rights and obligations of both Welsh- and English-speakers will be realized in tandem.

Extensive research based upon census and non-census sources in the past twenty years has produced a fairly detailed understanding of the interaction between Welsh and English. At the national scale, it suggests that there has been a persistent Anglicization of Welsh society and territory (Pryce and Williams 1988). As a result of a variety of factors which characterize contemporary society, many individuals are more autonomous, exercising language community without geographical contiguity. Well-understood processes such as the in-migration of non-Welsh-speakers, mixed marriages, language shift, the revolution in telecommunications and journey-to-work patterns have all contributed to the fragmentation of the Welsh heartland. Is fragmentation and collapse the inevitable future for the heartland? Should we be far less concerned with notions of domination, of territorial control and of resistance to externally-induced change? If we play down our concern with territorial heartlands we are led to depend on other factors, such as the mass media, to play a role in integrating Welsh-speakers within a communication network, comprising a post-modern community. To date, we are not entirely clear what the relationship is between the mass media and the reproduction of language and culture. For example, it is unlikely that an intermediate sensation derived from the passive reception of media culture can compensate for the loss of intimate face-to-face interaction in a local community. Different forms of language rules apply in non-face-to-face situations and the whole reinforcement experience of using language in society is reduced. Ineluctably, we conclude that no matter how comprehensive may be the new social communication system, Welsh-speakers will still need a region or a set of spaces wherein their language is dominant, or at the very least, co-equal with English. This is because the routinization of culture and economy can best be accomplished within familiar spaces. However, so many contemporary social processes are non-contiguous that experts are talking of the death of geography, because mass technology has overcome the barrier of space which distance conventionally represents. Heartlands, from this perspective, are *passé*. Attempts to introduce territorial language-planning measures based upon a set of shrinking cultural regions are doomed.

Thus it could be argued that the conquest of the 'tyranny of distance' means that our geographical framework for language analysis and planning will have to be totally rethought. However, if scale, place and regional context continue to be critical to the identification of linguistic practices, it is surely more a matter of integrating the newer perspectives in a far more sensitive manner, than of abandoning a spatial perspective (Ambrose and Williams 1981, 53–71). One of the determining factors influencing this choice will be the infrastructure currently being developed to support bilingual services.

Institutional bilingualism

It is evident that a rudimentary infrastructure supporting bilingual services already exists, based largely upon education and public administration. A promising development of late has been the renewed institutionalization of Welsh in public life, and a novel focus on language considerations within the private sector. If a strong institutional base can be constructed nationwide, then this will create new opportunities and domains wherein Welsh may be used as a matter of course. Conventionally, such usage is guaranteed either by reference to territorial language rights or to the personality principle of language rights. Institutionalization refers not only to the process of new domain construction, but also to the introduction of formal language planning in specific sectors via the creation of new agencies. From its inception, Pwyllgor Datblygu Addysg Gymraeg – the Committee for the Development of Welsh Education – performed a significant planning role in the field of education. The reconstituted Welsh Language Board looks set to become the most critical government agency yet in the social history of Welsh. Such status language planning allows for a measure of purposive rather than reactive thought and policy formulation. It also presages a new era of fresh initiatives and holistic interpretation of language in society which, though small-scale, do represent grounded local involvement in socio-linguistic issues. The emphasis on planning requires integrated action by a number of agencies and represents a more holistic approach than hitherto has been the norm. Additionally, rather than being exclusively concerned with the needs and interests of Welsh-speakers, we are beginning to address the concerns and involvement of second-language learners and non-Welsh-speakers in a more systematic fashion, thereby extending the bicultural nature of society from both ends of the spectrum.

In consequence, the Welsh language has entered a new phase of legitimacy, evidenced by the passage of the new Welsh Language Act (1993). Support for Welsh can no longer be interpreted as essentially a symbol of resistance to Anglicization, for it is itself deeply imbued in the process of state socialization. The language has become a contested instrument both of reform and of governance, of opposition and of authority. Welsh is increasingly incorporated into the machinery of government, of justice, of public administration and of civic control.

Contemporary society is being prepared for this new development in formal bilingualism through a variety of mechanisms. The first is the insistence on rerouting the relatively autonomous needs of Welsh culture into a more state-wide institutional design, so as to account for and control expenditure and subsidy. Many of the current reforms echo the demands of language activists since the early sixties and to that extent they are both welcome and long overdue. However, the ideological context within which such reforms are enacted is totally different. The new insistence on establishing an internal market in fields such as education, public health and the like runs counter to the conventional support for Welsh in public life as a service rather than as a good to be negotiated. It could be argued that much central government rhetoric becomes watered down by the time that pragmatic, county or local considerations of bilingual service provision are considered. Recent announcements about the reform of local government and the phasing out of county and local education authorities cast doubts on their ability to sustain a strong infrastructure which will enable the full implementation of language choice to be realized. Having examined this new dependency elsewhere I shall not pursue the argument here (Williams 1994b). The implication for civic rights is clear. With the strengthened Welsh Language Board determining priorities and polices from above, and an increasingly mobilized and expectant public demanding the extension of language rights from below, there will be a vacuum at the level of the local authorities who will be charged with implementing many of these new reforms. It is unlikely that significant amounts of additional capital will be available to local authorities to service such demands, thus rather than anticipate a stronger more uniform pattern of bilingual service provision throughout Wales, it is probable that we shall witness a new round of language-related tension. For some, this new round will be more localized and fractious because there will be significant examples of neighbouring local authorities who will have taken full advantage of the new regime to improve their bilingual services. Unless such services become a comprehensive statutory requirement underwritten by state financing then the bilingual programme will always be subject to competition from other sectors of local authority responsibility. And yet to approach language in such a fashion is misguided. It should not be seen primarily as a separate entity competing against road maintenance or hospital provision for scarce funding at that level. It is not ancillary to other services in a bilingual or multilingual society, but rather the democratic means by which such services are mediated to the constituent citizens. Unless and until that message is accepted in Welsh public life then the legitimacy of providing Welsh-medium services will always be subject to fierce debate about a contested social reality, namely the sort of Wales we are constructing together.

In many respects, the new institutionalization of Welsh consequent to the recent reforms promises to influence attitudes and behaviour patterns in a more constructive manner. The past decade has seen a more accommodating reaction on behalf of unilingual English-speakers and this bodes well for the future extension of services which seek to convince them that they also may benefit from sharing a bicultural community. However, the bilingual character of Wales is far more than the public, formal acknowledgement of language rights, public services and educational opportunities. There is a host of questions to which we need to know urgent answers if we are to come close to understanding the interaction of language and society in a more meaningful sense.

Unresolved questions

My concern in the remainder of this chapter is to highlight the paucity of sustained knowledge in a number of domains, and to relate these to extending our understanding of Welsh in a domestic and comparative international context.

Bilingualism was a necessary concomitant of the attempt to construct a distinct Welsh nation. J. R. Jones's vision of *cydymdreiddiad tir ac iaith*, the interpenetration of land and language, located the Welsh people as occupying a unique national space. The national plan of the cultural intelligentsia was to realize this space as being predominantly Welsh-speaking and hence separate in character from the rest of Britain and Europe. Self-government was favoured as the means whereby such a national plan could be achieved, for the early nationalists recognized that so much that was inimical to the success of Welsh was derived from state-inspired policies and actions.

The actions of the British state have been central to the process of Anglicization. I would contend that we know a great deal about the role of education, urbanization and mass industrialization in influencing patterns of bilingualism. Detailed work such as Sian Rhiannon Williams's (1992) study of the Rhymni Valley are confirming earlier generalizations (summarized in J. Davies 1993), and the current University of Wales project on the social history of

Welsh promises to provide excellent overviews of the effect of these processes on language choice. By contrast, we know a lot less about the detailed impact of, for example, warfare colonialism and the development of defence establishments on the social history of bilingualism. We can interpret what effect actions such as the Penyberth bombing incident had on the national psyche, and we have valuable testimonies on the role of pacifism and non-violent nationalism in Welsh political history. We can trace how demographic changes due to military requirements influence the patterns of stable bilingualism in Valley, Aberporth or Manorbier, through survey and socio-demographic means. All these studies require aggregate data which can be readily obtained with skill and effort. But it is quite a different matter to enquire into the socialization effects of voluntary or conscripted service in the armed forces on attitudes to Welsh and Welsh matters. Occasional biographical references may be found in the writings of poets, patriots and prisoners of war, but little explicit attention has been paid to the military factor in Welsh life. If we are to capture the experience of Second World War participants, we need to act now to transcribe their memoirs on such issues as British Army attitudes to using Welsh in personal affairs, POW camp life, political awakening and pacifism, else a generation's experience will be lost.

Organized religion
Similarly, although religious affiliation is often cited as one of the key pillars of a 'traditional' Welsh-speaking society, with its attendant emphasis on and high levels of cultural and scholarly achievement aided by a denominational press and cultural information network, much of the evidence is now dated, often clichéd and misleading. The church and chapel systems have been the historical mainstay of a Welsh communication system. Its personnel have been social leaders and local activists in all Welsh-medium causes. Consecrated buildings have been the original home of hundreds of Welsh nursery schools, debating societies and local amateur dramatic and choral societies. The relic landscape of Welsh Nonconformity houses the cultural infrastructure so essential to the voluntary sector. However, in contemporary Wales the impact of religion on culture is generation-linked. 'Welsh-Wales' is a secular society, most Welsh-medium chapels are struggling and the numbers coming forward for ordination and training as Anglican priests and

Nonconformist ministers is miniscule. The only saving grace in this context is that the few female ministers are finding appointments, and lively churches are spawning house fellowships and community action initiatives.

We need to know the current relationship between religious domains and Welsh cultural reproduction. We need to examine how early socialization in a particular church or chapel provides a context for adults to speak Welsh. In short we need a thorough reinvestigation of secularization, the faiths and the supernatural. Clearly, I am not suggesting that a transcendent God can be measured by the vagaries of mass social survey investigations, or that the mysterious can be deconstructed through textual analysis. I am merely asking how and to what extent organized religion currently expresses Welsh values in comparison with earlier generations of saints and sinners.

The individual and the para-public sector

A much neglected area is the para-public sector of administration, the health service and the 'caring sector' in general. We have little detailed research on the linguistic and social-psychological interaction involved in a number of contexts, whether that be the ordinary discourse at a post office counter or more specialist and tension-ridden situations. Thus we know little about the experience of patients in a predominantly Welsh-medium institution which specializes in psychiatric disorders, or even to gauge whether additional difficulties/traumas are meted upon patients or workers operating in an alien or second-language context. One might speculate that aged first-language Welsh-speakers could encounter difficulties in clinical and non-clinical institutions where English may prevail. This relates to the assumption that English is the language of authority within society. It would be interesting to know what effect the language of authority has on social experiences such as, recuperation, bereavement, imprisonment or occupational development. Here we are coming close to the concept of a 'cultural division of labour' so often interpreted in terms of either a privileged position or discrimination in diglossic situations. However, what I am searching for goes beyond the competitive element of economy and society to the deeper psyche of individual and collective adjustment to language dissonance in permanent, tension-ridden contexts. My concern is to know more about the processes creating individual and group alientation *in situ* so to speak, whether by reaction to historical events, such as exile or political pressure to conform, or contemporaneously by reaction to enforced captivity as prevention (mental hospital) or as punishment (prison).

The experience of previous generations of Welsh-speakers faced with authoritative specialists whether medics, engineers, scientists or government officials confirms that there is an established pattern of deferential language switching. This may be a severe impediment to the construction of an official bilingual society. The point is not that people cannot understand official conversations or transactions but that they *will* not entertain such transactions through Welsh. It may take a generation before such language switching is reversed. Thus one of the critical features to be addressed by the Welsh Language Board in constructing a fully functional bilingual social order, is the social psychological ramification of language choice. In my view social context and inter-group perception may be just as important as the creation of opportunity and legislative right in encouraging the normalization of bilingual services.

Thus rather than assess the efficacy of providing a whole range of official bilingual forms merely in terms of the number of printed forms distributed to the general public, we need to know the minute social-psychological processes which operate when an average Welsh-speaker is presented with a bilingual form. Does he/she read the whole form in Welsh solely/mainly/initially; or is it more a case of reading the principal themes in Welsh and then switching to English for the nuances and detailed instructions? If, as I suspect, the latter case is the norm, we need to identify what mechanisms education and the media can employ to increase confidence and concentration levels in such circumstances. It is vital that we know empirically what consumers actually do, rather than accept general claims about what they should do, before we embark on an expensive translation of most official forms. Despite the principle of equal validity of English and Welsh there are surely specific minimum thresholds which must be determined before some translations are authorized.

Experience to date in the supply and use of bilingual forms is of little practical use in predicting future demand, for often the forms which have been printed are unavailable at display counters, or requests for same cause interminable delays. However, under a more favourable climate and with the professional advice and experience of agencies such as the Welsh Language Board, it is likely that the supply and general usage of bilingual forms, advertisements, information and emergency signs will increase significantly. This in turn will give the appearance of inhabiting a bilingual country, even if the actual levels of functional biliteracy will always fall somewhat below the potential or optimum levels. We should not be surprised by this conclusion, for the same holds true of individual preferences exercised by students who have graduated from bilingual secondary schools: such is the reality of language choice in Wales.

Language choice also implies the selection of particular concepts to describe our linguistic predicament. A greater attention to the keywords we use in describing the bilingual character of Wales would surely repay intellectual and practical dividends. It is generally understood that 'class', 'ethnicity' and 'minority' are used in such a glib fashion that we often confuse fact and theory, reality and idealism in describing the genesis of our own identity. But what of our indigenous concepts, such as *cydymdreiddiad tir ac iaith* (the interpenetration of land and language), *cymrodor* (a fellow), *y werin* (everyday folk), *y Fro Gymraeg* (the Welsh Heartland)? It is debatable whether they are accurate representations or rather a sloppy shorthand for an ill-defined and ever-changing reality. There is also an ideological temptation to talk as if all Welsh-speakers formed an inclusive 'community' with all that concept's implication of warmth, integration and mutual dependence. By contrast non-Welsh-speakers are ascribed as belonging to a mass society, which is characterized as being aggregate, cold, functional and impersonal. There is also the practice of describing non-Welsh-speakers as *Saeson* (English), rather than as *Cymry di-Gymraeg* (non-Welsh-speaking Welsh). We need to be more self-aware of how the language of our language analysis influences our interpretation of inter-group relations.

Welsh stereotypes are another area of contention. The schoolteacher, minister of religion, wise shepherd and poetic slate-worker, so beloved as Welsh heroes and characters are in danger of being caricatured, not because they no longer form the 'pillars of Welsh society', but because their scarcity makes them simultaneously more essential and unrepresentative. Who are the new role models? The obvious answer is the TV guru and presenter, pop-artist and video-designer. They are undoubtedly attractive, but they play more distant roles for they cannot fulfil the duties of leadership laid on the old heroes. Not every village, hamlet or garden suburb can have a newscaster and crooner of its very own. It may be that in these transient post-modernist days we have no need of local heroes, for we can all share those beamed into our homes by the media. If so, that marginalizes those who conventionally served the basic need of the local community but provides opportunities for other identities to be validated.

Equally we need to know how the images of Wales are constructed and delivered both here and abroad. Good initiatives on symbolic interpretations of the landscape have been made by Prys Morgan (1983, 1986) and Pyrs Gruffudd (1989, 1990), among others, but it would be useful to have scholarly interpretations of the cumulative formation of the identity of Wales shaped by CADW: Welsh Historic Monuments, the Welsh Development Agency, the Welsh Rugby Union and the Wales Tourist Board, upon the landscape, its people and their idealization.

In short what we need is a set of *urban Welsh* identities which correspond to contemporary reality, not to the tired clichés of pit-worker, steel worker and quarryman. An attempt at such a construction is currently being undertaken by popular television serials such as *Pobl y Cwm* (The People of the Valley), and is reflected in television news magazines such as *Heno* (This Evening). However, unlike many of our European contemporaries, Welsh people seem so reluctant to embrace change and champion Welsh-medium advances even when they are patently the only worthwhile changes underway in our society.

The general drift away from a rural, farm-based social and economic order has altered the contemporary character of conventional Welsh-speaking society. Yet, the culture is heavily imbued with rural communal values and patterns of behaviour, which is not surprising given the history of Welsh ethnic mobilization so superbly analysed by David Howell (1993). Rural – urban migration has been the dominant tendency in modern Europe, and has given rise to a wide range of counter-movements celebrating the pristine nature of rural social life. Intellectuals such as Iorweth Peate continued a tradition of investing the true qualities of 'Welshness' (however that elusive concept was defined) in the yeoman farmer and noble peasant stock of the heartland. It was a general European celebration of rural communal interdependence which mass industrialization was threatening to destroy. Such genuine fears were foreshadowed by Oliver Goldsmith when he wrote in 'The Deserted Village'

> Ill fares the land to hastening ills of prey,
> Where wealth accumulates and men decay.
> Princes and lords may flourish or may fade,
> A breath can make them as a breath has made.
> But a bold peasantry, a country's pride,
> When once destroyed can never be supplied.

Today most Welsh people, bilingual or not, inhabit urban communities. It is due time that our popular culture not only recognized that fact but celebrated it, for only then will Welsh culture appeal to the vast majority of disaffected youth. The over-concentration on historical themes of struggle and despair, understandable as they are to a minority who share a mission-destiny view of the world, are hardly likely to make young people glad to be alive in Wales. They already have the double burden of being stigmatized in a marginal community. It would appear that we are overdue our share of joy, excitement, passion and adventure. Writing this chapter from my current home in Canada convinces me more than ever that the future belongs to the dynamic, vibrant individuals who recognize the value of their history and origins but are not prepared to imprison themselves in a cul-de-sac, destined to relive the anguish and pain of their forefathers.

Reconstructions and re-searches
The role of the Welsh diaspora has been critical to the development of Welsh identity in times past. Today, however, they are a relatively neglected phenomenon. It would be fascinating to have data on Welsh-speakers worldwide. But even data for our closest neighbour is patchy. We have little published material on the Welsh in London, Birmingham, Liverpool, Manchester and Bristol where there are centres of Welsh activity and innovation (cf. Y Cymmrodorion). Such communities have nurtured prominent politicians, intellectuals and public servants, for example, Saunders Lewis, born in Wallasey; K.O. Morgan, born in Wood Green; Gerald Morgan, born in Brighton; Harri Williams, born in Liverpool; to name but a few. Neither do we have informed detailed studies on how Welsh diaspora communities operate in such cities today and with what degree of ethno-linguistic vitality.

There are good historical accounts of the Welsh diaspora ('Y Cymry ar Wasgar') in specific countries, for example, the excellent studies on Patagonia by R. Bryn Williams (1962) and Glyn Williams (1975, 1991); on Scranton, Pennsylvania by William Jones (1993); on Canada by Wayne Davies (1985), Muriel Chamberlain (1985) and Carol Bennett (1985); and on Australia by Lewis Lloyd (1988). There are also very fine works on rates of emigration from Wales in the nineteenth century (Johnston 1993), initial Welsh settlements in maritime North America (Thomas 1986) and the relocation of settlers from Patagonia to the Canadian Prairies (Jones 1989). Scatterings of prose and newsletter material appear in *Y Drych* and *Ninnau*, and more systematically in the quarterly magazine *Yr Enfys*. Little of this material constitutes a sustained comparative analysis of the contemporary diaspora. We need to know more than the statistical profile of who lives where; we must seek to understand what it means to be Welsh in multicultural societies. It is time that we had a collected work on the Welsh in the world!

Because of the paucity of published evidence it is difficult to know what form the exilic interpretations of the Welsh diaspora would take. We do not know whether their experience is seen as a blessing, or punishment, an opportunity or a cost. Neither do we have survey evidence of the attitudes and expectations of people of Welsh descent in North America, Australia, South Africa or even England, though the latter should not be difficult to undertake given the will. Unlike the highland clearances or pre- and post-repression migration from Scotland and Ireland, the exilic Welsh have been driven by economic rather than political motives. Thus it would be revealing to know what are the expectations for the future of Welsh within such overseas communities. It is possible that the experience of living in predominantly multilingual societies such as North America and Australasia may make diaspora members value their Welsh heritage more. But it is equally likely to leave them satisfied by a sanitized transatlantic pastiche of Welshness. These are important issues, for diaspora ideas, finances, political pressure and involvement have proved critical in the modern development of other small nations such as the Estonians, the Basques, Ruthenians and Israelis.

As an illustration, it would be interesting to know who were the 23,395 self-identified Welsh/Gallois who responded to the 1986 Canadian Census question: 'What is your ethnic origin?' It would also be revealing to ascertain just how many of the 6,332,725 of the British Canadian/Britaniques were Welsh but chose not to be self-identified as a subgroup of the British majority. Little is known of the nature of their Welshness and how it has changed over time. Some of their organized and informal contacts with Wales and with fellow Welsh-Canadians may be gleaned from Bennett (1985) or more currently from *Yr Enfys*, *Y Drych* and *Ninnau*. But there is surely more to Welsh-Canadian social life than an occasional *gymanfa ganu*, rugby match or visiting choir — but how much more and with what effect on the next generation of Welsh-Canadians? Turning to Europe, now that we have an internal labour market, are we to assume that the migrant Welsh are a net loss to the Welsh-speaking community, or are there promising signs to the contrary? Were there equivalent concerns expressed about out-migration and the Welsh language in 1850 or 1894, and if so how were they mediated or turned to advantage?

To estimate the Welsh elsewhere in the UK, we may mine data on place of birth, migration estimates and occasional gems from the Office of Population Census Survey. But we need far more accurate data on marriage patterns, child-rearing practices, communication flows, mobility studies and network analyses on contemporary Welsh-speakers, wherever they live in these isles. In the absence of routine, geographic continuity, it becomes doubly difficult to 'stay in touch' with friends and interests in Wales. In the past, Radio Cymru has performed an invaluable integrative role, as, in a small way, did the regular transmission of *Pobl y Cwm* on BBC2. In the future one can imagine the diaspora Welsh, and others, being able to subscribe to satellite transmission of S4C programmes for news and entertainment from the homeland. For the present this is a slightly whimsical notion, as S4C does not yet penetrate the whole of Wales, but in less than ten years I suspect it will be a reality.

An international perspective on bilingualism
There are useful comparisons to be made with other bilingual contexts in Europe, particularly with Friesland, Euskadi and Friuli. Shared involvement in the construction of a new Europe, suggests that are we constraining ourselves if we only make common cause and comparisons with lesser-used language regions, rather than with smaller states such as Norway and Denmark, or overseas proto-states such as Quebec. In the past we may have been guilty of over-

emphasizing the Pan-Celtic nature of comparative bilingualism and language analysis to the detriment of socio-economic and political comparisons elsewhere. Today we are in danger of compounding this narrow vision of a bicultural Wales by emphasizing questions of marginality, peripherality and relative deprivation. I do not believe that this is the lasting reality of Wales. European, Japanese and American inward investment suggests otherwise.

Ultimately, it is the political construction of reality which will shape the contours of a bilingual Wales. Bilingualism and biculturalism have been mediated predominantly through a 'nationalist' paradigm of Welsh-medium discourse and analysis. This can lead to a neglect of many other commonalities of British and European life, and to the hijacking of the 'language issue' by a small interest group. We are beginning to see fissures within the nationalist-language lobby over the legitimacy and utility of the Welsh Language Board. The debate surrounds appointed members, senior officers and their perceived lack of accountability, as a quango, to any person other than the Secretary of State for Wales. Behind the rhetoric is a deeper debate between idealists and pragmatists as to how best to advance the cause of a bilingual Wales within a democratic framework. Accommodation and working within the present Conservative system are interpreted by some critics as evidence of accepting a sop. To others it is an opportunity to determine issues from within the system, a political calculus which may yet pay off. This debate is a sign of a healthy, vibrant society searching for better, more representative ways of shaping the near future. However, we are now poised to enter a technical, planned era of societal bilingualism, when professionalism will characterize aspects of language behaviour more than ever before. In consequence, we need the sharp voice of individual dissent, criticism and monitoring so that the future of our culture is not commodified and directed by the professional planning élite, however sincere or well placed they may be to shape events. Constructive *criticism* and energetic, intelligent *support* are the twin watchwords of the language struggle, if we are to develop a worthwhile bilingual existence in Wales.

Acknowledgements

An earlier version of this chapter was presented at the University of Wales Staff Colloquium on 'The Welsh Language in the History of Wales', Gregynog, 16–18 September 1992. The revised version was written whilst I was a Resident Scholar at the Multicultural History Society of Ontario, Toronto and a Visiting Professor at the University of Western Ontario. I wish to thank H. Jones of the Statistical Section of the Welsh Office for supplying me with the 1992 Social Survey data, and J. D. Lewis of Gwasg Gomer for his permission to reproduce W. R. Evans's poem 'Yr Ysgol Gymraeg'.

References

Aitchison, J. and Carter, H. (1993). 'The Welsh language in 1991 – a broken heart and a new beginning?' *Planet* 97, 3–10.
Ambrose, J. E. and Williams, C. H. (1981). 'On the spatial definition of minority: scale as an influence on the geolinguistic analysis of Welsh', in *Minority Languages Today*, E. Haugen, J. D. McClure and D. Thomson (eds.) (Edinburgh, Edinburgh University Press, 2nd ed. 1990), 53–71.
Bennett, C. (1985). *In Search of the Red Dragon* (Renfrew, Ont., Juniper Books).
Chamberlain, M. E. (ed.) (1985). *The Welsh in Canada* (Swansea, Canadian Studies in Wales Group).
Davies, J. (1993). *The Welsh Language* (Cardiff, The University of Wales Press).
Davies, W. K. (1985). 'The Welsh in Canada: A Geographical Overview', in *The Welsh in Canada*, M. E. Chamberlain (ed.) (Swansea, Canadian Studies In Wales Group), 1–45.
Evans, W. R. (1983). *Awen y Moelydd* (Llandysul, Gwasg Gomer).
Gruffudd, P. (1989). *Landscape and Nationhood: Tradition and modernity in Wales, 1900–1950*, unpublished Ph.D. thesis, Loughborough University.
Gruffudd, P. (1990). 'Uncivil engineering: nature, nationalism and hydroelectrics in north Wales' in D. Cosgrove and G. Petts (eds.), *Water, Engineering and Landscape*, London, Belhaven Press, 159–73.
Howell, D. (1993) 'A "less obtrusive and exacting" nationality: Welsh ethnic mobilisation in rural communities', D. Howell (ed.), *Roots of Rural Ethnic Mobilisation* (Aldershot, Dartmouth Publishing), 51–99.
Johnston, J. R. (1993). 'The Welsh diaspora: emigrating around the world in the late nineteenth century', *Llafur*, 6, 2, pp. 50–75.
Jones, J. R. (1966). *Prydeindod* (Llandybïe, Llyfrau'r Dryw).
Jones, R. O. (1989). 'From Wales to Saskatchewan via Patagonia', in C. Byrne, M. Hanry and P. O. Siadhail (eds.), *Celtic Languages and Celtic Peoples* (Halifax, N.S., Proceedings of the North American Congress of Celtic Peoples).
Jones, W. D. (1993). *Wales in America* (Cardiff, University of Wales Press).
Lloyd, L. (1988). *Australians From Wales* (Caernarfon, Gwynedd Archives).

Mackey, W. (1988). 'An introduction to geolinguistics', in C. H. Williams (ed.) *Language in Geographic Context*. (Clevedon, Avon, Multilingual Matters), 20–46.
Morgan, P. (1983). 'From a death to a view: the hunt for the Welsh past in the Romantic period', in E. J. Hobsbawm and T. Ranger (eds.), *The Invention of Tradition* (Cambridge, Cambridge University Press), 43–100.
Morgan, P. (1986). 'Keeping the legends alive', in T. Curtis (ed.), *Wales: the Imagined Nation* (Bridgend, Poetry Wales Press), 17–41.
Pryce, W. T. R. and Williams, C.H. (1988). 'Sources and methods in the study of language areas: a case study of Wales', in C. H. Williams (ed.), *Language in Geographic Context* (Clevedon, Avon, Multilingual Matters), 167–237.
Sopher, D. (1974). 'A Measure of Disparity', *The Professional Geographer*, XXVI, 389–92.
Sopher, D. (1980). *An Exploration of India* (London, Longman).
Sopher, D. (1983), private correspondence, 27 April.
Southall, J. E. (1892). *Wales and Her Language* (London, D. Nutt).
Thomas, P. (1986). *Strangers From a Secret Land* (Toronto, University of Toronto Press).
Welsh Office (1981). *The Welsh Language in Wales* (Cardiff, HMSO).
Welsh Office (1992). *County Monitors of the 1991 Census* (Cardiff, Welsh Office).
Welsh Office (1993). *Welsh Social Survey* (Cardiff, Statistical Section of the Welsh Office).
Williams, C. H. (1980), 'Language contact and language change in Wales, 1901–1971: a study in historical geolinguistics', *The Welsh History Review*, Vol. 10, 2, pp. 207–38.
Williams, C. H. (1985). 'Public gain and private grief: the ambiguous nature of contemporary Welsh', *The Transactions of the Honourable Society of Cymmrodorion*, 27–48.
Williams, C. H. (ed.), (1993). *The Political Geography of the New World Order* (London, Belhaven).
Williams, C. H. (1994a) *Called Unto Liberty: On Language and Nationalism*. (Clevedon, Avon, Multilingual Matters).
Williams, C. H. (1994b), 'Development, dependency and the democratic defecit', *Journal of Multilingual and Multicultural Development*, Vol. 15 Nos 2 and 3, (1994), pp. 101–28.
Williams, G. (1975). *The Desert and the Dream: A Study of Welsh Colonization in Chubut, 1865–1915*. (Cardiff, University of Wales Press).
Williams, G. (1991). *The Welsh in Patagonia: The State and the Ethnic Community*. Cardiff, University of Wales Press).
Williams, R. B. (1962). *Y Wladfa* (Cardiff, University of Wales Press).
Williams, S. Rh. (1992). *Oes y Byd i'r Iaith Gymraeg* (Cardiff, University of Wales Press).

4

SCHOOLS AND SPEECH COMMUNITIES IN A BILINGUAL SETTING

Bob Morris Jones

Introduction

This chapter examines the contribution that schools can make to the maintenance and restoration of a minority language. It concentrates upon a situation, found in Wales, where the school and community languages of some pupils are different: for many pupils in Welsh-medium education, the school is the only domain which provides opportunities for the use of the minority language, Welsh. Given the overall aims of language maintenance and restoration, the school in effect takes on the role of a speech community. This chapter asks to what extent schools are organized to fulfil this function and so provide their pupils with opportunities for language development. To this end, three issues are considered: the community languages of pupils in Welsh-medium education; the language used in classroom teaching; and extra-curricular ways of promoting language development. But, to begin with, an introductory examination will be made of the term 'Welsh-medium education'.

Welsh-medium education

As will become clear from the following discussion, Welsh-medium education can occur alongside English-medium education in the same school, especially in secondary schools. Consequently, in referring to Welsh-medium education, the labels 'bilingual education' or 'bilingual schools' are also in general use. As the discussion in this chapter is concerned with Welsh-medium education, this latter term will be preferred in most instances.

On the face of it, Welsh-medium education means using Welsh to teach the subjects on school curricula. Although this explanation is adequate in general terms, two problems emerge on a closer examination. One is that the number of subjects which are taught through the language can vary from school to school. The other is that even where a subject is available through the medium of Welsh, in some schools pupils may have the option of English-medium teaching for that subject. Consequently, Welsh-medium education varies from school to school according to the number of subjects and the numbers of pupils involved. In general terms, we can only grossly define Welsh-medium education as a curriculum design in which pupils are taught *wholly or partly* through the medium of Welsh. The above points are particularly relevant to secondary schools.

This variation makes it difficult to gain a precise statistical picture of Welsh-medium education, but Table 1 gives an indication of the numbers of children involved in Welsh-medium education at September 1991. These figures should only be taken as rough guidelines for two reasons. There are secondary schools which do not come within the criteria set out in the table but nevertheless offer some subjects wholly or partly through Welsh. And, as already mentioned, not all the pupils in secondary schools necessarily opt for Welsh-medium teaching where a choice of languages exists.

Table 1: Numbers of pupils in Welsh-medium education in maintained schools, 1991–1992

	Numbers	*Percentages*
Primary schools		
Solely/mainly through Welsh	43984	15.78
Partly through Welsh	10522	3.78
Welsh-medium total	54506	19.56
Total of all children	278657	100.00
Secondary schools		
Welsh-medium*	29990	15.87
Total of all children	189002	100.00
All schools		
Welsh-medium total	84496	13.79
Total of all children	467659	100.00

Source: These figures are compiled from *Statistics in Education and Training in Wales: Schools* for 1991–92, pp.30, 36, 107 table 11.08, 109 table 11.12

* '... more than half of the following subjects, namely religious education and the subjects other than English and Welsh which are foundation subjects are taught wholly or partly in Welsh.' (p. 109)

By today, there are two types of school which offer Welsh-medium education at both primary and secondary levels (the former extends from five to ten years of age, and the latter from eleven to sixteen, or optionally eighteen, years of age). Firstly, there are schools which have been established specifically to teach through the medium of Welsh. Historically, these are formally known as 'designated bilingual schools' but are also commonly referred to as 'Welsh schools'. They are located mainly in English-speaking areas — the primary and secondary designated schools in Cardiff are good examples. But designated bilingual schools are also found in Welsh-speaking areas — instances are the schools in the towns of Carmarthen, Bangor and Aberystwyth. Secondly, there are schools which are not designated to teach through the medium of Welsh but do so because the intake is mainly Welsh-speaking. They are sometimes popularly called 'natural Welsh schools' — but this is an unfortunate term which suggests the existence of 'unnatural Welsh schools'. This chapter will refer to them as 'non-designated bilingual schools'. They are found mainly in Welsh-speaking areas — particularly in Gwynedd (in the north-west of Wales). Following the Education Reform Act (1988), the expression 'Welsh-speaking schools' has emerged, and it refers to all secondary schools which meet the criteria quoted in Table 1. It thus includes the designated and non-designated schools.

Welsh-medium schools of both types have two main functions. Firstly, like English-medium schools, they have to teach the subjects on the curriculum. At the time of writing, these subjects are largely determined by the National Curriculum as laid down by the Education Reform Act (1988). Secondly, they seek to promote language development. This second aim of Welsh-medium schools is complex for two reasons. One reason is that they have to address two languages, Welsh and English. This chapter will concentrate upon the promotion of Welsh. The other reason is that their pupils come from varied linguistic backgrounds. By today, both types of Welsh-medium schools have a mixed intake of Welsh- and English-speaking children. This is particularly so of the designated bilingual schools in English-speaking areas. But it also applies to non-designated schools in traditionally Welsh-speaking areas: the proportion of first-language Welsh and first-language English pupils has been influenced by the in-migration of English-speaking families and the out-migration of Welsh-speakers. In view of their mixed intakes, Welsh-medium schools have a dual function in respect of Welsh: to *maintain* the Welsh of pupils who have a Welsh-speaking background; and to *restore* Welsh through promoting its acquisition as a second language by children who come from a non-Welsh-speaking background (which is predominantly English-speaking).

From a wider perspective, these linguistic aims are also shared by English-medium schools. They also seek to promote a language – English. Further, there are English-medium schools in the United Kingdom that also have to cater for pupils whose language backgrounds are different to the variety of English used in the school – be it a community language or an urban or regional variety of vernacular English. (A particularly interesting example of the relationship between school and community languages is given in Bekos (1993) who analyses the language use of children of Greek families in countries to which they emigrated, and compares this with their language use on their repatriation to Greece.) However, our concern in this chapter is entirely with Welsh-medium schools.

The community languages of pupils in Welsh-medium schools

This section focuses upon the use of language outside classroom teaching. For convenience, this general context will be referred to as the 'domain of the community'. An account will be given of the language choices made by pupils attending two designated and two non-designated secondary schools: the former are located in mainly English-speaking areas and the latter in traditionally Welsh-speaking areas. This account is based on a study recorded in B. M. Jones (1992) which involved a total of 212 pupils in Year 10 (these were pupils of fourteen to fifteen years of age in the fourth form, to use traditional terms). These pupils are not offered as a representative sample of all children in Welsh-medium education, but I suggest that the account indicates trends which are found to varying extents in schools offering Welsh-medium education.

A questionnaire was used to obtain information about the pupils' use of Welsh outside classroom teaching. This was done by exploiting a common technique which identifies general types of interlocutors in spontaneous discourse (this type of technique is seen in Sharp *et al.* 1973 and is discussed in Baker 1985, 69–73):

1. Mother
2. Father
3. Brothers and sisters
4. Grandparents
5. Friends in school
6. Friends at home
7. Neighbours
8. Shopkeepers
9. Staff in the local Post Office

As we are comparing languages used in teaching with languages used outside teaching, school friends have been placed in the community domain. They provide peer-group interlocutions which belong to the latter, even though the interlocutions occur in school. The languages spoken by the pupils in these interlocutions were identified by asking them whether they used: A – mainly Welsh; B – Welsh and English; or C – mainly English. It is acknowledged that there are weaknesses in this approach both in the use of self-assessment and in the broad categories of language choice. For instance, no attempt was made to assess the frequency and intensity of the interlocutions in 1 to 9, nor to quantify how much was 'mainly' in respect of A to C. But more rigorous methods were not practical, given the numbers of subjects which were involved in the study, and the use of school time and rooms.

Where we are concerned with discussing one type of interlocutor, identifying the language choices as in A, B and C above is informative enough. But where the discussion considers a group of interlocutors which form a wider domain, a general picture can be obtained by quantifying the use of Welsh as follows:

(a) each choice is scored arbitrarily but proportionally – 10 for mainly Welsh, 5 for Welsh and English, and 0 for mainly English;
(b) the extent of the use of Welsh in the whole domain can then be expressed as a percentage based on the total potential score.

Both these approaches are used in the following discussion.

The pupils' first language can be established on the basis of their choices with the members of the immediate family. This information is given in Graphs 1 and 2. Graph 1 gives the individual percentages of the use of Welsh. It can be seen that there are eight separate groups but the two biggest groups by far are the 0 per cent use of Welsh and the 100 per cent use of Welsh. Graph 2 presents a broader picture by conflating these individual percentages into four groups. Both approaches show that there are two different linguistic groups: there are those who mainly use English and those who mainly use Welsh. In the rest of this chapter, we shall concentrate upon the two extreme groups in Graph 2: the low and high users of Welsh will be referred to as English-speakers and Welsh-speakers respectively. In terms of percentages, 42 per cent are English-speakers and 46 per cent are Welsh-speakers. It is now obvious from these graphs that many pupils in these schools were English-speakers: in the immediate family at least, their language choices outside school did not develop the use of Welsh.

In discussing the linguistic aims of Welsh-medium education, an important consideration is the extent to which the community outside the family also provides opportunities for the use of Welsh. An indication of this can be obtained by comparing the pupils' first language, as determined by family usage, with their language choices outside the family. This is particularly crucial for English-speakers in Welsh-medium education. Graphs 3 to 7 include information about the extent to which the English-speakers use

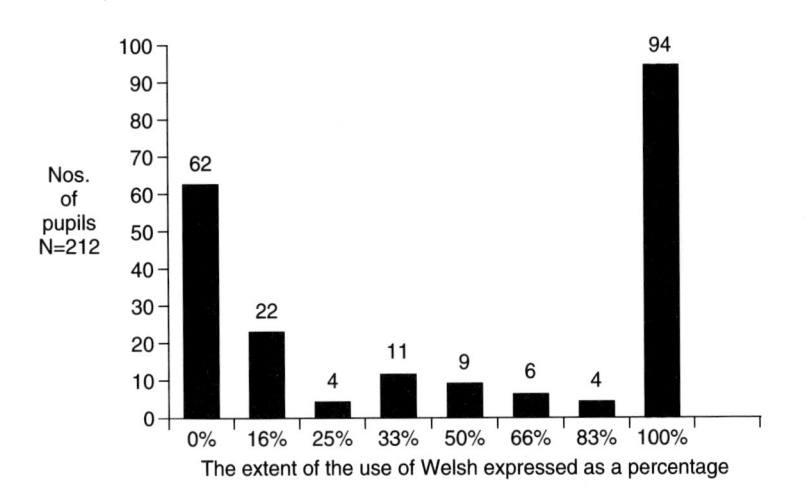

Graph 1: The use of Welsh in the immediate family

Graph 2: The use of Welsh in the immediate family

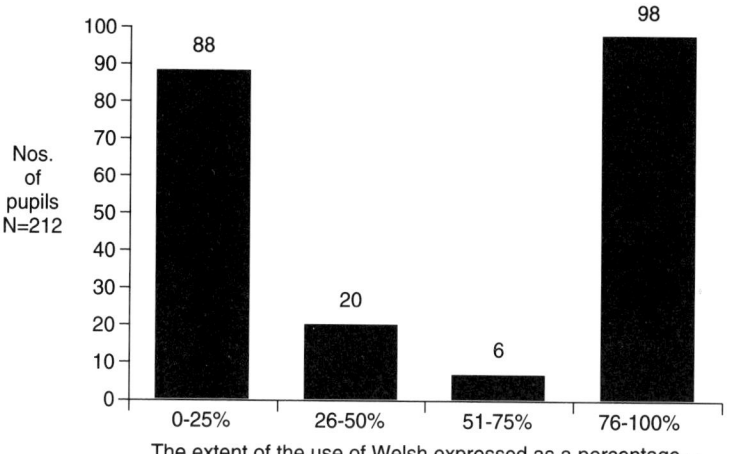

Nos. of pupils N=212

Bar values: 0-25%: 88; 26-50%: 20; 51-75%: 6; 76-100%: 98

The extent of the use of Welsh expressed as a percentage – conflated into groups

Welsh away from the family and the curriculum. It can be seen that, in general, it is very low. The general trend for the majority of English-speakers is to use their first language and not Welsh in non-curricular domains of use. In this light, it is clear that they either do not have the opportunity to use Welsh or, if they do, they do not exploit it. Either way, Graphs 3 to 7 show that English is very dominant in the community for those pupils in Welsh-medium education for whom it is their first language. As with the family domain, the wider community does not help to develop their use of Welsh. These graphs indicate that Welsh-speakers have more opportunities than English-speakers to use Welsh in the community. On this basis, it is reasonable to suppose that they enjoy linguistic advantages, but this supposition needs to be made guardedly for two reasons. Firstly, it is a common observation in socio-linguistic discussions of Welsh that the domains of the language have been historically restricted to domestic, religious and cultural contexts (e.g. Williams 1986, 189; Thomas 1987, 107). The more varied opportunities that exist today for the use of Welsh in a variety of new domains are unique to recent times. The exploitation of these domains probably lags behind their availability for some speakers. Further, in-migration into Welsh-speaking areas has contributed to the increase in the numbers of monolingual English-speakers and, where they figure in the interlocutions which are considered in this chapter, the opportunity to use Welsh disappears. Secondly, as already mentioned, the designated bilingual schools are located in English-speaking areas, and their Welsh-speakers will not have the array of domains which are found in Welsh-speaking areas. It is interesting to compare the Welsh-speakers in the two types of school. It should be borne in mind that although we are using labels based on types of school, we are essentially comparing the linguistic character of the areas in which the schools are located.

The examination of the language choices of Welsh-speakers outside the family, and away from the curriculum, reveals that the family usage of some of them is not maintained in all interlocutions. Graphs 3 to 7 supply the details. Grandparents reflect the family usage, as might be expected (Graph 3). For the Welsh-speakers in the designated schools, it is the immediate and extended family which maintains Welsh. Away from these two domains, differences between Welsh-speakers in the two types of school begin to emerge. An interesting contrast occurs with interlocutions with peers (Graphs 4 and 5). The Welsh-speakers in the non-designated schools

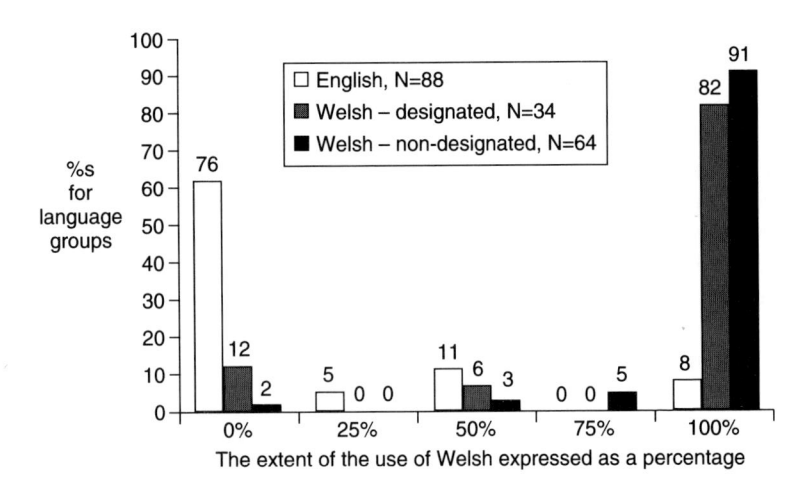

Graph 3: Welsh- and English-speakers' use of Welsh with grandparents (the percentages for the language groups are based on the total for each group)

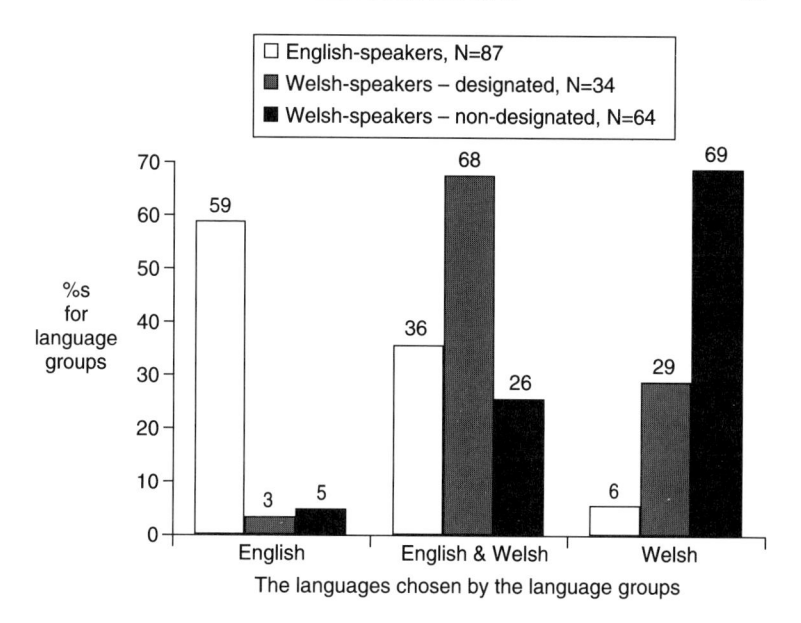

Graph 4: Welsh- and English-speakers' language choices with school friends (the percentages for the language groups are based on the total for each group)

use far more Welsh with their school friends while those in the designated schools opt more for Welsh and English. For the Welsh-speakers in the non-designated schools, friends at home are even more supportive of the use of Welsh. But the Welsh-speakers in the designated schools use less Welsh with home friends. Graph 6 shows that interlocutions with neighbours differentiate these two groups even further: the use of Welsh is much higher by the pupils from the non-designated schools than by those from the designated schools. Graph 7 shows that the domain of shops has a quite dramatic influence on the use of Welsh for both groups. The language choices of the Welsh-speakers in the designated schools is not very different from that of English-speakers – English is markedly dominant. This domain also significantly reduces the use of Welsh by Welsh-speakers in the non-designated schools. Although this aspect of the questionnaire is crude, the much lower use of Welsh in this domain reflects the historical difficulty of establishing the language in commercial domains.

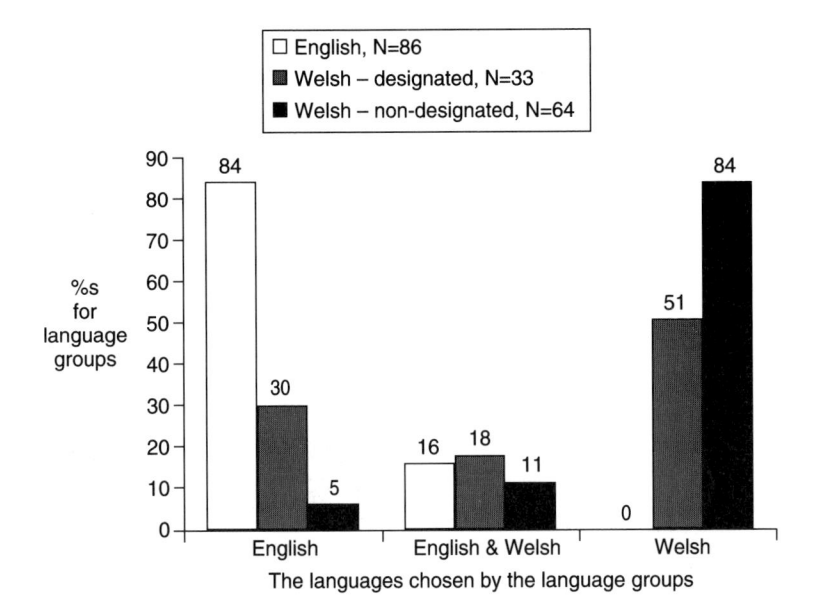

Graph 5: Welsh- and English-speakers' language choices with friends at home (the percentages for the language groups are based on the total for each group)

Graph 8 summarizes the use of Welsh in the individual domains outside the immediate family. It is based on the option of mainly Welsh and ignores the use of Welsh in the mixed option of Welsh and English. The weak use of Welsh by English-speakers is clearly apparent, as are the differences between Welsh-speakers in the two types of school. This graph also indicates the influences of the different domains: it demonstrates the strength of the language in domestic and peer-group domains but shows that it is much weaker outside these domains − shops are the least supportive of the use of Welsh.

Graph 9 combines all community domains outside the family. The different uses of Welsh are again apparent. English-speakers and Welsh-speakers in the non-designated schools occupy the two poles, with the Welsh-speakers in the designated schools occupying the middle ground.

The preceding domains involve at least two interlocutors who have the opportunity to share the roles of speaker and listener. We

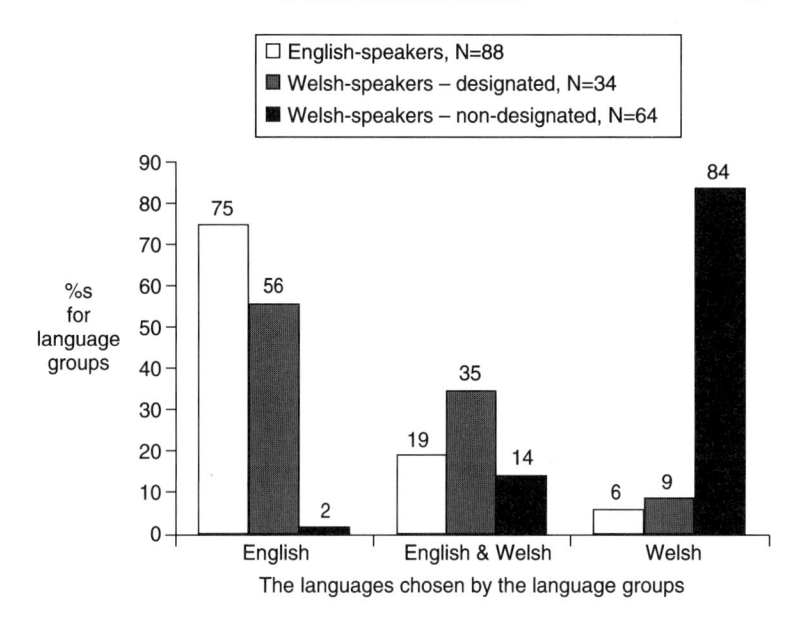

A BILINGUAL SETTING 89

□ English-speakers, N=88
■ Welsh-speakers – designated, N=34
■ Welsh-speakers – non-designated, N=64

%s for language groups

	English	English & Welsh	Welsh
English-speakers	75	19	6
Welsh-speakers – designated	56	35	9
Welsh-speakers – non-designated	2	14	84

The languages chosen by the language groups

Graph 6: Welsh- and English-speakers' language choices with neighbours (the percentages for the language groups are based on the total for each group)

□ English-speakers, N=88
■ Welsh-speakers – designated, N=34
■ Welsh-speakers – non-designated, N=64

%s for language groups

	0%	25%	50%	75%	100%
English-speakers	84	7	3	2	3
Welsh-speakers – designated	79	15	6	0	0
Welsh-speakers – non-designated	0	9	30	28	33

The extent of the use of Welsh expressed as a percentage

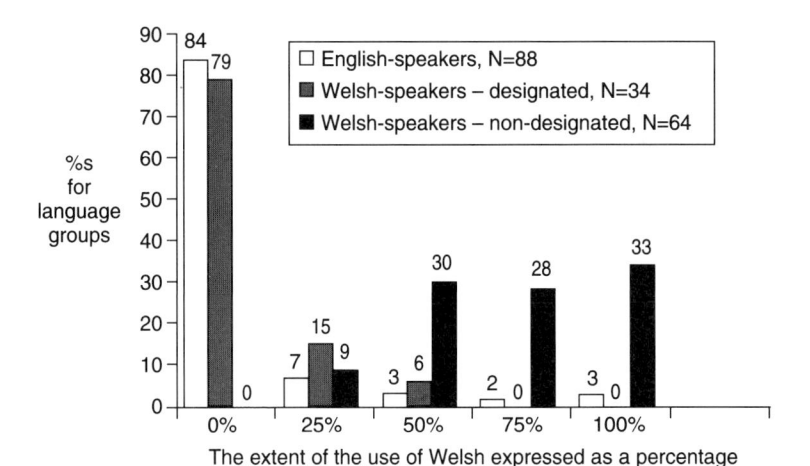

Graph 7: Welsh- and English-speakers' use of Welsh in shops (the percentages for the language groups are based on the total for each group)

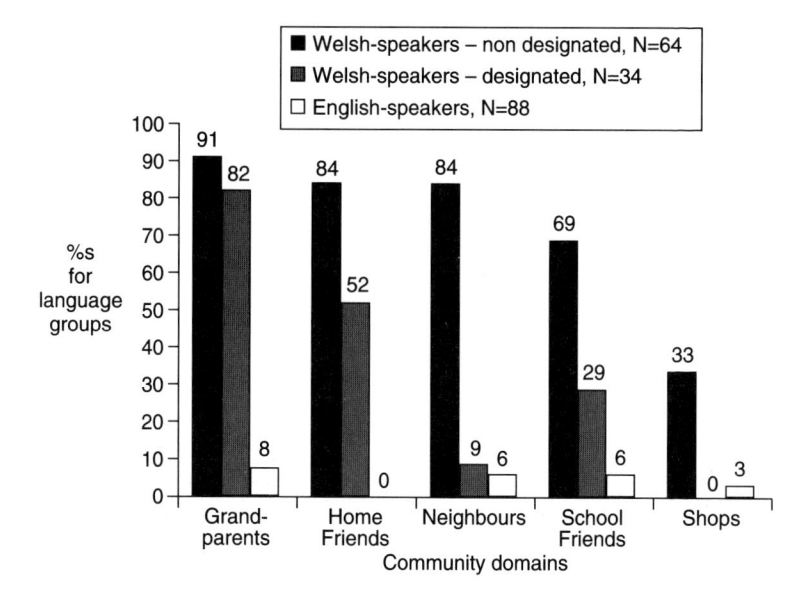

Graph 8: Welsh- and English-speakers' use of Welsh in community domains outside the family (the use of English and Welsh & English are not considered; the percentages for the language groups are based on the total for each group)

shall now examine two uses of language in which the role of pupils is essentially to receive language produced by someone else – namely, as readers of books and magazines, and as viewers of television programmes (in the context of this study, it is their roles as listeners which is important). These details were collected through two items on the questionnaire of the original study. One item asked the children to give the titles of books and magazines which they had read during the last fortnight. The other asked them to name their favourite television programmes. Their responses were scored in the manner previously described (although the choice Welsh and English did not occur). The details are given in Graphs 10 and 11. The general pattern is the same for both reading and watching television. The English-speakers in the main are very low users of Welsh. With both reading and watching television, the highest users come from the Welsh-speakers in non-designated schools. But overall, the Welsh-speakers are spread over the four user groups, although there is a tendency for them to be low to mid users of

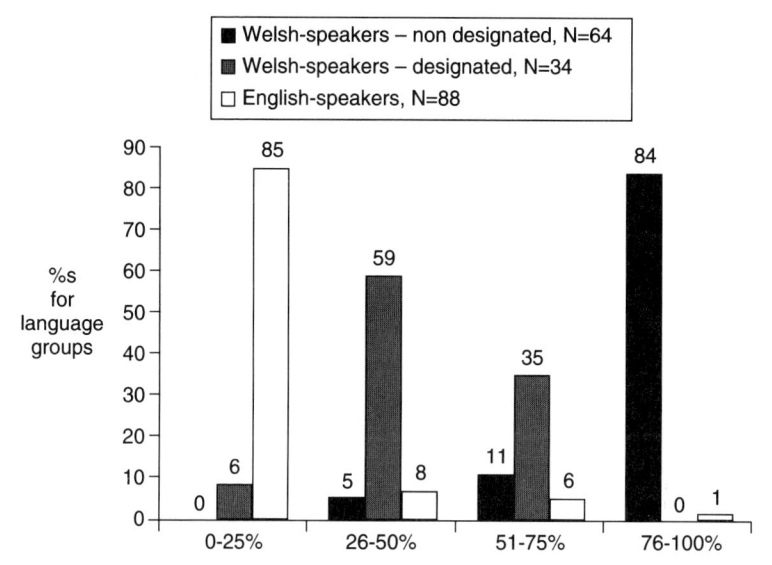

A BILINGUAL SETTING 91

Graph 9: Welsh- and English-speakers' use of Welsh in all community domains except the family (the percentages for the language groups are based on the total for each group)

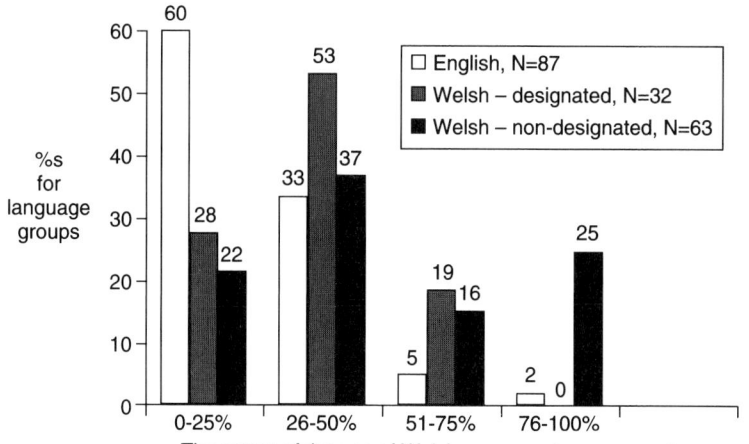

Graph 10: Welsh- and English-speakers' use of Welsh in reading books and magazines (the percentages for the language groups are based on the total for each group)

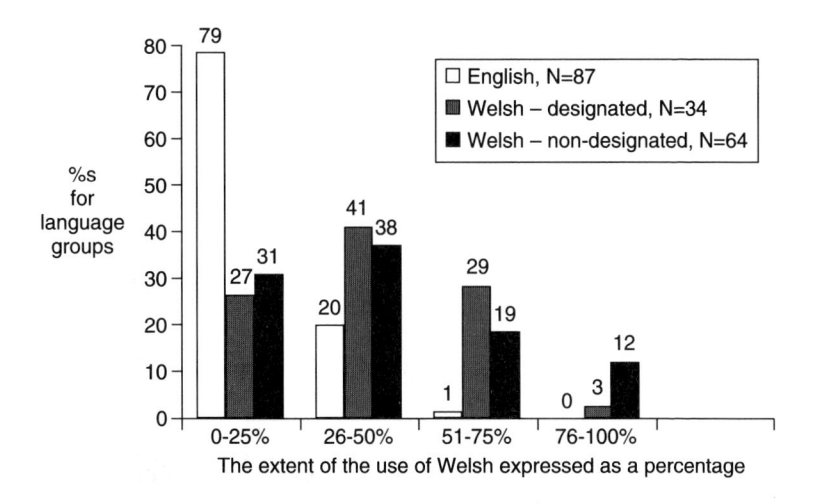

92 SCHOOL AND SPEECH COMMUNITIES IN

Graph 11: Welsh- and English-speakers' use of Welsh watching TV programmes (the percentages for the language groups are based on the total for each group)

Welsh. Their use of Welsh for reading and viewing television does not reflect their use of the language in the family.

From the overall picture which has emerged in the foregoing discussion, it is seen that the English-speakers have hardly any support for the use of Welsh outside teaching. The Welsh-speakers in the non-designated schools have a much higher use, particularly in the immediate and extended family, and with home friends and neighbours. For the Welsh-speakers in the designated schools, the use of Welsh is confined mainly to the immediate and extended family.

Language on the curriculum

Having outlined language choices in a variety of interlocutions outside the curriculum, we can now examine language choices on the curriculum, and compare the two. This assessment is based on a questionnaire which asked the same pupils individually to indicate the medium of teaching for each of their subjects on the curriculum. The same options were used: mainly Welsh, Welsh and English, mainly English. The responses were scored in the same fashion as previously described. The results are given in Graph 12, which illustrates four groups on their basis of the strength of their use of Welsh:

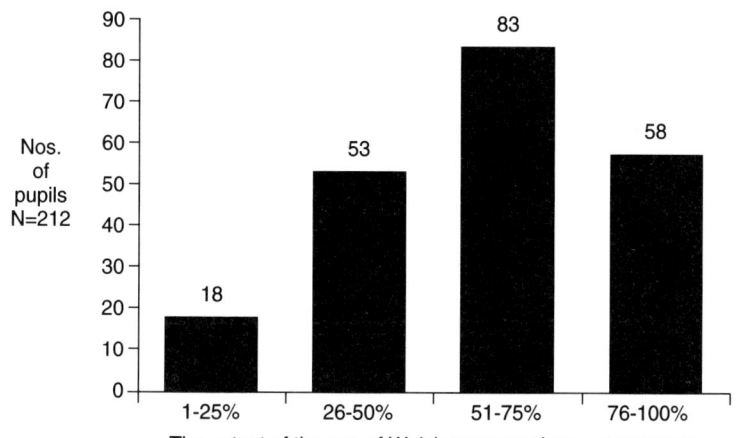

Nos. of pupils N=212

Extent of use of Welsh	Number of pupils
1-25%	18
26-50%	53
51-75%	83
76-100%	58

The extent of the use of Welsh expressed as a percentage

Graph 12: The use of Welsh on the curriculum

1. high users (76–100 per cent of teaching through Welsh)
2. mid-high users (51–75 per cent of teaching through Welsh)
3. low-mid users (26–50 per cent of teaching through Welsh)
4. low users (0–25 per cent of teaching through Welsh)

Unlike the non-curricular domains, we do not have polarized groupings. This figure shows that the favourite choice is the mid-high range – that is, 51 per cent to 75 per cent of the teaching is done through the medium of Welsh.

Graph 13 gives the curricular choices of Welsh- and English-speakers, and other notable differences emerge. The general picture which emerges can be summarized as follows:

1. whereas English-speakers have a very low use of Welsh in the community, their use of Welsh on the curriculum is much higher – 47 per cent of them are mainly in the mid-high range and 18 per cent of them are amongst the high users of Welsh;
2. Welsh-speakers from the non-designated schools had the highest use of Welsh in community domains, but on the curriculum, they mainly occupy either the low-mid group (42 per cent of them) or the

SCHOOL AND SPEECH COMMUNITIES IN

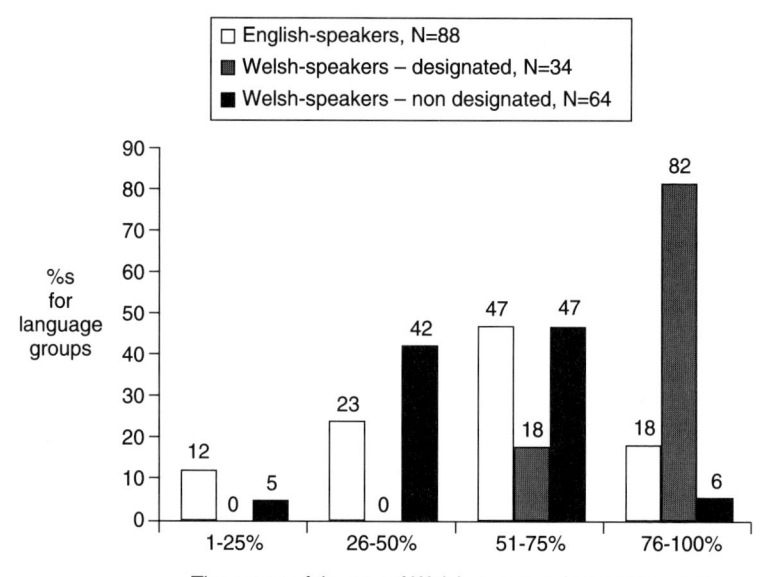

```
□ English-speakers, N=88
■ Welsh-speakers – designated, N=34
■ Welsh-speakers – non designated, N=64
```

[Bar chart: %s for language groups vs. extent of use of Welsh as a percentage]

- 1-25%: 12, 0, 5
- 26-50%: 23, 0, 42
- 51-75%: 47, 18, 47
- 76-100%: 18, 82, 6

The extent of the use of Welsh expressed as a percentage

Graph 13: Welsh- and English-speakers' use of Welsh on the curriculum (the percentages for the language groups are based on the total for each group)

mid-high group (47 per cent of them); there are only 6 per cent of them who belong to the high usage group;

3. the Welsh-speakers in the designated schools are the highest users of Welsh on the curriculum – they are found only in the top two groups – 82 per cent of them in the high group and 18 per cent in the mid-high group.

We see here that language use on the curriculum tends to reverse community usage in different ways for the three language groups. For the Welsh-speakers in the designated schools, their use of Welsh on the curriculum reflects their use of Welsh in the immediate and extended family but it is not reflected by their use in the wider community, which is much lower.

The Welsh-speakers in the non-designated schools have the highest use of Welsh in the community and, on this basis, they might be thought to be the best equipped to choose Welsh-medium education. But Graph 13 shows that they have a much lower use of Welsh in classroom teaching. The incongruous relationship of their curricular and community choices partially reflects the history of the role of Welsh in schools in Welsh-speaking areas: historically, Welsh was used in the community and English was used in the classroom (see, for instance, Jac L. Williams 1979). Although the non-designated schools do not exclude Welsh, its use on their curricula is still more limited than its use in the communities where these schools are located. The non-designated schools make less use of Welsh than the designated schools.

For the English-speakers, we have a very clear reversal of community usage: the curriculum provides the only domain which promotes the use of Welsh. In this respect, it is significant to note that interlocutions with their school friends indicate the highest use of both Welsh and English and mainly Welsh outside classroom teaching (see Graph 4). This further underlines the role of the school in promoting the use of Welsh. An interesting comparison arises between the Welsh-speakers in the non-designated schools and the English-speakers: for both, family and curricular language choices are incongruent, but the difference is greater for the English-speakers. Further, the Welsh-speakers have access to both English and Welsh outside school, whereas the majority of the English-speakers have little opportunity to develop Welsh in the wider community.

Graph 13 is interesting in another respect, namely the extent of *immersion* as a method of second-language teaching. This graph shows that only 18 per cent of the English-speakers are amongst the high users group, and in the original study of these children, B. M. Jones (1992, 83) notes that no pupil, Welsh nor English, had more than 90 per cent of the teaching through the medium of Welsh. In the secondary sector, it is unlikely that immersion is total, neither in terms of pupils nor the curriculum. But it is likely to be more extensively used in primary schools, particularly in designated bilingual schools.

We shall now examine the extent to which the school can promote language maintenance and restoration against the background of language usage outlined above. In respect of the second-language speaker of Welsh, several questions arise about the effectiveness of the use of the curriculum as a method to promote language acquisition. In acquiring a second language, learners have to master two main aspects of language, traditionally referred to as 'form' and 'use'.

Firstly, they must acquire the forms (and related functions) of its structural features. These include pronunciation, vocabulary, morphology and syntax. The effectiveness of the acquisition of structural features has been the subject of limited formal study (see, for instance B. M. Jones, 1988, 1990b, 1992; P. W. Thomas 1991; Price *et al.* 1989) but far greater anecdotal comment. There are two serious obstacles which hamper objective assessment. One is the task of obtaining appropriate data on second-language Welsh, and the other is the availability of a model of Welsh which can act as a norm against which second-language Welsh can be assessed. Traditional grammars of Welsh cannot be accepted as a norm of spoken Welsh as they are based mainly on literary Welsh, as is discussed below. Descriptions of spoken Welsh have been limited mainly to dialectological studies. These studies are usually concerned with specific features which demonstrate regional variation and rarely give systematic and uniform accounts of spoken Welsh (see Ball 1988, 7−23, and Thomas and Thomas 1989 for discussion and illustration of the methods and achievements of Welsh dialectology). More systematic treatments have emerged in recent decades from both linguistic and socio-linguistic standpoints (see Ball 1988 for examples of the latter). Spoken norms are considered in an assessment of language development in B. M. Jones (1992) but it is yet to be seen whether assessors of second-language Welsh will commit themselves to a consideration of spoken norms. A case in point is the dropping of prefixed personal pronouns as in *car chi* (your car) and *bwrw chi* (hit you) (instead of *ych car chi* and *ych bwrw chi*). This pattern is a common object of popular disapproval. But evidence has emerged that it is no stranger to vernacular Welsh, particularly the latter example (Watkins 1977; B. Thomas 1980; B. M. Jones 1990a, 1990b; Awbery 1992).

Secondly, second-language learners have to be able to experience the use of Welsh in a variety of domains and for a variety of purposes. We have seen that this is not the case. We must therefore ask whether the schools, and the curriculum in particular, can compensate for their limited exposure to different uses of Welsh. This chapter will concentrate upon the use of Welsh rather than its form. We shall examine three points: stylistic varieties of Welsh; general use of language; and particular characteristics of classroom discourse.

Stylistic varieties of Welsh
It should not be thought that Welsh-speakers are necessarily equipped with the linguistic skills to meet the challenges of classroom teaching. There are two reasons for this. One reason has already been discussed and concerns the availability of Welsh-speaking domains outside school – this applies particularly to Welsh-speakers in designated schools who rely mainly on the immediate and extended family. The other reason concerns the type of Welsh found outside the school. Conventional educational conceptions of language are based on the tradition of the codifications of John Morris-Jones (1913, 1922, 1931). This tradition has its origins not in the spoken varieties of the Welsh of Morris-Jones's time but on a tradition of literary Welsh of previous centuries. There are two types of entry into this tradition – one is cultural and is achieved mainly through higher education, and the other is religious and is achieved through chapel or church activities. These two influences can work together or separately to equip speakers with the conventions of the traditional written language. Outside these two spheres, it is the vernacular varieties of the language which dominate. The linguistic analysis of Welsh-speaking children in B. M. Jones (1992) indicates that the majority of them bring their colloquial conventions to school. An educational system which uses the John Morris-Jones tradition is out of step with the vernacular tradition of the pupils. Welsh-speaking pupils, then, are not necessarily stylistically equipped to follow classroom teaching which is based on literary Welsh.

An interesting consideration today, however, is the extent to which schools can recruit staff who have themselves been exposed to the traditional cultural and religious domains, and are able to use the conventions of traditional literary Welsh. It can be speculated that the growth of Welsh-medium education, both in terms of numbers of pupils and in terms of subjects on the curriculum, has necessarily extended recruitment to include first-language Welsh-speakers whose linguistic repertoire may not include the traditional style. Some teachers, then, may be happier with a more vernacular style which is more similar to that of the pupils.

General functions of language

Teaching has two major influences on language: it determines the general purposes for which language is employed and it shapes the types of interactive exchange which can occur. These two consequences are related and we shall discuss the former in this sub-section and the latter in the following sub-section.

Studies of semantics emphasize that there are different types of language functions. Lyons (1977, 50–56) refers to the following uses of language:

1. to handle factual content – the *descriptive* function;
2. to establish and maintain social relationships – the *social* function;
3. to express attitudes and personality – the *expressive* function.

Halliday (1973, 22–46) makes similar distinctions, as does Leech (1981, 9–23), although the labelling of these functions varies. Lyons points out that social and expressive functions are related, and uses Halliday's term 'interpersonal' as a label for their common features (Halliday's term for the descriptive function is 'ideational'). Indeed, Lyons concedes that the descriptive and interpersonal functions are not completely inseparable. This two-term distinction, however, is very useful in contasting language use in the classroom and in the community. The contexts and purposes of communication in the latter are many and varied, and this domain allows both descriptive and interpersonal functions. However, subject teaching is mainly concerned with the descriptive use of language; the essential role of the teacher is to bring factual information to the pupils. Within this general emphasis, there is emphasis on the communication of propositional meaning, and skills of argument and persuasion are particularly admired. The latter aspects of language use are often employed in the promotion and assessment of language development (see, for instance, a report by Price *et al.*, undated, which describes the use of the 'speech functions' *describing*, *persuading*, *explaining*, and *instructing* in the Welsh Oracy Survey of 1985).

Following Lyons, it must be acknowledged that the descriptive use of language can also involve the development and maintenance of social relationships, and the expression of attitudes and personality – and this applies to the relationships between teachers and pupils. It should also be conceded that the younger children in primary schools warrant a more child-centred teaching style which involves greater interpersonal uses of language. But in the curriculum-centred approach of the secondary schools, the interpersonal function of language is secondary to the descriptive function. A lesson on the War of Jenkins's Ear may be delivered spiritedly but it does not provide the pupils with the linguistic experiences of informal peer-group discussion on matters of interest to them. In the community, however, language use can be wholly social, or at least the factual content is secondary to the interpersonal aims. There are many uses of language which are found away from the curriculum but not within it − the banter of peers about unpredictable topics, the use of agreement and disagreement, the forthright issuing of commands, rubuttals, and disclaimers. These uses are not typically found in the language of pupils in the teaching domain.

The nature of classroom discourse
A much fuller portrait of classroom language can be achieved through contemporary discourse analysis. An account of the ways in which teachers and pupils play their parts in classroom discourse shows further limitations on the language experiences of pupils. Classroom discourse is geared to teaching and, as such, has two characteristics:

1. the teacher imparts knowledge to the pupils − this means that the teacher speaks and the pupils listen;
2. the teacher elicits information from the pupils − this means that the pupils can only act as speakers through the initiation of the teacher; and in large classes, each pupil has only a limited share of the speaker role.

A detailed account of classroom discourse is found in the work of Sinclair and Coulthard (1975) and Sinclair and Brazil (1982). The model that they have developed is based on classroom discourse which is largely produced and directed by the teacher − that is, teacher-centred discourse. It does not account for small-group work lightly overseen by the teacher, but reflects a more traditional style of class teaching. Nor does it necessarily account for approaches to the teaching of infant children. However, bearing in mind these limitations, it gives an informative picture of teacher-driven discourse.

The central aspect of the Sinclair view of classroom discourse is the concept of the initiation of discourse exchanges (or interactions). The teacher initiates exchanges in four ways:

1. by telling things to pupils – labelled as an *informative* discourse act;
2. by getting pupils to do things – labelled as a *directive* discourse act;
3. by getting pupils to say things – labelled as an act of *elicitation*;
4. by enquiring about possible problems – labelled as a *check*.

In traditional class teaching, it is the teacher who initiates in these ways. The opportunities for pupils to initiate are limited. The main role of the pupils is to *respond* to the teacher's initiations by: *replying* to elicitations; *reacting* to directives; and *acknowledging* initiations. The dominant role of the teacher is further underlined by other discourse acts, namely the teacher *accepts, evaluates* and *comments* upon the pupil's repsonse as a *follow-up*. Taking all these points together, there are three parts to classroom discourse which can be summarized and illustrated as in Figure 1 (the examples are taken from Sinclair and Coulthard 1975, 68). These examples show how the pupil's contribution is sandwiched between the dominant and controlling contributions of the teacher: the teacher not only elicits a response but also evaluates and comments upon it when one is given.

The teacher's authority and domination is further displayed by other discourse acts which support the initiation. Where a response is not forthcoming, the teacher can offer *clues* and also deliver *prompts* which seek a response. In the example in Figure 2, taken from Sinclair and Coulthard (1975, 68–9), the teacher *reinitiates* the original elicitation with two prompts and, finally, a clue. The teacher's control over the discourse is further underlined by the fact that pupils have to *bid* for a turn in the discourse with expressions such as 'sir', 'miss' and by raising a hand. The teacher, in contrast, can control the pupils' contributions by *cueing* a bid, ('hands up'), and *nominating* a pupil to contribute.

Around the central interchange of Initiation, Response and Follow-up, there are other ways in which the teacher shapes and directs the discourse. As each new point in the lesson is introduced, the teacher can *mark boundaries* in the discourse with a small set of expressions that include 'well', 'ok', 'now'. A *metastatement* can then indicate what the content of the discourse will *focus* upon.

Initiation	Response	Feedback
What makes a road slippery?	You might have rain or snow on it.	Yes, snow, ice.
Anything else make a road slippery!	Erm, oil	Oil makes it very slippery when it's mixed with water, doesn't it? The oil skims on top of the water.

Figure 1: The organization of teacher-centred classroom discourse
(Based on data in Sinclair and Coulthard 1975, 68)

Initiation	Response	Feedback
– but did you notice the difference between the first quiz you did and the second quiz?	One was words and the other was ...	One was words.
and one was just –	Signs.	Signs.
or –	Meanings.	They have meanings. Yes.
	Warnings.	They are all warnings.
I was thinking of a much simpler word than that.	Pictures.	Pictures! ....

Figure 2: The teacher's control over initiation in teacher-centred classroom discourse
(Based on data in Sinclair and Coulthard 1975, 68–9)

Where a boundary marker ends a chunk of discourse, a *conclusion* can summarize the preceding content. The illustration in Figure 3 is an adaptation of data from Sinclair and Coulthard (1975, 63–68).

Well [silent stress]	*Boundary marker*
Today I thought we'd do three quizzes.	*Metastatement*

(Intervening teaching exchanges have been omitted)

Right [silent stress]	*Boundary marker*
So that's the first quiz and I think you got that all right.	*Conclusion*
Right [silent stress]	*Boundary marker*
Here's the next quiz then if you're ready	*Metastatement*

(Intervening teaching exchanges have been omitted)

Yes good.	*Boundary marker*
So those are all caution signs.	*Conclusion*

Figure 3: The teacher's overall control over the direction and content of classroom discourses
(Based on data in Sinclair and Coulthard 1975, 63–8)

Thus, both in terms of the type of language functions described in the preceding section and the exchange roles outlined here, classroom discourse imposes limitations on the pupils' use of language both qualitatively and quantitatively. This general view of language in the classroom means that second-language speakers who rely upon the school for the use of the second language have restricted opportunities to develop language for social purposes. Their main experience of language is that of handling information and not that of maintaining social relationships and expressing attitudes and personality. Further, the exchange roles with which they are most familiar are those of responding when questioned, prompted or nominated, and not those of spontaneous initiation.

An account of the free conversations of even five-year-old children in B. M. Jones (1987/88) indicates that their range of discourse acts is greater and more spontaneous.

Ways of going beyond the classroom

The previous section has examined the limitations of teaching as a way of promoting interpersonal uses of language. In this section, we shall examine the extent to which these limitations can be countered. There are many traditional ways whereby teachers and pupils can go beyond classroom discourse. Sports, music, drama, discos, field trips, day trips and holidays organized through the school are extracurricular activities which place the teachers and pupils in different discourse roles, and introduce more interpersonal functions. But there are two points which are relevant here. First, there is still a hierarchical relationship of adult to child/adolescent rather than one involving equals from the same peer group. Second, anecdotal evidence suggests that teachers may have curtailed their extracurricular contributions following the teachers' strike of 1985–6 in Wales and England.

There are two other ways in which experiences away from teaching and the classroom can be in Welsh. One is through the Urdd (Urdd Gobaith Cymru – the League of the Hope of Wales). This is a youth movement whose origins are cultural and religious but which, by today, also caters for sport and outdoor activities. The main cultural events are the regional *eisteddfodau* and an annual national *eisteddfod* for the winners of the regional events. The central experiences are the cultural ones of poetry, prose, drama and music. The experiences are prepared ones and the linguistic skills can be learned for a one-off occasion, or may even be non-linguistic in the case of instrumental competitions. But there are wider contextual activities arising from practices and organization which can involve the use of Welsh. However, I suggest that more extensive social experiences are involved in the outdoor activities. The Urdd has two notable outdoor centres in north and south-west Wales. In these centres, pupils can experience a whole variety of activities away from the more formal context of the classroom. Where these activities are supervised by adults, a superior/subordinate relationship may exist, but the context of the language is generally more spontaneous and relaxed than that found in classroom teaching.

A recent development which enlarges linguistic opportunities for second-language speakers is seen with so-called enterprises like Menter Taf Elái based on an area to the north of Cardiff extending to Pontypridd, and Menter Cwm Gwendraeth based on Llanelli. The whole purpose of these enterprises is to provide experiences in Welsh outside school. The promotion of Welsh in society is not a new phenomenon. Since the 1960s, there has been sustained pressure to promote the use of Welsh in non-educational contexts; Cymdeithas yr Iaith Gymraeg (The Welsh Language Society) has been particularly prominent in campaigns to extend the use of the language. Local and national government agencies now present a range of services in both Welsh and English. In the private sector, banks and building societies variously provide Welsh-medium services at the counter, through their cheque books, and their cashpoints (many of which can offer a variety of European languages, of course). But these uses of Welsh are not based on informal social and pleasure activities, and many are typically found in Welsh-speaking areas. There remains a gap for providing more ordinary experiences through the medium of Welsh, particularly in areas where Welsh is not strong.

The Taf Elái project is not confined to school pupils but also offers opportunities for adults to use Welsh. The general aim of Menter Taf Elái is to encourage the use of Welsh in a variety of contexts in society. There are a number of aspects to its work (the following account is based on Prosser 1993). Of particular relevance to this chapter are those which come under their heading of Leisure and Youth (*Hamdden a Ieuenctid*). The project promotes a whole range of Welsh-medium activities including walking, playing snooker and golf, gigs for young people and play sessions during the school holidays. There is also an attempt, in co-operation with local authorities, to arrange Welsh-medium training sessions in karate, football, swimming and aerobics. An interesting development is the introduction of Welsh in local supermarkets by identifying Welsh-speakers on the staff, particularly at checkout points. This social and sporting provision may seem prosaic and mundane in comparison with the traditionally perceived gravitas of educational and cultural uses of language (some of which are also catered for by Menter Taf Elái), but the ordinariness of these activities is the very strength of the project. They make up for the limitations of the use of the school curriculum to maintain and restore a language; these uses are the very uses that the school is not equipped to provide.

It is well to be aware of reservations about such projects. Firstly, we must await an adequate assessment of their work to see how successfully the aims and objectives are achieved in practice. Secondly, the activities described are all organized activities. They do not necessarily represent spontaneous options in peer groups and social networks. Despite these reservations, enterprises like Menter Taf Eláí should be recognized as significant and important developments in language maintenance and restoration in Wales. It indicates a growing awareness of language use beyond the curriculum, and the importance of catering for the use of Welsh in society. This is an important development which cannot be underestimated. If the progress in setting up a bilingual education system can be matched by setting up bilingual domains of use in the community, then the two together produce complementary vehicles for the promotion of Welsh.

Conclusions

The weaknesses of bilingual education as outlined above are not specifically the weaknesses of Welsh bilingual education. These weaknesses arise because of the general limitations which schools have in influencing behaviour away from the curriculum. When pupils move away from the school they are subject to the social norms of the wider community and, in particular, their own peer group. Schools can be reasonably expected to equip their pupils with the ability to use a language for the purposes of the curriculum (see Baker in this volume for evidence of this), but away from the curriculum, the school can have only an indirect influence.

Language maintenance and restoration cannot rely on education alone. The achievement of such goals must involve a partnership of schools, families and the wider society. The schools are doing their bit. We have now reached a point where other partners in this process must lend a helping hand. Ideally, parents who want their children to acquire Welsh should encourage the use of Welsh in the home. In this respect, there are two other organizations — Pont and CYD — which do much to promote the acquisition and use of Welsh by adults (and, indeed, teaching Welsh to adults is another of the activities of Menter Taf Eláí). The advent of Menter Taf Eláí and similar movements is of enormous significance; if developed effectively they can contribute significantly to extra-curricular Welsh, which will do much to support the work of the schools. The Welsh achievement is the impressive one of establishing a dynamic system of Welsh-medium education, mainly within the last three decades. It is a system which is essentially based on grass-roots enthusiasm allied to middle-class expertise in skilful lobbying. Welsh-medium education is currently an expanding system, exhibiting growing confidence and maturity. However, it is sometimes criticized for not paying sufficient attention to assessment of its methods through research programmes (see the comments of Baker and Colin Williams in this volume). We are reaching a time when more considered appraisals are possible, and hopefully this chapter provides a contribution to the assessment of Welsh-medium education.

References

Awbery, G. M. (1994). 'Echo Pronouns in a Welsh Dialect: A System of Crisis', *Research Papers in Linguistics*, Volume No. 5, (Bangor, Linguistics Department, University of Wales), 1–29.
Baker, C. (1985). *Aspects of Bilingualism in Wales* (Clevedon, Avon, Multilingual Matters Ltd.).
Ball, M. J. (ed.) (1988). *The Use of Welsh* (Clevedon, Avon, Multilingual Matters Ltd.).
Bekos, Joannis D. (1993). *A Study of Language Skills in Bilingual Education in Athens*, unpublished M.Phil. Thesis, University of Wales, Aberystwyth.
Halliday, M. A. K. (1973). *Explorations in the Functions of Language* (London, Edward Arnold Publishers Ltd.).
Jones, B. M. (1987/88). 'The Discourse Acts of Five-Year-Olds Speaking Welsh', *Studia Celtica* XXII–XXIII, 176–99.
Jones, B. M. (1988). *Beth Yw Gwall Mewn Iaith Plant?* (Aberystwyth, Canolfan Astudiaethau Addysg).
Jones, B. M. (1990a). 'Variation in the use of pronouns in verbnoun phrases and genitive noun phrases in child language', in M. J. Ball *et al.* (eds.), *Celtic Linguistics*, (Amsterdam, Philadelphia, Benjamins B.V.), 53–76.
Jones, B. M. (1990b). 'Linguistic Causes of Change in Pronominalization in Children's Welsh', *Bulletin of the Board of Celtic Studies*, XXVII, 43–70.
Jones, B. M. (1992). *Linguistic Performance and Language Background*. Aberystwyth, Canolfan Astudiaethau Addysg).
Leech, G. (1981). *Semantics* (Harmondsworth, Penguin).
Lyons, John (1977). *Semantics*, Vol. 1 (Cambridge, Cambridge University Press).

Morris-Jones, John (1913). *A Welsh Grammar* (Oxford, The Clarendon Press).
Morris-Jones, John (1922). *An Elementary Welsh Grammar* (Oxford, The Clarendon Press).
Morris-Jones, John (1931). *Welsh Syntax, an Unfinished Draft* (Cardiff, University of Wales Press).
Price, E., Powel R., Griffith C. Ll. (undated). *Children Talking*, commissioned by the Welsh Office.
Price, E., Powel R., Griffith C. Ll. (1989). *Survey of Welsh Reading and Writing among first and second language pupils aged 13+*, report commissioned by the Welsh Office, Cardiff, and undertaken by the NFER (National Foundation for Educational Research).
Prosser, Helen (1993). 'Menter Taf Elái', paper read at the half-yearly meeting of Cylch Astudiathau Tafodieithol, November 1993, University of Wales, Cardiff.
Sharp, D., Thomas, B., Price, E., Francis, G. and Davies, I. (1973). *Attitudes to Welsh and English in the Schools of Wales* (Basingstoke/Cardiff, Macmillan/University of Wales Press).
Sinclair, J. McH. and Coulthard, R. M. (1975). *Towards an Analysis of Discourse* (Oxford, Oxford University Press).
Sinclair, J. McH. and Brazil, D. (1982). *Teacher Talk* (Oxford, Oxford University Press).
Statistics of Education and Training in Wales: Schools, No. 1 1993, (Cardiff, The Welsh Office).
Thomas, A. R. (1987). 'A Spoken Standard for Welsh: Description and Pedagogy', *International Journal of the Sociology of Language* 66, 99–113.
Thomas, B. (1980). 'Cymrêg, Cymraeg: Cyweiriau iaith siaradwraig o Ddyffryn Afan', *Bulletin of the Board of Celtic Studies* XX, 579–92.
Thomas, B. and Thomas, P. W. (1989). *Cymraeg, Cymrâg, Cymrêg* (Cardiff, Gwasg Taf).
Thomas, P. W. (1991). 'Children in Welsh-medium Education: Semilinguals or Innovators?', *Journal of Multilingual and Multicultural Development*, Vol. 12, 1 & 2, 45–53.
Watkins, T. A. (1977). 'The Welsh Personal Pronoun', *Word* 28, 146–65.
Williams, G. (1986). 'Recent Trends in the Sociology of Wales' in I. Hume and W. T. R. Pryce (eds.), *The Welsh and Their Country* (Llandysul, Gomer Press in association with the Open University) 176–92.
Williams, Jac L. (1979). 'The Welsh Language in Education' in Meic Stephens (ed.), *The Welsh Language Today* (Llandysul, Gomer Press), 93–111.

5

THE EFFECTS OF SECOND-LANGUAGE EDUCATION ON FIRST/SECOND-LANGUAGE DEVELOPMENT

C. J. Dodson

Introduction

For Professor Jac L. Williams it was self-evident that pupils had the right to be educated through the medium of their own language, and throughout his working life he did everything in his power to turn this principle into reality as far as Wales was concerned.[1] Yet his vision was not only focused on Wales. Through correspondence and overseas visits he attempted to give hope to other language communities who were struggling to realize the same aims under conditions which in many cases were even more difficult than those found in his own homeland. The truth is that the principle of education through one's own language in multilingual countries has never been accepted universally, whether on account of linguistic prejudice, politics, economics or plain fear.

Professor Williams felt concerned about two main situations. On the one hand he obviously had in mind countries such as Wales and Brittany, where the language spoken by the original inhabitants is eroded by the immense force of a more powerful language, to the point of becoming a minority language on its own territory. As a consequence minority-language pupils find themselves in classrooms where the language used exclusively as a medium of instruction is *not* the language of the hearth. At times, the only speakers of the majority language are the teachers, who may not even know the language of their pupils. Even if they do, they, like their pupils, may be forbidden to use it. This situation was a familiar one in Wales for the vast majority of Welsh-speaking pupils from the start of compulsory, English-medium, education in the middle of the nineteenth century right up to the end of the Second World

War. On the other hand, Professor Williams also had in mind the situation found in countries with large influxes of political and economic refugees or invited workers (*Gastarbeiter*) and their families. Germany is a good example of this particular category. Before the civil wars in various parts of Africa and the former Yugoslavia set into motion successive waves of refugees, Germany already had several million, mainly Turkish, guestworkers and their families. Their children have had to attend German schools where the medium of instruction across the whole curriculum is German, despite the fact that they cannot speak a word of German at the outset. They are expected to pick up German as fast as possible so that they can participate in the various subject-lessons alongside their German classmates. As early as the 1960s, during informal discussions, Professor Williams constantly made the prophetic point that this type of education would ultimately lead to trouble. He related their plight to that of the majority of Welsh-speaking pupils who at that time still found themselves in a similar situation to that of the Turkish children from a linguistic point of view. (For further details on the teaching of German as a second language to immigrants in Germany, see Reich 1979 and Hoffmann 1991).

Immersion

The second-language (L2) immersion education in which both categories of pupils find themselves has three consequences: firstly, although the pupils achieve a good level of fluency, they are in danger of developing what could be called a fossilized interlanguage (FI), when errors, even basic grammatical errors, made by L2 learners during communicative L2 acquisition gradually become 'frozen' or fossilized and are almost impossible to eradicate once established. FI can be characterized as a simplified form of the target language where pupils' use of vocabulary is limited, redundant language features are ignored, and many grammatical devices such as gender, number, tense, mutations, articles, etc. are avoided, eliminated or used wrongly, whilst at the same time a great deal of transfer from pupils' mother tongue causes interference. Some of the main reasons for this fossilization are given later in this chapter. (For further information on fossilization of errors and interlanguage, see Selinker (1969, 1972), Schumann (1978, 367–80)) and Spolsky (1989, Ch. XI). FI is by now a well-known phenomenon, although in countries where L2 (second-language) immersion education is found, the authorities have in the past tended to underplay its effects, while teachers themselves are often only too glad that their pupils are saying anything at all. I have observed this type of faulty use of language not only in International Schools where English is the sole medium of education for intakes of children who initially do not know any English and who speak a language other than English after school hours, but also in German state schools among even second-generation Turkish pupils whose parents went to German schools and who have lived in a German-speaking environment all their lives. (Also see Ferguson 1975, and James 1986.).

Secondly, although the pupils may find it relatively easy to understand the gist of what they hear from the teacher or from other more proficient pupils, since they can rely a great deal on non-verbal cues, this superficial understanding does not lead to the development of clear and unambiguous concepts and concept chains relating to the subject in question. Experiments conducted in Birmingham primary schools with ethnic minority children showed this quite clearly (Dodson, in preparation). For example, in a situation where Year 2 children with some knowledge of English were asked to retell in their own (English) words a story told them previously in simple English (with and without visual aids), they found this extremely difficult and most faltered after the first two or three sentences. When this same story was repeated in their mother tongue, they were able to retell the complete story in English without hesitation, although their speech contained grammatical errors. Not understanding some of the words or word clusters whilst listening to the story in English had caused interruptions in their attempt to process the successive concepts making up the story as a whole, thus making it more or less unintelligible for them. On further investigation it was found that some of the vocabulary not properly understood consisted of high-frequency items often spoken by the teacher in the classroom. However, in hindsight it was also realized that pupils had never used this high-frequency vocabulary themselves in their interactions with teachers. Similar experiments were made with topics relating to history, science and number work appropriate to their age level and background, and the same results were obtained (Dodson, in preparation). Rehbein (1987) made a similar story-retelling experiment in Germany with Turkish pupils and obtained the same results. It should be stressed that even if pupils clearly and accurately grasped the meanings of the sentences spoken by others, this would not by itself lead to accurate and fluent speech production. 'Comprehensible input', contrary to Krashen's view (1982), does not seem to be sufficient for effective second-language acquisition.

Thirdly, because of these pupils' inability to acquire the correct structures of their second language, they are loath to participate in spoken classroom interactions,[2] and as a consequence they tend to fall behind in the acquisition of curriculum knowledge and skills. It is a truism nowadays that successful education requires a great deal of active verbal interaction between teacher and pupils, and that a predominance of teacher talk in the classroom tends to slow down pupils' learning rate in all subject areas. If this is combined with mere gist understanding on the part of the L2 pupils, then their rate of understanding and processing subject knowledge will be even slower. Poor receptive and productive skills at the aural/oral level will be compounded at the written level, since inaccuracies which might pass unnoticed in speech become glaring, and worse still, virtually ineradicable when they appear in writing. Less easy to detect, and hence correct, is any inaccuracy in the pupils' reading comprehension; yet this will affect their ability to study across the whole curriculum (Dodson and Thomas 1984). It can be postulated that initially monoglot Welsh-speaking pupils taught entirely through the medium of English from the middle of the nineteenth century experienced the same linguistic insecurity in the use of English, causing them the same difficulties in the acquisition of knowledge and skills. Three generations after the introduction of English in schools as a medium of instruction, a considerable number of individuals, depending on their exposure to English after leaving school, still failed to eliminate FI and to reach a reasonable level of native-like competence in that language (T. Williams 1989). Turkish and other ethnic minority-language pupils, in Germany and elsewhere in Europe, who have little or no initial knowledge of the target language used as a medium of instruction, are a further case in point.

It should be noted that nothing said above refers to the development of speech fluency. Even first-generation learners may acquire L2 fluency reasonably quickly, given enough language contacts, but they become fluent speakers of incorrect speech. Nor are we referring here to the retention of the L1 accent which first-generation learners are unlikely to lose if they have not started to acquire the second language before the age of thirteen or so, depending on their capacity to mimic sounds. We are concerned here merely with the development and persistence of inaccurate syntax and vocabulary.

However, there is a further drawback if pupils experience monolingual L2 immersion education. Even before they leave school, they may find it increasingly difficult to communicate in their original first language, and if the L2 environment persists, some of them may lose their original language altogether by the end of their lifetime. Their children at least or their grandchildren are certain to lose that language, unless they receive original L1 reinforcement. This loss of language could be tragic; if immigrant parents are determined that their children learn the language of the new country, and have every intention of staying in that country, the damage done is perhaps not too great, as the language of their country of origin has not been lost to the world. The children, however, may find it very difficult when they are older to return to the old country without a feeling of being outsiders. Yet there are situations where the loss of an individual's L1 through L2 immersion education could have a much more devastating effect, for instance, in countries such as Wales where the language has no firm base elsewhere, and where its loss would consequently be final.

When Professor Williams advocated the introduction of Welsh-medium education for Welsh-speaking pupils, he was aware of the dangers of a mongolot educational system in a bilingual country, and always emphasized that pupils educated through the medium of Welsh should also be competent in English. He did not want Welsh first-language speakers to be at a disadvantage when it came to matters of employment and public life in Wales and throughout Britain. His aim was for schools to produce competent bilinguals and this, he believed, could only be achieved through bilingual education in one form or another. Professor Williams also held the view that the provision of Welsh-medium or bilingual education solely in Welsh-speaking areas, that is, where there was a sufficient concentration of pupils to allow the establishment of appropriate schools, would merely perpetuate the isolation of these pockets of Welsh, which would have difficulty in sustaining themselves in the long term. What he wanted to see in addition was a bilingual education system intended for *non*-Welsh-speakers in the Anglicized areas of Wales, so that Welsh could eventually be used in all regions. The Gittins Report advocated such a system in 1967, and two years later the Gittins recommendations for bilingual education in primary schools were implemented in some seventy schools in anglicized areas in the form of a Schools Council Project, whilst a further Bilingual Education Project for Secondary Schools was started in 1974. Professor Williams was extremely glad that the evaluation of the bilingual primary schools project as well as the direction of the bilingual secondary schools project was in the hands of members of his department at Aberystwyth. He and the Schools Council teams were hoping that the experience gained from these two projects would enable local authorities to set up their own bilingual schools for Welsh learners.

In the mean time the demand for Welsh-medium education for Welsh-speakers grew beyond the wildest expectations, until a point was reached when there were no longer enough Welsh-speakers in the various local areas for authorities to make the establishment of further Welsh-medium schools viable. However, during the 1970s many parents who had lost their Welsh were determined to send their monoglot English-speaking children to Welsh-medium schools, with the result that by the end of the decade some of the newly established Welsh-medium schools, both primary and secondary, began to receive more monoglot English-speakers than Welsh-speakers, and the movement towards the establishment of bilingual schools on a larger national scale, as envisaged by Gittins, came to a halt.[3] The pressure for total Welsh-medium, rather than bilingual, schools was fuelled by the apparent success of French-medium 'immersion' schools in Canada and the United States, where *all* the intakes consisted of monoglot English-speaking children. It was considered that if the French immersion programmes worked satisfactorily, then Welsh-medium schools with mixed intakes of both Welsh-speakers and originally monoglot English-speakers would be even better for Welsh-learners from a linguistic point of view. The development and fossilization of non-standard forms of Welsh among L2 speakers had not been envisaged at that stage.

Yet it should be pointed out that as early as the beginning of the 1970s researchers dealing with Canadian French immersion programmes were noting that pupils found it difficult in immersion teaching to acquire native-like French structures in normal L2 interactions. Baetens Beardsmore (1986, 128–9) refers to two of these researchers who at the time found that as soon as the L2 pupil in an immersion class realizes that he can make himself understood in the second language with incorrect structures, he will continue to use these structures in subsequent interactions,

> so that his strategy of communication becomes fossilized at the stage where he no longer needs to progress any further in the weaker language. Harley & Swain (1977, 75–6) show how this happens with English-Canadian children learning French. Their communicative needs in the classroom are orientated towards the conveyance of cognitive meaning and once the children have reached a point in their cognitive development where they can make themselves understood to the teacher and their classmates there is no strong social incentive to develop further towards native-speaker forms.

Cummins and Genesee (1985, 45), when analysing their observations of pupils made during the 1970s, state that 'although immersion students have developed a high level of communicative competence, certain types of grammatical errors persist in their speech and have proved extremely difficult to eradicate'. Carey (1984, 256), in a paper reflecting on a decade of French immersion, states that 'This study is consistent with other studies that have shown that immersion students speak a French that is highly discriminable from native French.' Hammerly (1989, 29), after years of research and observations, confirms in a review of French immersion education that

> listeners to a second language interpret what they hear on the basis of the language or languages they know, eliminating what seems redundant, such as certain endings, little unstressed words like articles and prepositions, and so forth, even though they are important in the second language. Of course, the listener as *listener* cannot be corrected by anyone, so without saying a word faulty second language structures are internalised.
>
> I think that by the time [French immersion] pupils start to speak French, at the end of Grade 1 or Grade 2, they have mentally stored so much incorrect and oversimplified material (mixed, in their minds, with English) that inevitably they will start speaking in a very faulty classroom 'pidgin'.

When comparing first- and second-language acquisition, Hammerly argues that young children acquiring their mother tongue face a very different situation, so for them subvocal memory storage or incorrect language – which, in any case, turns out to be only temporary – is not a problem. For the older child or adult, however, classroom learning conditions are such that the subvocal memory storage of faulty language very easily becomes permanent. And by then it is too late; extensive exposure to the language and intensive correction will result in some improvement, but much long-term harm is already done.

It was stated previously that mere gist understanding does not lead to accurate language at the productive level. During listening, pupils are focusing primarily on the 'messages' being sent, rather than on the form of the utterances, especially when speech is directed at them personally. During normal interactions with L1 speakers there is just not sufficient reflection time available to them to focus on both, although their level of concentration is extremely high in such situations. As stated by Hammerly, many utterances or parts of utterances spoken by others are of necessity filtered out and discarded by L2 listeners, so as to enable them to grapple with the overall message of the interaction, that is, the gist, or to make themselves ready for focusing on the next utterance to be spoken by the interlocutor. As such enforced and often random selectivity prevents the listeners from focusing to any great extent on both the message *and* the form of the utterances heard, it is extremely difficult for utterances to be reproduced accurately in subsequent speech, especially if they are of what native speakers consider to be normal length.

One of the difficulties L2 listeners have is that they cannot recognize what is the end of one word and the beginning of another. In an investigation into the problem of accurate L2 meaning acquisition using audio-visual courses, carried out in Aberystwyth in 1963 with pupils who did not know any French, it was found that a large percentage of them assumed that for the utterance 'il est sept heures', 'il est' meant 'seven' and 'sept heures' meant 'o'clock' (Dodson, 1974). Likewise, in experiments focusing on the same problem with ethnic-minority children learning English as a second-language in a Birmingham school, one of the children assumed that 'very hot' meant the single concept 'hot' (Dodson, in preparation). Although superficially this might be considered a small error, it can nevertheless cause linguistic nonsense as soon as the pupil attempts to apply this meaning-set to subsequent utterances. A London inner-city teacher reports[4] that one L2 pupil assumed that 'hit me' meant 'hit', after having heard the utterance 'He hit me'. When this pupil approached the teacher to complain that someone had hit another pupil, she said, 'He hit-me him'. Another example showed that a pupil took 'go home' to mean 'go'. These are merely a few examples taken from a large number of similar instances concerning pupils' faulty meaning acquisition. Although the majority of these meaning errors are dependent on an individual child's specific language environment, his/her linguistic pre-perceptions and the type of mother tongue, some errors seem to be universal.

However, in all these cases pupils find it extremely difficult, if not impossible, to substitute and/or extend utterance elements correctly, so as to create utterances with new and functionally appropriate meanings. The problem is compounded by the fact that many of the learners are not able to recognize the underlying structural grammar of the second language from the mere speech of others around them. On most occasions they will make do with 'what they have' by producing utterances which approximate normal L2 speech, and which they can retrieve from their internal store of imperfectly heard and remembered L2 utterances. The alternative is for them to say nothing at all and bring any interaction to an abrupt halt. As a matter of fact, developing bilinguals often find themselves in situations where they have to postpone the satisfaction of their personal needs of the moment, perhaps for many months, because they lack the linguistic tools (Dodson, in preparation). To make the task of acquiring a second language easier, some pupils will resort to bilingual help from other more proficient L2 learners, from bilingual dictionaries and phrasebooks or from parents and friends outside school. However, this help is not always available. Where the philosophy of the classroom actually dictates total avoidance of the pupils' mother tongue, many pupils will perhaps conscientiously avoid such bilingual activities — or make them surreptitiously and no doubt develop a sense of guilt in the process.

Given the above problems relating to ESL ethnic-minority learners or those found in French immersion programmes it would have been surprising had the same problems not arisen in Wales, and in fact it did not take long before L2 pupils began to use an L2 FI in

Welsh-medium schools. At the same time teachers reported[4] that the speech of their L2 learners even affected the way their first-language Welsh-speakers began to express themselves not only to their L2 peers but also among themselves. This is, perhaps, only a temporary phenomenon for a child with rich language contacts outside school or after leaving school. Potentially more damaging for these first-language Welsh pupils is the situation where teachers themselves simplify their language, or even (as reported by one Head of Department[4]) use FI Welsh to speed up and clarify their L2 pupils' understanding, thus depriving their L1 pupils of access to a sophisticated and structurally sound model of their own language. The same has been noted in inner-city schools in England where there is a high proportion of ethnic-minority pupils. In London and Birmingham schools, for example, first-language English-speaking teachers and L1 pupils alike have been heard to take on aspects of their L2 pupils' speech by wrongly omitting definite articles or at times by applying peculiar non-English substitutions or using an odd word order. Yet, it is important to note that no matter how correct the speech of teachers and L1 pupils, this is not sufficient by itself to help L2 learners avoid FI.

Assuming the second language is *actively* taught, which is not always the case in immersion programmes, the development of FI in L2 immersion education is ultimately due to the fact that the mother tongue of the pupils is avoided in the teaching of the second language as a help in L2 meaning acquisition. This methodology is based on the pedagogical principle that the learning of a second language should imitate as closely as possible the learning of one's first. This principle is a convenient one when teachers have little or no knowledge of their pupils' language. In other circumstances it is convenient for political or social reasons. However, the principle has proved suspect from the L2 learning point of view.

Medium- and message-orientated activities

Some aspects of L2 acquisition are indeed identical to L1 acquisition. However, others are not, and it is these differences which are crucial in an analysis of L2 acquisition and classroom practices. Of interest here are the performative strategies exhibited by both L1 and L2 learners, not merely because they are relatively easy to observe, but also because they are important for pedagogical reasons to be explained later.

Weir (1962) recorded the speech of her two-year-old *monolingual* child when alone in his cot before going to sleep. She found that her child operated at two main levels, both in private and public speech. At one level he played with language as if it were toy or a game. Here the focus was on the language itself or on his own language-learning process. In this game he generated utterances of four types: i) he imitated and repeated utterances heard previously; ii) he substituted utterance elements with other known utterance-elements in order to create hitherto unexpressed utterances or even new concepts; iii) he added elements to known utterances in order to extend their meaning or function; and iv) he chained together a number of known utterances in a flow of speech. He made these various types of utterance to himself rather than during communicative interactions with others. In addition to imitating isolated utterances heard previously he would on occasions combine two or more of the various utterance types described above in a linguistic order and in a connected flow of speech (Weir 1962, 109). For example he would combine imitation with substitution and extension:

a) What colour
   What colour blanket
   What colour mop
   What colour glass

b) I go up there
   I go up there
   I go
   She go up there

In a keynote conference lecture Bruner (1983) gives several examples of such speech activities, for example, where a little girl says, 'the hat − the blue hat − the blue blue hat [= the very blue hat]', as if learning to extend the length of utterances. She is, as it were, playing or practising with language by herself, outside normal communicative events. This form of pleasurable play, like any other form of play, is part and parcel of a child's learning how to cope with the world, both in the present and in the future. It can be said that she is rehearsing for a performance yet to come. Wells (1975, 53) calls these speech activities 'practice':

> *Practice* covers play with linguistic patterns at the level of sound, syntax or lexis, and substitution routines where attention is on the pattern rather than on the content of the utterance. (This category would include many of the utterances that Ruth Weir recorded and presented in 'Language in the Crib').

Butzkamm (1993, 64) gives several examples spoken by his own fifteen-month-old monolingual daughter as well as by the children of other researchers, including Lindner (1898, 47), Pilch (1966, 54), Ramge (1976, 80) and Miller (1977, 89). At times children 'rehearse' aloud in front of others, although their speech is not necessarily directed at others around them. Butzkamm (1993, 66) quotes Holt (1970, 71–2) who mentions the strategies used at mealtimes by his two-year-old daughter. She would say 'Pass the sugar. Pass the pepper. Pass the toast. Pass the jam.' When these items were handed to her, the other members of the family realized that she did not really want any of them and that she was in fact practising or testing her own use of language.

For very young children this enjoyable language game is, like any other play activity, an end in itself, since they will not be conscious at the time of its ultimate developmental purpose. When playing with language in the situations quoted above, the children's minds are focused on language or the language-learning process, so that such strategies can be called *medium*-orientated activities. They are, as it were, continually preparing themselves through verbal exploration and discovery for any future verbal interactions with other people. These interactions with others are *message*-orientated communication, because in those situations the message takes precedence over *how* to use the language or the medium. The more children learn how to cope at message-orientated levels, the greater their language proficiency, and the fewer are the occasions on which they will need to resort to medium-orientated speech activities. However, they will never disappear completely in later life, as can be seen, for instance, when a competent native speaker searches for a word during a conversation: at that moment the individual is reverting once more to a medium-orientated level. In terms of the above strategies first-language acquisition can thus be seen as a fluctuating process between medium- and message-orientated communication, with medium-orientated communication decreasing as an individual's language proficiency increases (see Dodson, 1985b).

Before dealing with the language strategies used by developing bilinguals, it should be noted that one of their languages will always be stronger (in terms of 'ease of use') than the other for given areas of experience, even though this difference might be extremely small in some of these areas. It should also be noted that either language could be the stronger for given areas. For the sake of clarity the weaker language will here be referred to as the second language.

Bilingual strategies of language acquisition

When strengthening their second language, developing bilinguals will, on the one hand, use the medium-orientated strategies described above for the first-language learner. On the other hand, when using these strategies they will often make use of their stronger language to consolidate the functional meaning of particular utterances by speaking them in both languages one after the other, as if they were acting as interpreters for their own purposes, especially if they are young children (see, for example, Leopold 1939–49; Burling 1971; or Fantini, 1976). Comparing and contrasting utterances across two languages also helps the developing bilingual to keep the two language systems apart. Depending on the amount of initial interpreting practice done for any language item, this strategy eventually disappears altogether, by which time the sentence-meaning has become fully welded to the second-language utterance. These bilingual interpreting activities occur with the strategies relating to imitation, substitution and extension.

However, naturally developing bilinguals have two major additional bilingual strategies in medium-orientated speech which are not available to first-language learners. On the one hand, whenever necessary they will ask for the functional meaning in their stronger language of words and sentences in the second which they have not understood or only partly understood. On the other hand, they will constantly seek, through their stronger language, models for correct and appropriate second-language utterances to satisfy the pressing needs of the moment, so that they will be able to express themselves correctly during subsequent message-orientated speech.[5] Adults regularly use the same bilingual medium-orientated strategies when they find themselves in a country whose language they do not know. Although language acquisition of both naturally developing monolinguals and bilinguals includes medium-orientated speech activities, for developing monolinguals these activities are *monolingual,* but for developing bilinguals they are *bilingual*; they are crucial for the L2 learner in his proper development of fluent and accurate monolingual L2 message-orientated communication. However, in many L2 immersion programmes such activities are taboo. The question must be asked whether the appropriate model for L2 teaching and learning ought to be the natural language-learning process of the young bilingual, or that of the young monolingual who by definition has no experience whatever of acquiring a second language.

If in the initial stages of second-language learning bilingual help is withheld or not available, as in L2-medium education, the individuals will have to guess the meaning of the L2 utterances they hear. It is obvious that at first they will guess incorrectly on many occasions, and as a consequence many of them will switch off and retreat into their shell, even if it is for that situation only. They will have to possess quite strong personalities to persevere in such interactions after having experienced a number of similar failures in the past. On many occasions the L2 learners must at best be satisfied with mere gist understanding through non-verbal cues and the previous acquisition of some L2 vocabulary.

As mentioned earlier, when pupils begin to speak in their second language in the classroom, the teacher is often so glad that the target language is being used, that any faulty language produced will not be corrected. This, of course, is a signal for the pupils concerned that they have made themselves understood, and as no correction was made, that the utterance spoken was linguistically correct. If the teacher does correct a pupil's utterance, this is often done rapidly in order to avoid an interruption in the verbal interaction, with the result that the pupil is not aware that a correct version has been given. I have observed many classroom situations in English-medium international schools in South America and Europe, as well as in state schools in Birmingham and Wales, where the teacher did, in fact, make a deliberate and slow correction of a pupil's faulty utterance, before continuing with the interaction. In less than five minutes, however, the pupil concerned would once again produce the same utterance with the same errors. It is clear that merely listening to correct forms does not help the pupil a great deal in the development of native-like utterances. It is also clear that a second language cannot be learnt properly through 'osmosis' only, that is, where the learners are plunged into a monolingual 'second-language bath'. In that situation most of them will drown.

L2 pupils receiving L2 education must not only be allowed to make use of bilingual medium-orientated strategies when by themselves, like their naturally developing bilingual counterparts, but they ought to be given active help by the teachers to apply these strategies properly. If this is done, pupils' L2 communicative competence increases more rapidly, and the development of FI is kept to a minimum and eventually almost totally eliminated. Without such help, pupils develop a 'façade' competence, where speech is faulty and individual utterances are often ambiguous as far as meaning is concerned. This is a most unsatisfactory state of affairs when the target language is being used for academic purposes, where accuracy in the expression of concepts is of prime importance.

When individuals' second-language speech consists more or less of FI utterances, it is often the case that a large number of their written sentences will also be in FI. I have seen many essays of this type written by pupils in international English-medium schools and by ethnic-minority pupils in Britain and Germany. The errors made are not merely spelling errors which could in fact be made by any first-language writer, but errors in word order or the omission of words. Tenses are invariably expressed wrongly, with a heavy emphasis on the use of the infinitive. It was also found that in the scripts of pupils of different ages the same errors appeared again and again, as confirmed by Cummins and Genesee (1985) when dealing with French Canadian L2 immersion programmes in Canada. It seems that years of L2 immersion education, often as many as fifteen, do not enable pupils to acquire the second language effectively, and at the end of it all they are left with an L2 speech facility which cannot, and does not, allow them to participate fully in the employment and leisure activities granted to the native speaker.

It should not be assumed, however, that the application of bilingual medium-orientated strategies as a corrective measure solves all problems overnight. It was the aim in a small experiment made in Birmingham primary schools with intakes of five-year-old community-language pupils who spoke little or no English on entry, to ascertain how long it would take before specific high-frequency utterances used during bilingual medium-orientated play would be used freely at message-orientated level (Dodson, in preparation). The teachers in the experiment initially established what they considered to be high-frequency utterances used by the pupils' first-language peers, for example: 'Please, give me xxx', 'Can I have xxx?', 'Can I go to the toilet?', 'I've lost my xxx'. The ESL unit in the multicultural centre of the authority had made translations of these utterances into various community languages together with bilingual tapes for the teachers' use. The pupils learnt to say each

English utterance after hearing from the teacher or the tape the equivalent utterance in their own language. The utterance was then placed into a small playlet consisting of three or four utterances which became a 'basic situation' for role-playing. Although the pupils greatly enjoyed this medium-orientated activity, they were still not necessarily using the utterances in real situations as they arose during the school day. In the case of one utterance, 'Please, do up my coat', it took a whole week or more of daily role-play including the specific utterance before the first of the pupils began to speak this English sentence as a genuine request without any prompting from the teacher.

It is important to note that the basic utterances, such as those above, which pupils had mastered at medium- and message-orientated levels were also used as springboards in substitution and extension work so that they learnt the skill of creating, to them, entirely new English utterances to express their own thoughts. Teachers were surprised to find how quickly pupils began to create and use a whole range of new utterances at message-orientated level, without having to resort to FI. Yet none of this could have been achieved without the pupils' having initially received precise first-language functional equivalents, followed by medium-orientated activities relating to comparing and contrasting, as well as substitution and extension. (For further information on substitution and extentsion work, see Dodson 1985a, 171–2 or 1974, 102–12). Whenever a pupil used an incorrect English utterance during the practice phase, he or she would not only be given the correct version but would also practise the correct version there and then, often together with the whole class. In other words, if grammatical accuracy is not emphasized from the very outset, it is almost impossible to prevent the development of FI.

As stated previously, L2 immersion programmes have a further effect on L2 learners. If monolingual L2 programmes persist, the learners' use of their first language, especially in the subject areas dealt with in secondary schools, will remain at a rudimentary level. Some older pupils in Welsh-medium schools report[4] that they find it most difficult to discuss academic subjects with linguistic ease in their original first language after years of focusing on these subjects in their second language. Unless there is a great deal of sympathetic help at home, there is a danger that at least a small minority of pupils in L2 immersion programmes will not only develop FI, but will also see the use of their first language atrophy in given areas of experience. When they leave school, they will be disadvantaged in areas of employment which require accurate and fluent use of either or both of their languages, although they may have a greater than average native intelligence.

Summary

In summary, the concerns expressed in this chapter relate to two main aspects of L2 education. The first of these is the effect of L2 education on L2 pupils' development towards fluency and accuracy in their second language, that is, towards competent bilingualism. As far as I know, no systematic study has been made of L2 pupils' proficiency in Welsh when they leave secondary school at the age of eighteen, that is, after thirteen years of Welsh-medium education.[6] These studies have, however, been made on Canadian French immersion programmes. Hammerly (1989, 16–17), for example, quotes Pellerin and Hammerly (1986), who made a study in 1984 with eighteen-year-old Grade 12 pupils from two secondary schools in the Vancouver area. The pupils had received French-medium immersion education from the age of five. The researchers had tape-recorded and transcribed informal, unstructured interviews on very familiar topics. Hammerly writes that

> the average number of incorrect sentences among these twelfth grade students was 53.8 per cent when only grammar and vocabulary were counted and 55.3 per cent when errors in the use of *liaison* and major pronunciation errors were included. There were, of course, considerable individual differences: the strongest student had 40.3 per cent incorrect sentences and the weakest 72. 48 per cent. This was after nearly thirteen years – or 7,000 hours of French immersion.

Hammerly (1989, 18) also makes the observation that

> although the students managed to communicate nearly all of their ideas, they did so in Frenglish, not French. Frenglish is not a language, nor a dialect, but an embarrassment. A 6-year old may sound cute coping with communication needs in very faulty French but would you say the same of a 30- or 40-year old?

In Wales one has to rely largely on anecdotal evidence from teachers, parents and university departments of Welsh. It would seem that specific and systematic investigations into the Welsh proficiency of L2 school leavers are much overdue. Internal or external examinations in subject areas are not an ideal way of measuring these factors, although they will give some indication.

Greater focus should be placed in schools on correct L2 speech right from the outset. As soon as new intakes begin to express themselves in faulty Welsh, corrective measures should be taken immediately. The precise meanings of those sentences with which pupils have difficulty should be given through pupils' L1, followed by interpretation and substitution practice at medium-orientated level. Pupils should be encouraged to find out from teachers the correct way or ways of expressing sentences they might need in Welsh at message-orientated level, but which they have not yet heard or been taught, together with subsequent speaking practice of these sentences. Teachers should also be fully aware that initially many sentences they speak have not been heard or consolidated by their pupils. Ideally teachers themselves should be given an opportunity to cope with a hitherto unknown L2 in an academic environment where this foreign/second language is spoken by the natives and used as a medium of education. This would show them how easy it is to slip into L2 FI if help of the kind mentioned above is not available. As this is not feasible, teachers will have to use their imagination to gauge how much empathy is required to satisfy the linguistic, and consequently personal, needs of their pupils.

Many Welsh-medium schools do have language preparation sessions during the preceding summer of their pupils' entry into their schools. It is suggested that such activities should be continued at least for the first two years or so, after the pupil has entered school. This would also give teachers time to gain precise information about their pupils' individual linguistic difficulties, and ensure that their L2 interlanguage does not become fossilized. Wherever possible, pupils' linguistic difficulties should also be tackled in specific lessons set aside for this purpose during term time. Whilst L2 pupils will have to be withdrawn from their L1 peers during these lessons, the advantages gained would more than compensate for any disadvantages, especially if the school took the necessary steps to ensure that no pupil suffered academically.

The other main concern in L2 education was the deterioration of L2 pupils' first language in given subject areas. The only way to overcome this is by introducing bilingual education for at least some subjects. The proportion of first-language teaching for L2 pupils of the subjects chosen need not reach 50 per cent. One lesson in five, carefully planned, would be sufficient to allow L2 pupils to acquire any new L1 vocabulary and, equally importantly, to develop a linguistic L1 fluency and syntax equivalent to that of their peers in monolingual schools for the same areas of experience. Inversely, bilingual education would also help L1 Welsh-speakers in the same classroom to express themselves fluently and accurately in what to them is their second language. This is precisely what Professor Jac L. Williams had in mind when he constantly reminded us that the future of Wales and its language depended on its population learning to become competent bilinguals.

Notes

1 Professor R. M. Jones, formerly Professor of Welsh at the University of Wales, Aberystwyth, confirms that Professor Jac L. Williams held the views attributed to him in this paper. At the time Professor Jones was Research Lecturer in Professor Williams's Department of Education.
2 'An "immersion school" for the first few months is painfully silent.' When L2 pupils begin to participate more in verbal interactions at a later stage, initially through one- or two-word responses, 'they don't always use it [the L2] correctly, of course; they make basic errors. The idea is to pick out these major errors and to drill them to eliminate faults of structure. This is difficult in the immersion situation...' (Swain, 1972, 26) Many of these errors thus become fossilized. This problem is compounded when L2 pupils find themselves in the same class as L1 speakers, especially when subject syllabuses have to be followed in a given time.
3 This development is confirmed by Eric Evans who was formally Language Adviser for the old County of Glamorgan and at the time was Director of the National Language Unit, Wales, and Director of the Schools Council Primary Schools Project in Bilingual Education during its final years, subsequently becoming Senior Lecturer in Education, University of Wales, Cardiff.
4 The evidence in all these instances is anecdotal, but it was offered to me directly by individuals who are familiar with this field.
5 Butzkamm (1993), when dealing with *bilingual* medium-orientated (private and public) speech activities of developing infant bilinguals, refers to a number of researchers (e.g. Kielhöfer and Jonekeit 1983, 57; Leopold 1949, 14; Porsché 1983; Ronjat 1913; Saunders 1980/82, 143, 195; Taeschner 1983, 42; Zierer 1977, 147) who have recorded the various types of bilingual medium-orientated speech activities of developing bilingual children. These include: a) repeating a word, phrase or sentence (depending on age) in the other language; b) asking for an L2 equivalent for an L1 utterance for immediate or later use when speaking in their L2;

c) asking in L1 for meanings of L2 sentences heard but not understood, and d) asking for confirmation in the stronger language to ensure that the meaning of L2 words, phrases or sentences heard has been correctly grasped.

6 Whilst writing this paper I was made aware of a study in progress by Dr Tim Williams who is investigating the Welsh proficiency of seventeen/eighteen-year-old final-year sixth-form L2 pupils as well as L2 school-leavers from Welsh-medium schools. Dr Williams records the speech of these pupils in small focus groups of six pupils during informal discussions. This work is ongoing. In a personal letter he writes that 'these pupils speak in a pidgin-like Welsh. My early findings show that the main errors are as follows:

a) tendency to use simple verb forms (*"Rydwi i wedi gwneud"* instead of *"Fe wnes i"*, that is, the perfect instead of preterite) and the over-use of the periphrastic present tense in Welsh;
b) avoidance of mutations;
c) deficiency of subject specific vocabulary in L2 (Welsh);
d) considerable interference from L1 in L2, in terms of sentence structure and vocabulary;
e) deficiency of general vocabulary in L1 (English);
f) tendency to 'reach for words' in L1 and malapropisms.

References

Baetens Beardsmore, H. (1986). *Bilingualism: Basic Principles*, 2nd edn., (Clevedon, Multilingual Matters).
Bruner, J. (1983). *The Challenge of Diversity*. Keynote lecture given at the 22nd Annual Conference of the Pre-school Playgroups Association, Llandudno, March 25, 1983.
Burling, R. (1971). 'Language Development of a Garo and English Speaking Child', in A. Bar-Adon and W. F. Leopold (eds.), *Child Language* (New Jersey, Prentice Hall), 170–85.
Butzkamm, W. (1993). *Psycholinguistik des Fremdsprachenunterrichts* (Tübingen, Francke Verlag, 2nd edition).
Carey S. (1984). 'Reflections on a Decade of French Immersion', *The Canadian Modern Language Review*, 41, 2, 246–59.
Cummins, J and Genesee, F. (1985). 'Bilingual Education Programmes in Wales and Canada', in C. J. Dodson (ed.), *Bilingual Education: Evaluation, Assessment and Methodology*, (Cardiff, University of Wales Press), 37–49.
Dodson, C. J. (1974). *Language Teaching and the Bilingual Method* (London, Sir Isaac Pitman and Sons). Reprint of paperback edition 1972, first published 1967.
Dodson, C. J. (1985a). (ed.) *Bilingual Education: Evaluation, Assessment and Methodology*, (Cardiff, University of Wales Press).
Dodson, C. J. (1985b). 'Second language acquisition and bilingual development: a theoretical framework', *Journal of Multilingual and*

Multicultural Development, Vol. 6, No. 5, 325–46.
Dodson, C. J. (In preparation). *The Bilingual Method: a Handbook for Foreign/Second Language Teachers.*
Dodson, C. J. and Thomas, S. E. (1984). *Multilingual Aids in the Classroom* (Aberystwyth, BALEC International).
Fantini, A. E. (1976). *Language Acquisition of a Bilingual Child: A Sociolinguistic Perspective,* (Battleboro, Vermont, The Experimental Press).
Ferguson, C. A. (1975). 'Towards a characterisation of English foreigner Talk', *Anthropological Linguistics* Vol 17, No. 1, 1–14.
Gittins Report (1967). *Primary Education in Wales* (Cardiff, Central Advisory Council for Education (Wales) HMSO).
Hammerly, H. (1989) *French Immersion: Myths and Reality* (Calgary, Alberta, Detselig Enterprises Ltd.).
Harley, B and Swain, M (1977). 'An analysis of verb form and function in the speech of French immersion pupils', *Working Papers in Bilingualism,* 14, 31–46.
Hoffmann, C. (1991). *An Introduction to Bilingualism* (London, Longman).
Holt, J. (1986) *How children learn* (Harmondsworth, Penguin).
James, C. (1986). 'Welsh foreigner talk: breaking new ground', *Journal of Multilingual and Multicultural Development,* Vol. 7, No. 1, 41–54.
Kielhöfer B. and Jonekeit S. (1983). *Zweisprachige Kindererziehung,* (Tübingen, Stauffenberg Verlag).
Krashen, S. D. (1982). *Principles and Practice in Second Language Acquisition* (Oxford, Pergamon Press).
Leopold, W. F. (1939–49). *Speech Development of a Bilingual Child,* Vols. 1 to 4, (Evanston, Illinois, Northwest University Press).
Leopold, W. F. (1949). *Diary from Age Two,* Vol. 4 of *Speech Development of a Bilingual Child: A Linguist's Record* (Evanston, Illinois, Northwestern University Press).
Lindner, G. (1989). *Aus dem Naturgarten der Kindersprache,* (Leipzig, Th. Grieben).
Miller, G. A. (1977) *Spontaneous Apprentices: Children and Language,* (New York, Seaburg Press).
Pellerin, M. and Hammerly, H. (1986). 'L'expression orale après treize ans d'immersion française'. *The Canadian Modern Language Review,* Vol. 42, 592–606.
Pilch, H. (1966) *Sprache als Spiel und Methode* (Freiburger Dies Universitatis).
Porsché, D. C. (1983). *Die Zweisprachigkeit während des primären Spracherwerbs* (Tübingen, Narr Verlag).
Ramge, H. (1976). *Spracherwerb und sprachliches Handeln,* (Düsseldorf, Schwamm).
Rehbein, J. (1987). 'Diskurs und Verstehen. Zur Rolle der Muttersprache bei der Textverarbeitung in der Zweitsprache', in E. Apeltauer, *Gesteuerter Zweitsprachenerwerb: Voraussetzungen und Konsequenzen für den Unterricht,* 113–172, (Munich, Hueber).

Reich, H. H. (1979). 'Deutschlehrer für Gastarbeiterkinder: Eine Übersicht über Ausbildungsmöglichkeiten in der Bundesrepublik', *Deutsch Lernen*, No. 3, 3–14.
Ronjat, J. (1913). *Le Développement du Langage Observé chez un Enfant Bilingue* (Paris, Librairie Ancienne, H. H. Campion).
Saunders, G. (1980/82). *Bilingual Children: Guidance for the Family*, (Clevedon, Multilingual Matters).
Schumann, J. H. (1978). 'The relationship of pidginization, creolization and decreolization to second language acquisition', *Language Learning*, No. 28, 367–80.
Selinker, L. (1969). 'Language Transfer', *General Linguistics*, No. 9, 671–92.
Selinker, L. (1972). 'Interlanguage', *IRAL* Vol. 10, No. 3, 209–31.
Spolsky, B. (1989). *Conditions for Second Language Learning*, (Oxford, Oxford University Press).
Swain, M. (ed.) (1972). *Bilingual Schooling* (Ontario, The Ontario Institute for Studies in Education).
Taeschner, T. (1983). *The Sun is Feminine: A Study on Language Acquisition in Bilingual Children*, (Berlin, Springer Verlag).
Weir, R. H. (1962). *Language in the Crib* (The Hague, Mouton & Co.).
Wells, C. G. (1975). *Coding Manual for the Description of Child Speech* (Bristol: University of Bristol School of Education).
Williams T. (1989). *Patriots and Citizens: Language Shift in a Liberal State: The Anglicisation of Pontypridd, 1818–1920*, Ph.D. thesis, the University of Wales, Cardiff.
Zierer, E. (1977). 'Experiences in the bilingual education of a child of preschool age', *IRAL*, Vol. 2, 143–9.

6
BILINGUAL EDUCATION AND ASSESSMENT

Colin Baker

Introduction: The aims of the chapter

The aim of this chapter is to analyse the commencement of National Curriculum assessment of the Welsh language in schools and its relation to bilingual education. Commencing with brief details of the Welsh Language National Curriculum and its attendant assessment procedures, the aims of Welsh-language assessment are then discussed followed by a consideration of recent research. The chapter concludes by integrating Welsh-language assessment in the National Curriculum with international concerns about the effectiveness of bilingual education. A criterion-referenced approach to language assessment on a national scale is relatively novel. The experience gained over the last five years in Wales is generalizable to other national contexts where national criterion-referenced assessment may be entertained.

Education reform

The National Curriculum in England and Wales was initiated by the 1988 Education Reform Act. The Act instituted the most radical change in British state education since Butler's 1944 Education Act. Alongside a National Curriculum, a National Assessment Programme was created. Pupils were to be tested at ages seven, eleven, fourteen and sixteen.

Both the National Curriculum and National Assessment procedures were designed to raise *educational standards* by defining what every child aged five to sixteen should be taught in specific curriculum subjects. For the first time in over a century of compulsory schooling, pupils' entitlement in the curriculum became statutory. Surrounding the radical reform was also a concern for a broader and more balanced curriculum. Until the National Curriculum was introduced, local schools and local education authorities could determine themselves what was to be taught. Local initiatives led to many progressive educational ideas and much creative development. At the same time, it created unintentional secrecy, idiosyncrasies in curriculum design and delivery, a lack of accountability and, in some schools and some curriculum areas, standards which needed to be raised. For example, in many primary schools in Wales, little or no science was taught. Whether Welsh was taught as a second language at primary and secondary level was left to local variations, local pressures and sometimes simply the changing tide of teacher supply and motivation.

Premature specialization also deprived many pupils of a broad and balanced curriculum. For example, over 60 per cent of pupils were not studying a modern foreign language beyond the age of fourteen. Another example of premature specialization was the strong gender bias in the curriculum, with very few girls electing to study science and craft subjects, and very few boys studying foreign languages. The high failure rate of less academic pupils in examinations, and the low examination entry rate of less able children, also produced a situation where many children were failing in the system and the reservoir of talent was not being fully or properly developed. The government's solution to such a situation was a National Curriculum and a national assessment programme.

The National Curriculum and National Assessment

The National Curriculum in Wales is currently composed of four core subjects and eight foundation subjects. The core curriculum areas of the National Curriculum are mathematics, science and English. Welsh is a core subject in schools in Wales where Welsh is the main medium of instruction. The foundation subjects of the National Curriculum are: technology, modern foreign languages, history, geography, art, music and physical education. Welsh is a foundation subject in schools in Wales where Welsh is not a main medium of instruction. Religious education has been a compulsory element of the curriculum of England and Wales since the 1944 Act. In each subject, Statutory Orders describe the knowledge, skills, concepts and processes to be taught (Welsh Office 1990, 1991; Schools Examination and Assessment Council 1991). Every subject is broken down into Attainment Targets. In the Welsh language as a curriculum subject, the Attainment Targets are three: listening/speaking, reading and writing (also handwriting in the early years). The Attainment Targets are defined by a series of ten developmental levels. The description of what constitutes a level attempts to avoid age-specific criteria. Within each level, *goals* and objectives (called Statements of Attainment) are defined for children to master. At around seven years of age, an average child is expected to be on Level two; most eleven-year-old pupils are expected to be at Level four (National Curriculum Council 1992). Thus, the underlying model for National Curriculum assessment is similar to the 'non-behavioural objectives' model of the curriculum used in the United States with accompanying criterion-referenced testing. This is explained and discussed further in the next section.

The Statements of Attainment are an important step forward in defining the Welsh-language curriculum. Such Statements of Attainment mostly provide criteria that are clear enough to be used as teaching goals, but avoid being so prescriptive as to trivialize the teaching and the assessment process. The Statements of Attainment have avoided the much criticized approach of the 1960s and the 1970s in over-defined and minutely specific behavioural objectives. While there are some Statements of Attainment that need to be redefined or placed at different levels, the overall majority of Statements of Attainment have been welcomed by teachers (GWASG (the acronym for an Evaluation Project in which the author was Research Director — see Appendix 1 at the end of this chapter) Report 25, 1993; GWASG Final Report, 1993). This appears to be because the Statements of Attainment provide a standard set of *goals* that is neither over-prescriptive nor too wide and ambiguous to be of value. The view of language contained within the Statements of Attainment admirably captures linguistic, functional and social communicative language goals. The Statements of Attainment do not just produce language skills, but also lend themselves to language concepts, language knowledge and language understanding, the basis of the full National Curriculum approach. Such goals and objectives (Statements of Attainment) are directly linked to a *criterion-referenced assessment system*. All children (except exempted Special Needs children) are required by law to be assessed by teacher assessment and/or by standard assessment tasks or tests at the ages of seven, eleven, fourteen and sixteen. The results for individual pupils on the criterion-referenced tests and teacher assessments are intended partly for internal school feedback (for example, formative information on individual pupils), partly for publication (for example, consumer information on the performance of individual schools). Thus, aggregated results for a class, school and local education authorities (LEAs) were sent to a central data bank (in 1991 and 1992) and performance data was published at a high level of aggregation (that is, at Local Education Authority level rather than at school level).

In 1991 and 1992, children taking Welsh as a core subject were tested at the age of seven (Key Stage 1). Pupils taking Welsh as a foundation subject (second-language Welsh pupils in the main) were assessed in 1992 solely by teachers. In 1992, pupils aged fourteen (Key Stage 3) in Wales were involved in the first pilot Welsh-language tests. Various analyses of this data are presented later. In 1993, in both primary and secondary schools, teachers' industrial action disrupted the National Curriculum testing arrangements. A boycott of the standardized tests was in part a reaction against perceived over-prescription in the curriculum, the manageability problems of dual teacher assessment and standardized task assessment; and was partly due to major concerns about the very rapid pace of change (Curriculum Council for Wales 1993). Following a Government report by Sir Ron Dearing (1993), future tests and tasks will simply assess basic skills in the core subjects. Teacher assessment is expected to cover the wider area of skills, knowledge and concepts throughout the National Curriculum.

National criterion-referenced testing

A criterion-referenced system can be simply defined as a comparison between a child and the subject matter of the curriculum (Rowntree 1987; Shepard 1991). What curriculum objectives has the child met and where is remedial action necessary? Such a criterion-referenced system aims at providing feedback and feedforward to the classroom teacher to enable classroom decisions about individual pupils, curriculum delivery and the effective use of curriculum resources (Brown 1981; Blenkin and Kelly 1992). The general argument is that criterion-referenced tests are more likely to increase standards of attainment in the curriculum than norm-based tests as they provide directly relevant and usable information for the teacher (Wood 1991). However, criterion-referenced tests can have a number of different purposes (Gipps 1990, 1992, 1993; O'Hear and White 1993; Wolf 1993). These are now explored in terms of National Curriculum assessment aims. Issues about language assessment are little different from general assessment issues. Hence, the following discussion treats assessment generally with language assessment being used as the example.

The purposes of assessment

It is important to define the aims of assessment. Such aims are the same for language assessment as for assessment in any other curriculum area. Teacher and task assessment via the Attainment Targets and their attendant Statements of Attainment may be concerned with the following ten overlapping and interacting aims:

1. The *diagnosis* of the mastery, or incipient mastery, of Attainment Targets and Statements of Attainment, with accelerated learning as a possible outcome. Diagnosis (or *formative* assessment) also reveals weaknesses of individual children on a specific Attainment Target or Statement of Attainment that need remediation and the further development of skills, concepts, knowledge or understanding.
2. The *summative* assessment of individual pupils. National Curriculum assessment through standardized tests and tasks occurs near the end of the school year. This provides a 'summing up' of an individual's level of achievement for that school year.
3. The *screening* of individual children who are in need of special help. For example, early detection of language weaknesses in a child may effect initiatives in the provision of curriculum resources and language teachers.
4. *Record keeping:* for example, the transferring of information to successive teachers within a school, in the transfer of achievement records from primary to secondary school, and in the transfer of information at individual pupil level to parents.
5. *Feedback to individual teachers* on their level of success with the children they teach and hence their classroom effectiveness. This may be information which allows a teacher to monitor parts of a reading or writing exercise that have been mastered or less well understood by children. Such feedback allows remedial teaching

action through, for example, a change in teaching materials, teaching style or classroom organization.
6. *Feedback to schools* on their performance relative to previous years and relative to other schools. When assessment data is standardized and aggregated, individual schools may evaluate their relative success and determine what developments may be needed to improve standards of teaching and learning.
7. *Feedback to parents* about their child's level of attainment and about progress during a school term and school year.
8. Assessment in the National Curriculum may be one source of data useful for examining *school effectiveness* and 'value addedness'. Aggregated feedback may be valuable to headteachers, governors, prospective parents and to institutions beyond the school (e.g. employers) who wish to monitor effective performance at a classroom or school level.
9. When *LEA monitoring* of schools and *national monitoring* occurs, assessment data from schools allows analysis across years and across schools.
10. Assessment in the National Curriculum can have other purposes: for example, as part of course assessment for *certification* (e.g. Key Stage 4) and for *selection* purposes (e.g. in grouping children).

Given such a range of purposes for National Curriculum assessment, it becomes important to examine whether criterion-referenced language tests can provide *valid* information to meet each and all of these purposes. Hence, this chapter now considers the validity of criterion-referenced National Curriculum assessment with a focus on the purposes of assessment.

Validity and reliability in National Curriculum assessment

Classically, validity concerns the extent to which a skill, concept or attitude, for example, is accurately and effectively measured. Validity is often assumed to be 'the extent to which a test measures what it says it measures'. Validity in National Curriculum assessment centres on how exactly pupil attainment on the Statements of Attainment and the Attainment Targets is measured. There is difficulty in precisely defining, and therefore exactly measuring, the language Attainment Targets (Listening and

Speaking, Reading and Writing). Only on the surface are the language targets of oracy, reading and writing 'obvious' and 'straightforward to measure'. As soon as we ask what constitutes these competences, differences of definition and classification occur (Baker 1993a). Does pronunciation and dialect matter in oracy? How should context play a part in measuring reading and listening? How important is spelling in writing? Answers to such questions vary among teachers, academics and over decades as they reflect values, attitudes and beliefs.

The justifiable avoidance of highly specific behavioural objectives and the goal-based nature of Statements of Attainment mean that measurement cannot be as exact and precise as traditional norm-based standardized measurement. The specification of language goals necessarily invites personal interpretation. The defensible ambiguity of Statements of Attainment such as 'Write a range of passages presenting information, and use vocabulary, phrases, sentence patterns familiar to them from their work across the curriculum' (Writing Attainment Target, Level 3, Statement of Attainment iii), means that assessment will require value judgements and the growth of common understanding among teachers. Accepted and standardized interpretations can only evolve among educationists. They cannot be imposed.

To estimate the validity of National Curriculum assessment tests and tasks, it has become customary to engage in a thorough inspection of test or task items and consider the extent to which these items logically measure the Attainment Target and relevant Statements of Attainment. This is *content validity*. Since there is human judgement required, this task can valuably be attempted by *expert groups*. Membership of such groups needs to balance language experts, expert teachers and assessment experts. Expert groups need to be independent of test-developing agencies yet maintain clear lines of communication with such agencies. Content validity can be assessed by a searching examination of the initial drafts of the tasks and tests for *content relevance and completeness*. A stronger version of content validity requires the post hoc examination of pupils' *answers*. Expert groups can judge a priori the face validity of items. Only after the test has been used can evidence be gathered about the extent to which the test has 'worked' effectively and fairly with pupils. Debriefing by teachers is insufficient. Examining a sample of pupil responses is required to see what answers were elicited within the context of actual National Curriculum assessment periods. This can be part of the role of a test-writing agency.

The extent to which a test is valid depends partly on *what it is expected to be valid for.* What uses are going to be made of the information gained from the test: for screening, diagnosis, record-keeping, curriculum feedback, selection or judgement about school effectiveness? National curriculum assessment is unlikely to be equally valid and valuable for each of these purposes. Thus, there is a need to define the way in which the test information is going to be used. Subsequently, the test constructor needs to build a test that is valid for that purpose. It then becomes important to gather evidence to show that decisions can be properly made on the basis of test results. For example, can such assessments be aggregated to give information about the effectiveness of a particular school? What inferences can be validly made on the basis of National Curriculum assessment? It is possible that, in Welsh-language assessment, content validity has become too central in discussions. It may be that the more important validity issue is whether the information from assessment is valid for the *purposes* to which the information will be put. This requires clear specification of the use (or uses) for which the assessment information. Is the information from assessment: for the diagnosis of pupil strengths and weaknessess; for the summative assessment of pupils; for screening; for record-keeping, reporting, transfer; for general teacher feedback; for general school feedback; for feedback to parents; for informing about school effectiveness; for local area and national monitoring; for selection or certification? It may be that *different forms of tests and tasks* are needed for these different purposes. This idea is now explored in more detail.

The curriculum and managerial uses of assessment

An important distinction can be made between the *curriculum* uses of teacher assessment and its *managerial* uses. (However, there are many overlaps and important interactions between the two uses.) The *curriculum* use of teacher assessment is to help the teacher ensure the constant progress of children in the National Curriculum, and to develop their own teaching performance. The *managerial* use of teacher assessment concerns providing information for the monitoring and performance of teachers, classes and/or schools. While the Task Group on Assessment and Testing (DES/Welsh Office 1988) suggested that teacher assessment could fulfil both the curriculum and managerial functions, experience of the National Curriculum has suggested that teacher assessment has greater value in curriculum feedback. The managerial uses of teacher assessment uses may be more problematic. The managerial functions of assessment appear to require highly reliable tests that can broadly sample pupil achievement with speed. Current National Curriculum assessment is trying to carry both curriculum and managerial functions — less successfully than may be desirable. The nature of curriculum and managerial assessment appears to require different forms of testing. The varying *strengths* of teacher assessment and standardized test and task assessment are summarized in Table 1. This table tends to oversimplify, overstereotype, overcategorize and contains 'pairs' that are not opposites. There is a false dichotomy in this table which hides many complex dimensions. However, the table makes an important point. The differences suggest *the value of both forms of assessment and their separation:*

Both the curriculum and managerial functions of assessment rely on the supply of data and evidence from individual pupils. This chapter therefore moves to outlining briefly the composition of pupil assessment data. This is necessary to an understanding of data analyses to be presented in a later section.

The National Curriculum assessment of an individual pupil will often result in a score and/or a level. Scores will be converted into levels. This level will represent an individual's attainment which may have depressed or accelerated performance. For example, such effects may relate to classroom practices, school policies, school environments (e.g. class size, resourcing) and school composition (e.g. entry characteristics and progress levels of other pupils), and the social, cultural and economic characteristics of the home, community and school. There will also inevitably be some invalidity and unreliability in measurement, in the testing environment, sometimes in the marking and aggregation, and in the mood (e.g. test anxiety) and motivation of the pupil. All human measurement will be prone to measurement error. Tests and tasks have to attempt to minimize sources of invalidity and unreliability.

Effective National Curriculum criterion-referenced language tests and tasks must closely reflect National Curriculum approaches

Table 1: Teacher assessment, and standardized test and task assessment

Teacher assessment when curriculum based	Standardized assessment when managerial based
1. Focus on curriculum goals, integrated with teaching.	1. Focus on managerial goals, integrated with central policy.
2. Responsive to individual pupils.	2. Responsive to customers and managers (governors, administration).
3. Focus on individual pupils' progress.	3. Focus on school effectiveness.
4. Assesses qualitatively and quantitively.	4. Assesses quantitatively.
5. Assesses skills, concepts, understanding, attitudes and higher order skills (e.g. problem-solving creativity).	5. Assesses foundational subject skills and concepts.
6. Assesses lengthy classroom processes.	6. Assesses classroom products.
7. Contextualized – adapted to varying classroom situations.	7. De-contextualized – standard across classrooms.
8. Assessment on multiple occasions.	8. Assessment on a single occasion.
9. Authentic performance assessment (e.g. practical work, homework).	9. 'Test conditions' assessment.
10. Individual level (pupil) analysis.	10. School and Area analysis (aggregated information).
11. Formative classroom feedback.	11. Summative departmental and school feedback.
12. Comprehensive and detailed competences (e.g. at Statement of Attainment level).	12. Representatice sample of pupils' achievements (e.g. in an Attainment Target such as Reading).
13. Multi-media approach possible.	13. Tendency to written tests.
14. Moderation by teacher consensus.	14. Moderation by experts.
15. Moderate reliability of assessments.	15. High reliability of assessments.
16. High validity of assessing curriculum.	16. Moderate validity of assessing curriculum.
17. Holistic, complex, cross-disciplinary assessment.	17. Explicit, defined assessment items.
18. Relatively time-consuming.	18. Speedy survey testing.
19. Profile reporting – criterion-referenced (e.g. by Statement of Attainment).	19. Test score results – comparative.
20. Internally organized.	20. Externally organized.

to language represented in the Statements of Attainment. As previously stated, the view of language contained within the Statements of Attainment combines linguistic, functional and social communicative language goals. Thus, pencil-and-paper tests, for example, will not reflect the partly communicative approach to the Welsh-language National Curriculum. Practical tasks, teacher observations of indvidual and group work are needed to assess oracy; tasks rather than tests. Measuring authentic language situations by assessment tasks is clearly difficult and is not represented in pencil-and-paper tests (Verhoevan and de Jong 1992). Oracy assessment needs to relate to genuine communication. Genuine communication is often unpredictable and creative, bounded by a relationship and a particular context, and has a purpose (e.g. trying to persuade or negotiate). Oracy assessment therefore requires authentic communication situations and should avoid contrived, simulated conditions. Such issues in oracy assessment suggest that *teacher assessment* is crucial. A teacher can observe and record throughout the year, use different situations and contexts, observe the child interacting with different people, and use the different functions of oral communication. The assessment of oracy is complex and lends itself to the continuous monitoring inherent in National Curriculum teacher assessment.

Before moving to the 'results' part of this chapter, it is important to note that there are many other important aspects of a national system of criterion-referenced assessment that cannot be discussed in the space of one chapter; these include:

1. the structure of language performance, defining appropriate language goals and objectives;
2. the complexities of allocating such goals to levels;
3. the integration of teaching and assessing oracy, reading and writing;
4. the nature of standard language tasks and their difference from standardized tests;
5. the nature and process of teacher assessment;
6. defining national standards;
7. the reliability of assessment,
8. the manageability of assessment in the classroom;
9. the aggregation from marks on tests to Statements of Attainment to Attainment Targets to Subject scores;

10. the integration of teaching and assessment;
11. the in-service education of teachers for assessment;
12. the production of tests and tasks, logistic arrangements and infrastructures for National Curriculum assessment;
13. the exemption or inclusion of children with special educational needs;
14. gender differences;
15. integrating first- and second-language assessment into a continuum;
16. comparability and compatibility in teacher assessment;
17. the moderation of assessment by teachers and examiners;
18. the relationship between levels and age of pupils;
19. the unintended positive and negative effects of testing on pupils, teachers, schools and the curriculum;
20. the number of levels possible to assess in any one task or test;
21. the importance of allowing for the different intake characteristics of schools before engaging in school comparisons;
22. the importance of measuring the progress of children and not just their current performance.

A consideration of the issues listed above was undertaken by the GWASG evaluation project based in the School of Education, University College of North Wales (March 1992 to September 1993). A full list of GWASG Reports is given in an appendix to this chapter; internationally generalizable aspects of the evaluation and its relationship to concerns about the effectiveness of bilingual education will be presented in Baker (forthcoming).

Having considered the background to National Curriculum assessment and the key issue of the purpose and validity of testing, this chapter now moves on to consider results from the assessment. Theses results focus on the language performance of bilingual pupils and bilingual schools in Wales. Linking with the first part of this chapter, the results are examined through the particular perspective of criterion-referenced assessment. Competence will become more important than contrasts.

The performance of bilingual children in the National Curriculum: a criterion-referenced perspective

As part of the Key Stage 3 (age fourteen) Welsh-language assessment trials in fifty-five schools, the National Foundation of

Educational Research team (based in Swansea, south Wales) collected data on children's language background which were made available to the GWASG project (NFER, 1992). In all fifty-five schools, Welsh was assessed as a first language only. All schools could thus be classified as Welsh-medium or 'bilingual' schools. Teachers were requested to record (alongside children's attainment in the Welsh-language Attainment Targets) the following information about each child assessed:

Siaradai Cymraeg cyn dechrau addysg ffurfiol   *neu*
Ni siaradai cyn dechrau addysg ffurfiol

Spoke Welsh before starting formal education   or
Did not speak Welsh before starting formal education

Children in this second group had thus learned Welsh at school and were taking their education mostly through the medium of Welsh. Using the data supplied by the NFER, children's attainment on the three language Attainment Targets was examined in terms of these two language background categories. Graphs 1, 2, 3 and 4 display the similarities and differences between Welsh home language, and English home language speakers in their attainment across the oral, reading and writing Attainment Targets.

It is possible to locate differences in these graphs between 'mother-tongue' Welsh-speakers and those speaking English before formal schooling. Although these differences are statistically significant, such statistical significance should not be confused with substantive significance as will be discussed later. The differences indicate that children who spoke Welsh before school are slightly more likely to achieve Levels 6, 7, and 8 in Welsh (first language) as a subject (i.e. an aggregation of oral, reading and writing attainment) than those speaking English (only) before school. For example, 19.8 per cent of Welsh 'mother-tongue' children achieved Level 6 compared with 13.8 per cent of English 'mother-tongue' children. There is a tendency for English 'mother-tongue' children to be represented in higher percentages at Level 3 than 'mother-tongue' Welsh children. At the 'Welsh as a first language' subject level (i.e. oral, reading and writing combined), 12.7 per cent of 'mother-tongue' Welsh children are at Level 3 compared with 22.5 per cent of English 'mother-tongue' children. A similar pattern is found with the oral, reading and writing assessment. While there are differences, it is important to judge the differences by two criteria:

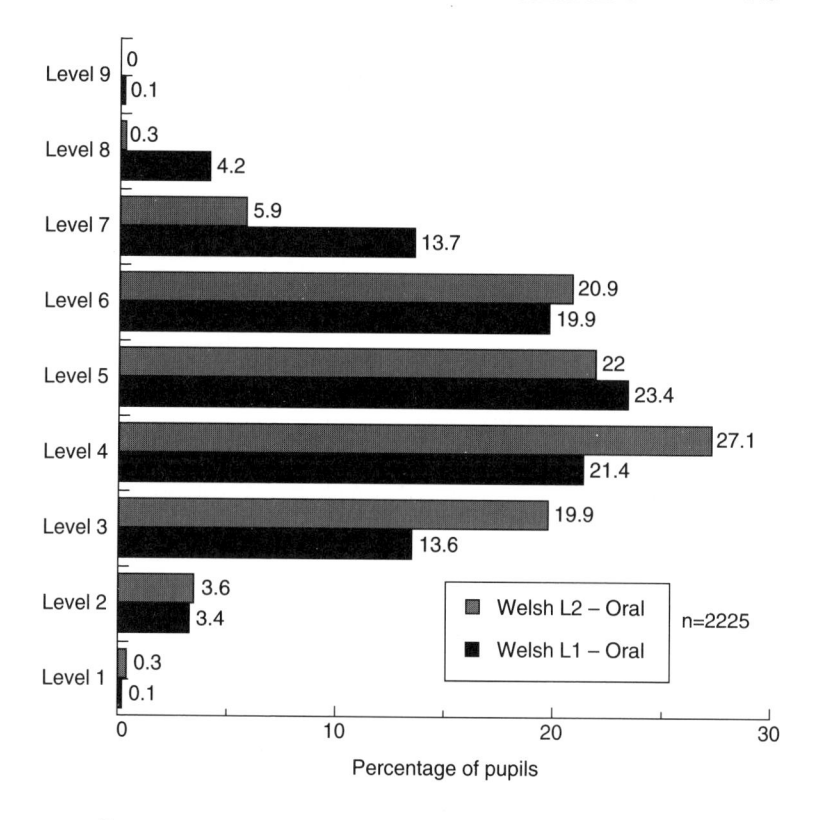

Level	Welsh L2 – Oral	Welsh L1 – Oral
Level 9	0	0.1
Level 8	0.3	4.2
Level 7	5.9	13.7
Level 6	20.9	19.9
Level 5	22	23.4
Level 4	27.1	21.4
Level 3	19.9	13.6
Level 2	3.6	3.4
Level 1	0.3	0.1

n=2225

Graph 1: Oral attainment in Welsh at Key Stage 3 by first- and second-language Welsh children

first, the distribution of English first-language and Welsh first-language speakers *within* their groups, and secondly, the *size* of the difference. When these two analyses are undertaken, *similarities between first- and second-language Welsh-speakers become more apparent.* In a criterion-referenced assessment system, the important focus is the distribution of pupils (e.g. 'mother-tongue' English and 'mother-tongue' Welsh) across levels, rather than a comparison of groups. So irrespective of differences, what levels did children with differing home languages attain?

The two most frequent levels for 'mother-tongue' English children are Levels 4 and 5. 32.2 per cent of English 'mother-tongue' children obtained Level 4, and 25.6 per cent obtained Level 5 at the subject level (i.e. oral, reading and writing combined). Given that

Reading attainment data

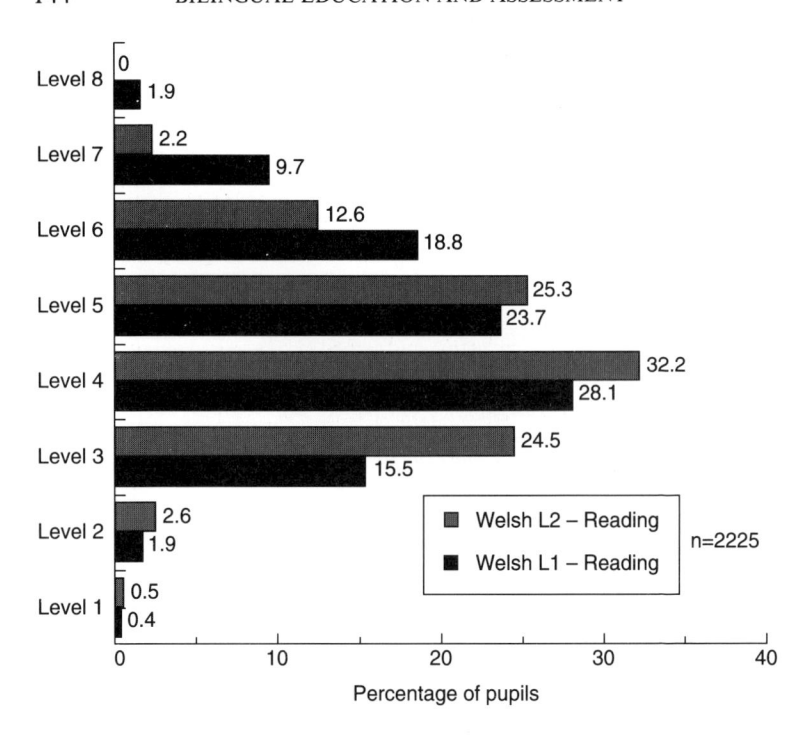

Level	Welsh L2 – Reading	Welsh L1 – Reading
Level 8	0	1.9
Level 7	2.2	9.7
Level 6	12.6	18.8
Level 5	25.3	23.7
Level 4	32.2	28.1
Level 3	24.5	15.5
Level 2	2.6	1.9
Level 1	0.5	0.4

n=2225

Graph 2: Reading attainment in Welsh at Key Stage 3 by first- and second-language Welsh children

Levels 4 and 5 are within the range of attainment appropriate to Key Stage 3, large numbers of Welsh second-language children appear to be performing at expected levels. Four out of every ten English 'mother-tongue' children are at Level 5 or higher, and three out of every four English 'mother-tongue' children are at Level 4 or higher. Those who are at level three and below will include those who started Welsh-medium education late (e.g. at age eleven, year 7) and those with special needs. If the focus on 'mother-tongue' English-speakers moves to Levels 6 and 7, it is clear that home language does not prevent achievement at these high levels. One hundred and twenty-six (out of 910) 'mother-tongue' English children achieved Level 6; eighteen pupils achieved Level 7. A home language which is different from school language is not an impediment to success in Welsh, even when first-language criteria are used for assessment. To summarize: in terms of the distribution of 'mother-tongue' Welsh children across the levels, there is evidence that such children are achieving levels in Welsh first language that are age appropriate.

When differences between Welsh and English 'mother tongue' are discussed, the crucial question is not whether there are differences, but the *extent* of those differences. It is important to ask whether home language has a large, medium or small effect on Welsh-language attainment in the National Curriculum. Table 2 presents the correlations between 'mother tongue' and attainment at Key Stage 3 in the three Attainment Targets. These correlations are small. A correlation of 0.2 on a scale of 0 to 1.0 must be regarded as low and not substantially (educationally) significant. Thus, while

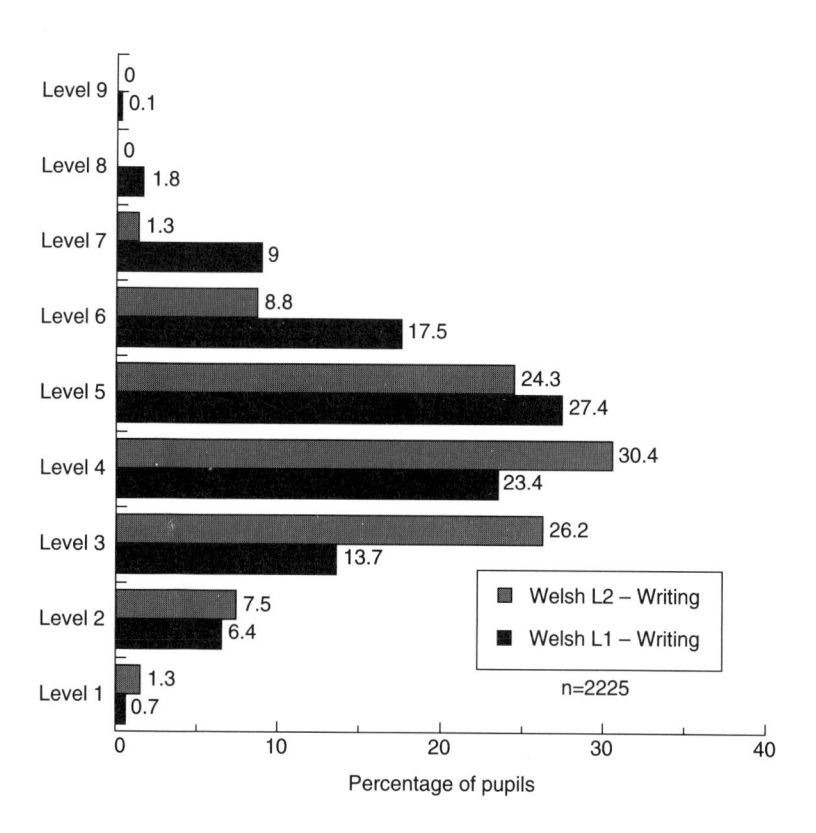

Level	Welsh L2 – Writing	Welsh L1 – Writing
Level 9	0	0.1
Level 8	0	1.8
Level 7	1.3	9
Level 6	8.8	17.5
Level 5	24.3	27.4
Level 4	30.4	23.4
Level 3	26.2	13.7
Level 2	7.5	6.4
Level 1	1.3	0.7

Percentage of pupils (n=2225)

Graph 3: Writing attainment in Welsh at Key Stage 3 by first- and second-language Welsh children

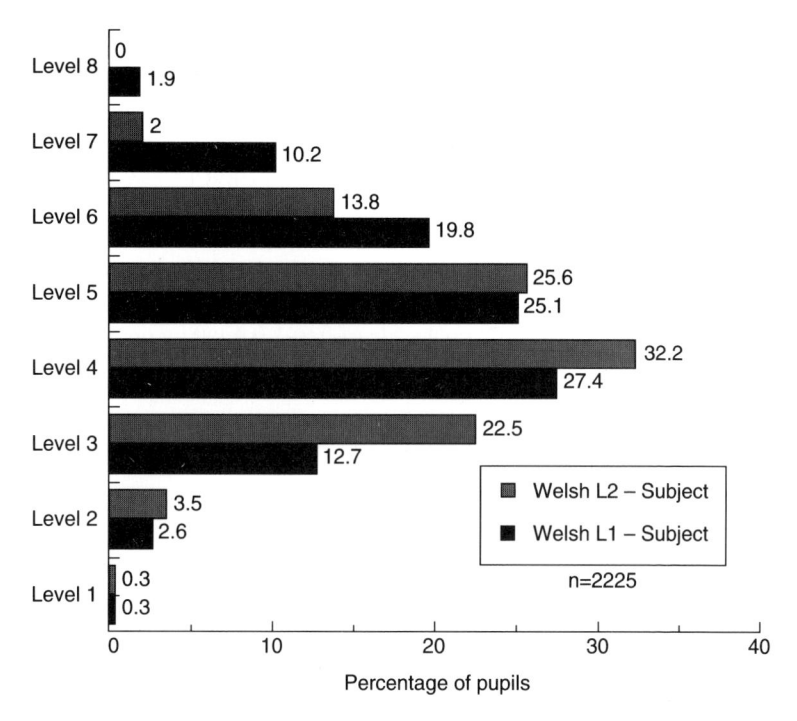

Graph data

Level	Welsh L2 – Subject	Welsh L1 – Subject
Level 8	0	1.9
Level 7	2	10.2
Level 6	13.8	19.8
Level 5	25.6	25.1
Level 4	32.2	27.4
Level 3	22.5	12.7
Level 2	3.5	2.6
Level 1	0.3	0.3

Percentage of pupils (n=2225)

Graph 4: Overall subject attainment in Welsh at Key Stage 3 by first- and second-language Welsh children

home-language Welsh children are performing slightly better than children from English-speaking homes, the difference is marginal.

These results suggest, firstly, that in a criterion-referenced system, the accent should be on 'absolute' rather than 'relative' achievement. That is, evaluation should be made against expected distributions rather than by directly contrasting the two language groups. The distribution of 'mother-tongue' English-speakers across the levels appears at least satisfactory. With significant percentages of 'mother-tongue' English-speakers achieving Levels 5, 6 and 7, there is clear evidence that home language (e.g. English) does not disadvantage Welsh-language National Curriculum achievement. Secondly, the results show that it could be expected that the potential advantage of having parents and siblings speaking Welsh at home would have an effect on children's Welsh-language

Table 2: Home language and Welsh (as a first-language) attainment

			Spearman correlation
(a)	Oral	Standardized tasks	0.15
(b)	Oral	Teacher assessment	0.19
(c)	Reading	Standardized tasks	0.19
(d)	Reading	Teacher assessment	0.20
(e)	Writing	Standardized tasks	0.24
(f)	Writing	Teacher assessment	0.22

The correlations are between Attainment Targets and Home Language. Home language is defined by a breakdown into two categories: 'Spoke Welsh before starting formal education'; 'Did not speak Welsh before formal education'. (Number of pupils = 2225)

school performance compared with children who experience English at home for most or all of the non-school week. However, such an effect is small as is indicated by the low correlations.

Key Stage 1 results

This chapter will now consider Key Stage 1 (age seven) results from research in 1991 by the University of Leeds and the NFER. These results are different from those presented for Key Stage 3 (age fourteen). First, the numbers are not large and may not be generalizable (the Leeds research contained sixty-four pupils fluent in Welsh and 258 not fluent; the NFER research used 413 Welsh-medium pupils and 495 English-medium pupils in Wales). Second, the exact language categorization of these pupils is not precise enough. The Leeds study compares those fluent and not fluent in Welsh. The fluent Welsh-speakers may not all be in Welsh-medium education. The NFER report concerns Welsh-medium school children (a mixture of first- and second-language children) compared with English-medium education in England and Wales.

The evaluation of National Curriculum assessment at Key Stage 1
A team from the School of Education from the University of Leeds in their report entitled 'The evaluation of National Curriculum

assessment at Key Stage 1' (Shorrocks 1992), analysed the performance of different pupils on teacher assessment and standardized task assessment at Key Stage 1. Section 8.5 of the report, entitled 'The performance of children from different ethnic background and the effect of home language', analysed children from varying ethnic origins on overall National Curriculum subject scores. For example, British Pakistani children tend to attain lower levels than other ethnic groups in English, Mathematics and Science. Also, Black British Caribbean and British Indian children tended to attain lower levels than white children in English and Mathematics but not in Science. The report explains the differences in terms of home language: 'A major factor in some of these differences was the fact that the home language of many of the children from different ethnic origins was not English' (page 101). Such a statement is at least controversial, and essentially lacks evidence to back it up. Casting home language as the 'cause' of ethnic group differences seems a naïve guess. International research literature indicates that language is not usually regarded as a direct 'cause' of underachievement (see Baker 1993a for a review). Rather, socio-economic differences, variations in cultural belief in the 'value of education', quality of schools and teaching, and a lack of collaboration between home and school will tend to be stronger (interacting) explanations.

In Wales, the schools used in the Leeds project were asked to indicate the fluency of children in Welsh. Classification was in terms of being either fluent in Welsh (presumably including fluent Welsh second-language speakers) or being non-fluent in Welsh. These two groups were compared on their performance in Science and Mathematics at Key Stage 1. Graphs 5 and 6 are derived from page 102 of the Leeds report showing levels of performance of Welsh-speakers.

Analysis by the Leeds Evaluation Team suggested that at subject PC (profile component) and AT (attainment target) levels (both teacher assessment and standardized task), the fluent Welsh-speakers performed better than the non-fluent Welsh-speakers (page 103). No explanation is given for this result. This leaves the crucial question unanswered: 'What is it about being fluent in Welsh that is connected with higher levels of National Curriculum attainment?' Only recourse to the international literature (see Baker 1993a) provides a set of possible answers. There is no current

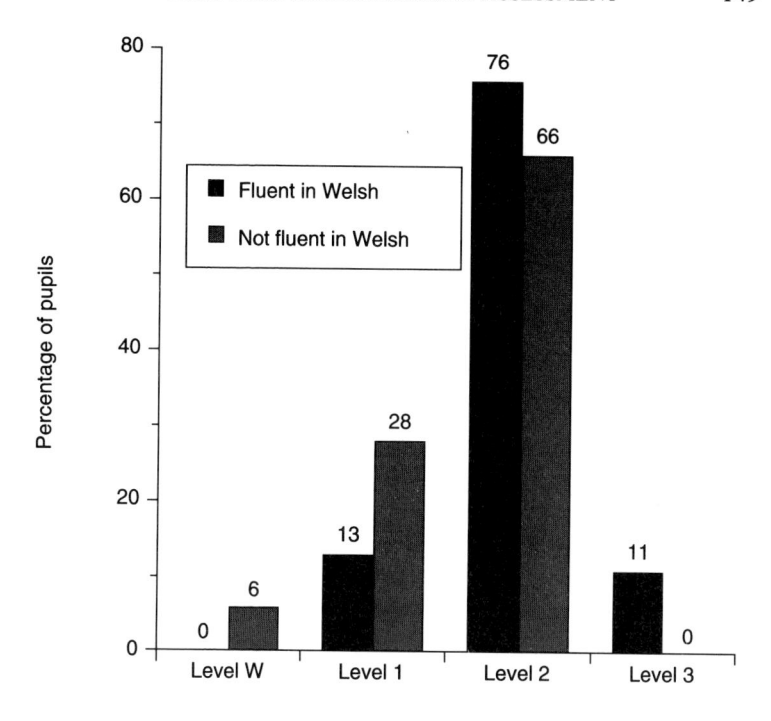

Graph 5: Key Stage 1 Mathematics: attainment of fluent and non-fluent Welsh children

research in Wales that allows an answer contextualized in Welsh-language performance.

The NFER evaluation of 1991 National Curriculum assessment
Report 4 of the Evaluation of the 1991 National Curriculum Assessment by the NFER (NFER/BGC, 1991) looked at the effect of the Welsh language on test and task performance at Key Stage 1. Section 17.4 of that Report entitled 'The Effects of the Language of the SAT', provides an analysis of language medium and attainment. In Mathematics, there tended to be proportionally more children in Welsh-medium schools at Levels 2 and 3 compared with English-medium schools. In Welsh-medium schools, there tended to be relatively fewer children at Level W (approaching level 1) and Level 1. In Mathematics, twice as many children in Welsh-medium schools achieved Level 3 compared with those in English-medium

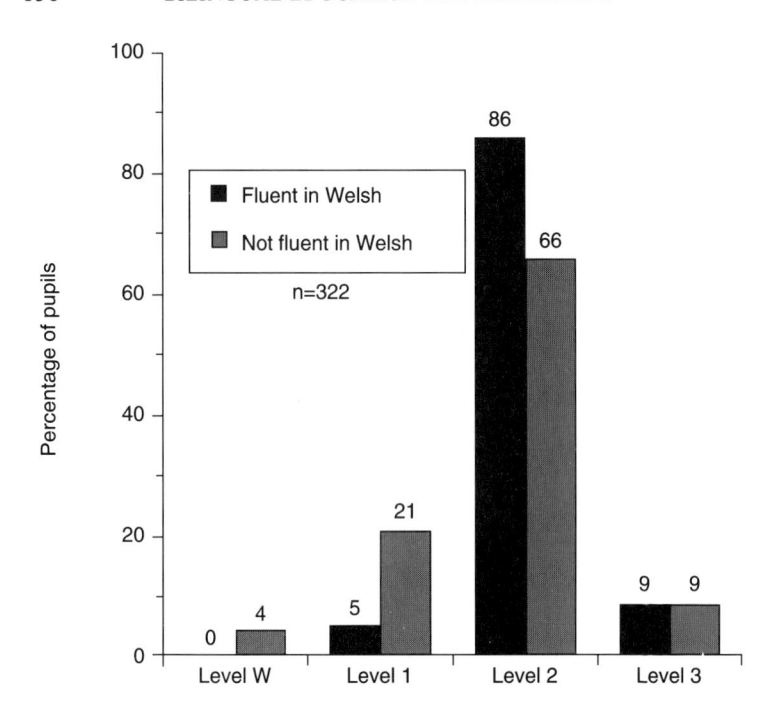

Graph 6: Key Stage 1 Science: attainment of fluent and non-fluent Welsh children

schools. In Science, 27 per cent of pupils in the Welsh-medium schools were at Level 3, compared with 22 per cent of pupils in the English-medium sample. At subject level, there were statistically significant differences between Welsh-medium and English-medium schools in Wales. Welsh-medium schools tended to show higher performance in Mathematics and in Science. These results are illustrated in Graphs 7 and 8.

Key Stage 1 conclusions
Two different sets of Key Stage 1 analysis, from two different evaluation teams, tend to suggest positive results at Key Stage 1 for Welsh-medium schools (NFER) and children fluent in Welsh (Leeds). At Key Stage 3, the evidence suggests only a small difference in Welsh-language attainment between English home-language and Welsh home-language speakers. There thus tends to

be evidence to support Welsh-medium education as a system. That system appears not to disadvantage children from English-language backgrounds in their Welsh-language performance. Such findings bear close resemblance to the dominant international (e.g. Canada, Spain, US) research findings (see Baker 1993a for a review).

The international findings with regard to bilingual education may be summarized as follows. Where children's two languages are both well developed, there tend to be no negative and mostly positive benefits for being educated in their home language when that language is a minority language such as Welsh. International evidence suggests that *language majority children* (for example, children from English-language homes) do not tend to suffer when educated through the medium of a minority language. Similarly, for

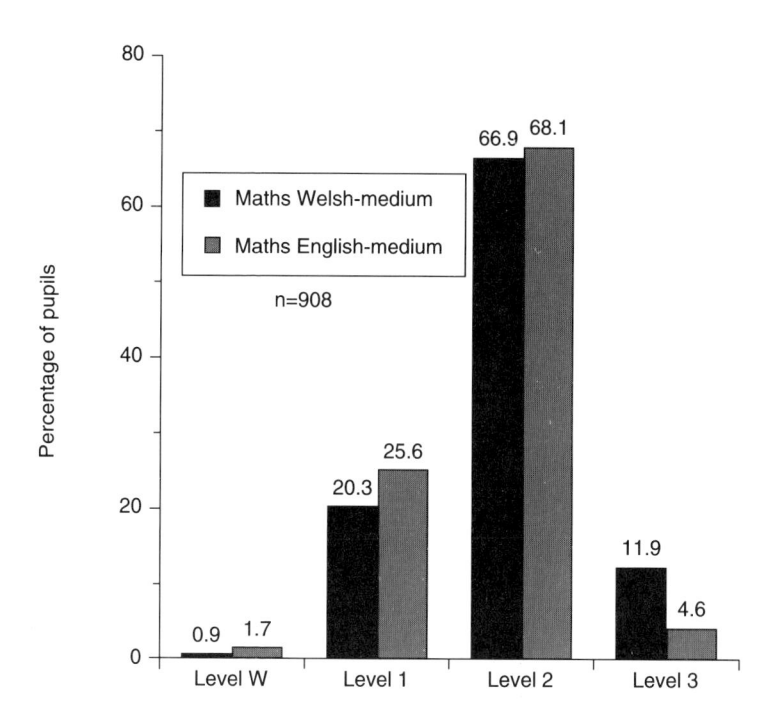

Graph 7: Key Stage 1 Mathematics: the attainment of children in Welsh-medium and English-medium education

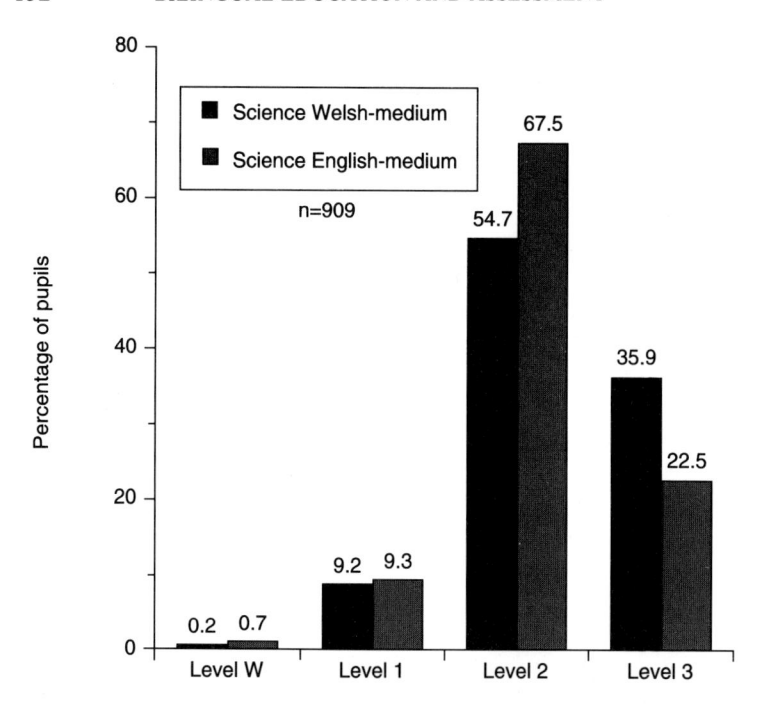

Graph 8: Key Stage 1 Science: the attainment of children in Welsh-medium and English-medium education

language minority children (for example, children from Welsh-language homes), education through their minority language tends to result in positive curriculum outcomes in a relative and absolute sense (Baker 1988; Baker 1993a). The evidence presented above is of fluency in Welsh, and Welsh-medium education itself, as tending to lead to positive outcomes in core curriculum areas.

However, there are limitations to this research and I will conclude by briefly indicating the constraints on the conclusions. For example, it is important to ask whether we are comparing similar groups. Were the children from English-language backgrounds and Welsh-language backgrounds at Key Stage 3 comparable in terms of social class, gender and ability? If, for example, the English home-language children had different characteristics to the Welsh home-language children, then the similarities and differences may be explained in these terms, as well as, or instead of the language background factor. Thus, in a piece of research, it is necessary to take into account other factors that could provide explanations of differences. We need to compare like with like. For example, the Welsh first-language and English first-language children need to be compared when (or if) any differences in social class background have been taken into account. While the results in this chapter are positive about Welsh-medium education and about children fluent in Welsh, a question remains. What are the factors that *explain* these results? As further National Curriculum assessment occurs, such results need monitoring and be capable of a more refined explanation.

For the moment, the evidence suggests three possibilities: first, that the effect of home language is small; second, and most important, the numbers of Key Stage 3 children from English-language backgrounds attaining Levels 4, 5, 6 and 7 is such that home language clearly does not create any impediment to success in the National Curriculum in Welsh as a subject. Indeed, the evidence of the tables suggests that English-language children educated through the medium of Welsh are *attaining levels in Welsh as a first language* in line with National Curriculum expectations. Third, at Key Stage 1, Welsh-medium education appears (from the early evidence) to be connected with higher performance in National Curriculum core subjects.

A comparative perspective

Wales has tended to lag behind some European and North American countries with bilingual education systems in analysing the effectiveness of its bilingual schooling arrangements. For example, in Canada there has been a long tradition of examining the effectiveness of immersion bilingual education. Core programmes have been compared with early total immersion, partial early immersion and late immersion programmes. Heritage language programmes in Canada, USA and Sweden, for example, have been evaluated for their relative effectiveness with children from minority language backgrounds (Baker 1991, 1993a). Recent research in Spain on Basque and Catalan bilingual education systems provided administrators, teachers and parents with evidence for the success of bilingual education (e.g. Sierra and Olaziregi 1989). In the United States, there has been a growing interest in comparing submersion with transitional with dual language bilingual education provision (e.g. Garcia 1991; Ramirez *et al.* 1991). Similarly in Australasia, research has examined the effectiveness of bilingual education both for indigenous groups of society and for major in-migrant language groups (e.g. Clyne 1988).

In North American and European evaluation studies of bilingual education,the assessment customarily reflects a norm-referenced model. Essentially, children are compared with other children in terms of curriculum performance. Standardized tests of language performance across the curriculum, attitudes and effective outcomes are used (e.g. in North American research) for comparison between different types of bilingual education. In the United States, for example, such tests aim to assess whether transitional bilingual education children are doing any better or worse than those in a submersion system (Baker 1993a).

As a review of bilingual education in Wales observed, the effectiveness of different types of bilingual education in Wales is a major unknown (Baker 1993b). This partly reflects the political struggle for bilingual education which has sometimes seen research as irrelevant to ideology, too expensive, and of low priority compared with curriculum development. When legal challenges have been mounted to bilingual education in north and south Wales, there is a search for research evidence, but no conscience or embarrassment at its absence. The Welsh bilingual education movement has much to offer the world in terms of teaching approaches, exciting curriculum developments and creative and imaginative styles of language teaching. It has much to learn from countries in Europe and North America as to why evaluations of bilingual education programmes are essential in understanding and improving, in decision-making and in gaining publicity for bilingual education.

With statutory assessment at the ages of seven, eleven, fourteen and sixteen, there is a possibility of evaluating the effectiveness of bilingual education provision in Wales. However, as this chapter has revealed, this is not the only purpose of National Curriculum assessment. National Curriculum assessment has taken on a dual purpose. It seems necessary to separate formative teacher assessment of individual pupils from 'school effectiveness' assessment. Current National Curriculum assessment is trying to do both things — less successfully than is desirable. The outcomes of such assessment unfortunately require different forms of testing. It would be preferable if one integrated system of assessment were viable. Despite valiant attempts in England and Wales to run an integrated system, curriculum-based and managerial-based assessment have two different languages and two different purposes, needing two complementary styles of assessment. The two general purposes of assessment are difficult and probably impossible to reconcile. Teacher needs and preferences are different from central political needs and preferences. Central bureaucracy requires information from the assessments of pupils for economic and educational planning. Assessment systems which support a formative curriculum approach to assessment and are weak on accountability are often of secondary interest to politicians and government officials. Assessment arrangements which do not support the aims of a powerful administration are unlikely to survive. Yet the assessments of individual pupils for managerial purposes provide researchers with data to evaluate the effectiveness of bilingual education in Wales. Given the criterion-referenced basis of such data, this allows Welsh research to make an important original contribution to international debates on the effectiveness of bilingual education.

Note

The author wishes to thank the University of Wales's Faculty of Education for a grant that enabled completion of this chapter.

Appendix: GWASG Project Reports

Twenty-six reports were compiled plus the Final Report. These are listed below:

GWASG Report No. 1, An interim Report from the Project 'An Evaluation of National Curriculum Assessment of Welsh and Welsh Second Language at Key Stages 1, 2 and 3'.

GWASG Report No. 2, 'Key Stage 3 Welsh Assessment Materials 1992 Report of an Expert Conference'.

GWASG Report No. 3, 'Key Stage 3 Welsh First Language Assessment (Cy) Analysis of Assessment Record Booklet Data'.

GWASG Report No. 4, 'Key Stage 3 Welsh Second Language Assessment (Ca) Analysis of Assessment Record Booklet Data'.

GWASG Report No. 5, 'Evaluation of the Bridges Assessment Pack for Key Stage 1 Second Language Welsh'.

GWASG Report No. 6, '1992 Key Stage 3 Welsh Second Language Assessment: Preliminary Findings'.

GWASG Report No. 7, 'Key Stage 1 Report 1992: Fieldwork (Cy)'.
GWASG Report No. 8, 'Key Stage 1: An Analysis of Data from Assessment Record Booklets'.
GWASG Report No. 9, 'Key Stage 1 Welsh First and Second Language Assessment 1992: Analysis of Attainment Target Level Data'.
GWASG Report No. 10, 'National Curriculum Assessment and Welsh Medium Education: Trends in Recent Results'.
GWASG Report No. 11, 'Key Stage 3 School Visits'.
GWASG Report No. 12, 'Adapting Test and Testing Arrangements'.
GWASG Report No. 13, 'Sampling of Welsh Statements of Attainment: Cy and Ca'.
GWASG Report No. 14, 'Stranding'.
GWASG Report No. 15, 'The Validity of Key Stage 1 Assessment Materials'.
GWASG Report No. 16, 'Gender and Assessment in the National Curriculum'.
GWASG Report No. 17, 'Assessment and Aggregation'.
GWASG Report No. 18, 'Ca Levels in the Welsh Order'.
GWASG Report No. 19, 'The Use of Marks and Aggregation'.
GWASG Report No. 20, 'Assessing Children's Writing'.
GWASG Report No. 21, 'School Level Stability in National Curriculum Results Key Stage 1 1991 to 1992'.
GWASG Report No. 22, 'Key Stage 1 Welsh Ca Assessment Materials: Report of an Expert Conference'.
GWASG Report No. 23, 'Key Stage 1 Cy The Compilation of a Welsh Spelling Test: Report of an Expert Conference'.
GWASG Report No. 24, 'Key Stage 1 (Cy) Report 1993: Fieldwork'.
GWASG Report No. 25, 'Questionnaire Survey of Teacher opinions about the National Curriculum Assessment of Welsh and Second Language Welsh'.
Occasional GWASG Report, 'GCSE Welsh and the National Curriculum'.
GWASG Final Report: 1993, 'Evaluation of the National Curriculum Assessment of Welsh and Welsh as a Second Language'. (Cardiff, Welsh Office & London, School and Curriculum Assessment Authority.)

References

Baker C. (1988). *Key Issues in Bilingualism and Bilingual Education* (Clevedon, Avon, Multilingual Matters Ltd.).
Baker, C. (1991). 'The effectiveness of bilingual education', *Journal of Multilingual and Multicultural Development,* 11, No. 4, 269–77.
Baker, C. (1993a). *Foundations of Bilingual Education and Bilingualism* (Clevedon, Avon, Multilingual Matters Ltd.).
Baker, C. (1993b). 'Bilingual education in Wales', in Hugo Baetens Beardsmore (ed.) *European Models of Bilingual Education* (Clevedon, Avon, Multilingual Matters Ltd.).
Baker, C. (forthcoming). *The Effectiveness of Bilingual Education* (Clevedon, Avon, Multilingual Matters Ltd.).

Blenkin, G. M. and Kelly, A. V. (1992). *Assessment in Early Childhood* (London, Paul Chapman).
Brown, S. (1981). *What do they know? A Review of Criterion-Referenced Assessment* (Edinburgh, HMSO).
Clyne, M. (1988). 'Bilingual education – what can we learn from the past?', *Australian Journal of Education,* 32, No. 1, 95–114.
Curriculum Council for Wales (1993). *The National Curriculum and Assessment Framework in Wales* (Cardiff, Curriculum Council for Wales).
Dearing, R. (1993). *The National Curriculum and Its Assessment: An Interim Report* (London, SEAC).
DES/Welsh Office, (1988). *National Curriculum: Task Group on Assessment and Testing: A Report* (London/Cardiff, DES/Welsh Office).
García, O. (ed.) (1991). *Bilingual Education: Focusschrift in honor of Joshua A. Fishman* (Amsterdam/Philadelphia, John Benjamins).
Gipps, C. (1990). *Assessment: A Teachers' Guide to the Issues* (London, Hodder & Stoughton).
Gipps, C. (1992). *Developing Assessment for the National Curriculum* (London, Institute of Education & Kogan Page).
Gipps, C. (1993). 'Equal opportunities and the Standard Assessment Tasks for 7 year olds', *The Curriculum Journal,* 3, No. 2, 171–83.
National Curriculum Council (1992). *Starting out with the National Curriculum* (York, National Curriculum Council).
NFER (Swansea), (1992). *Report on the 1992 Welsh KS3 Pilot* (Swansea, NFER).
NFER/BGC Consortium (1991). *An Evaluation of the 1991 National Curriculum Assessment: The Working of the SAT* (Slough, NFER).
O'Hear, P. and White, J. (eds.) (1993). *Assessing the National Curriculum* (London, Paul Chapman).
Ramirez, J. D., Yuen, S. D. and Ramey, D. R. (1991). *Final Report: Longitudinal Study of Structured English Immersion Strategy, Early-Exit & Late-Exit Programs for Language-Minority Children,* Report submitted to the US Department of Education (San Mateo, California, Aguirre International).
Rowntree, D. (1987). *Assessing Students: How shall we know them?* (London, Kogan Page).
Schools Examination and Assessment Council (1991). *School Assessment Folder: KS1* (London, SEAC).
Shepard, L. (1991). Interview on assessment issues with Lorrie Shepard, *Educational Researcher,* 20, No. 2, 21–7.
Shorrocks D. et al. (1992). *ENCA1 Project: The Evaluation of National Curriculum Assessment at Key Stage 1* (School of Education, University of Leeds).
Sierra, J. and Olaziregi, I. (1989). *EIFE 2. Influence of factors on the learning of Basque* (Gasteiz, Spain, Central Publications Service of the Basque Government).

Verhoevan, L. and de Jong, J. H. (1992). *The Construct of Language Proficiency* (Amsterdam, John Benjamins Pub. Co.).

Welsh Office, (1990). *Welsh in the National Curriculum* (Cardiff, Welsh Office).

Welsh Office (1991). *National Curriculum: Assessment Arrangements in English, Welsh, Mathematics and Science at Key Stage 1* (Circular 51/91) (Cardiff, Welsh Office).

Wolf, A. (1993). *Assessment Issues and Problems in a Criterion-Based System* (London, Further Education Unit).

Wood, R. (1991). *Assessment and Testing* (Cambridge, Cambridge University Press).

7
PSYCHOLOGY AND BILINGUAL EDUCATION: INTELLIGENCE TESTS AND THE INFLUENCE OF PEDAGOGY

Wynford Bellin

Introduction

This chapter deals with the way psychologists overlooked the major influence in bilingual education − the influence of pedagogy − as a result of regarding intelligence tests as a neutral measure of educability. The major omission was pointed out by Jac L. Williams of Aberystwyth in 1960 − see Williams (1960). Jac L. Williams emphatically told two diligent researchers on the relation between bilingualism and intelligence that their endeavours could never 'make a worthwhile contribution to the study of bilingualism or to the means of attaining a high degree of bilingualism where such an educational aim has been accepted'. Research on bilingualism and intelligence had been conducted in Wales by psychologists since the 1920s, but Jac L. Williams quoted the 'somewhat contradictory results' still emerging from the work of W. R. Jones (1960a) and D. G. Lewis (1960) as proof that the efforts were barren. The replies of both W. R. Jones and D. G. Lewis called for more participation in this 'most difficult field of enquiry' (Jones 1960b, 273), on the grounds that there had been progress mainly in statistical techniques and experimental design; but neither reply addressed the fundamental complaint. They had failed to address the importance of two kinds of factor. Psychologists of the time barely mentioned 'home background, not of necessity, linked with language spoken or parental occupation' (Williams 1960, 271). Nor had they done any more than ask head-teachers in general terms about how they implemented the language policy of the Welsh Department of the Ministry of Education. There was no investigation of 'variations in teaching time, methods of language presentation and usage, policy of language use for different subjects' (Williams 1960, 271).

There is a reason why the social position of children in such investigations and pedagogic practice in their schools were not given attention. Such particularistic details were not deemed part of the search for universal relationships and historical knowledge which the existence of mental tests were believed to have made possible. D. G. Lewis and W. R. Jones were steeped in a particular understanding of what psychology was about. The dominant tradition was the 'London' school or 'Galton-Pearson' school of psychology (Danziger 1990, 110–12) which had taken mental testing beyond phrenology, or 'feeling bumps', and physiognomy into a science with major developments in the mathematics of correlational analysis. Even the founding father of mental testing – Binet – could be dismissed by 1920 for 'adopting the easy-going attitude of the artist' (Ballard, 1920, 23–4) in not realizing that intelligence tests were for measuring 'inborn all-round mental efficency' or 'gauging a mind's capacity'. The standard works of Ballard (1920, 1923) had sharply distinguished measuring 'capacity' from 'content' or 'potential' from 'product'. So attainment tests (Ballard 1923) were for measuring what had been done with the potential. The original Binet notions of what mental tests could measure were regarded as 'nebulous' (Ballard 1923, 24). Despite tremendous advances in statistical thinking, in the basic conceptualization, results from mental tests on populations measured for 'adjustment', 'occupational success' and other variables were treated as a closed system allowing for detection of simple causal relationships. The general approach – uncritical reliance on correlational methodology – led to Welsh 'bilingualism' being quantified, as by Lewis (1960). This was done by adding up the number of circumstances in which Welsh was used according to self reports from children of different ages. A simple bivariate relationship with mental test results would show whether or not bilingualism resulted in intellectual disadvantage.

The general approach contrasted with the way in which experimental psychology was developed. In alternative general approaches to psychology a wide variety of test situations (cf. Bellin 1994) formed part of a formal procedure aimed at uncovering underlying processes in activities involving two or more languages. The pursuit of alternative directions called for by Jac L. Williams was not to bear fruit until later in the decade, but the more fruitful directions were actually proposed as a programme for psychologists by a major contributor to the development of the discipline during the 1920s.

A difficult field or psychologists in difficulty?

It is clear from both earlier psychology and more recent psychological advances that the almost obsessive pursuit of a simple relationship between mental test performance and bilingualism was a blind alley. Before psychologists went too far down that blind alley they were warned about what they were doing by the Russian psychologist Lev Vygotsky in an article on 'Multilingualism in children' dating from 1928 or 1929 but not published until 1935 – a year after his death. Unfortunately the warnings of Vygotsky were not translated until 1980. Vygotsky was remarkably far-sighted in pointing to the directions which were eventually taken up much later in the century and which cleared up much of the confusion. What he foreshadowed highlights the importance of social context and pedagogic practice. In the first place, Vygotsky said it was futile to 'ask whether multilingualism is a favourable or hindering factor always, everywhere, and in all circumstances, irrespective of those concrete conditions in which the child develops ...' There is an urgency about the way in which Vygotsky stressed this first point. Failure to accept that there could never be a simple universal answer to the question of advantages or disadvantages resulted from the way psychologists took extremely primitive concepts about language knowledge very seriously. Researchers were treating notions that bilingualism would cause 'mental confusion' or require too much 'mental effort' as if they could be part of 'the working out of a scientific method'. Such crude pre-theoretical notions should have been exposed as 'not justified from the point of view of modern scientific psychology'.

Instead, Vygotsky's second point proposed a direction for psychology which has turned out to be anything but a blind alley (cf., for example, Baker 1993, chapters 11–16). Vygotsky insisted that the 'influence of pedagogy is nowhere more decisive than in bilingual education'. Taking this direction 'for the organisation of research' was the 'necessary prerequisite' for finding the conditions when advantages or disadvantages might occur. Thirdly, he was not so impressed by the statistical sophistication which was then just developing in the field of mental testing, that he failed to detect the 'radical empiricism' which underlay the confidence that simple relationships could be given a causal interpretation. He refused to accept mental tests as devices for providing ahistorical measures. As he put it, 'Tests and norms based on them appear to be none other than empirically discovered research devices which arrive at empirically fixed, more or less constant results under the preservation of basic conditions in an invariable way'. They could not therefore be applied uncritically to 'socially heterogenous groups'. Vygotsky seems far-sighted concerning the applicability of normative data. Even though large numbers of people may be used in developing 'norms', the social categories they represent have to be regarded as 'fixed' factors rather than 'random' factors, to use more recent terminology (cf. Goldstein 1987). Although the norms are based on 'populations', they are not randomly selected representatives of all the populations on which the tests are likely to be used. Fourthly, Vygotsky refused to believe that mental test results could just be used without deeper consideration of what problem-solving behaviour led up to the answers given to particular items in the tests. As he put it: 'applying the majority of tests, we do not know the psychological nature of these functions which are activated in the resolutions of the tasks brought out by the test ... For example, we cannot determine any closer ... the intellectual operations [employed] in solving the Binet tests.' Fifthly, he would readily accept any relationships between bilingualism and mental test performance that may be demonstrated. But he could not accept the linkage to the 'unjustified' notions of 'mental confusion' or bilingualism straining people because of too much 'mental effort'. Instead he would want to ask: 'Is it only the factor of bilingualism or much more important factors determining the general course of child development in play?' Particular findings would have to be related to the 'overall complex of social conditions'.

Vygotsky's five points can be readily applied to research on Welsh bilingualism. The work of W. R. Jones eventually vindicated Vygotsky's insistence that underlying social factors might well be overlooked when comparing mental test results for different groups (see Jones 1963; 1966). W. R. Jones demonstrated the confounding of rural/urban and social position effects with the categorization of children as bilingual or otherwise. However, decades of following the quest which Vygotsky warned against obscured the central importance of pedagogic practice in the 'overall complex of social conditions'.

Correlation and causal influences

In fairness to researchers in the original correlational paradigm, there was advance in the direction of attention to the 'complex of social conditions'. Figure 1(a) depicts the kind of relationship envisaged by Saer (1922, 1923) and Saer, Smith and Hughes (1924), where an arrow represents a causal influence. In the case of Welsh bilingualism the influence was regarded as negative, representing a disadvantage. By the time of the book by W. R. Jones (1966), there was a much better appreciation of the distinction between correlation and causation. Correlations, it was acknowledged, could be obtained as a by-product of more basic social influences. So the line without the arrow head in Figure 1(b) indicates that a correlation was obtained, but the arrows indicate that deeper social background factors were more important than the bilingualism itself.

During the 1960s, there was much more caution in general psychological writing about what intelligence tests actually measured, and about the use of test norms on heterogeneous populations. There is a tremendous contrast between books like those of Ballard (1920, 1923) and Vernon (1960). The early unshakeable confidence that intelligence tests measured inborn intellectual aptitude waned, although it regained strength in the 1970s (see Block and Dworkin 1977). In the 1920s any social group found lacking — whether for reasons of bilingualism or because of assumed racial differences — had no option but to accept the verdict from the tests (see Karier 1972, Kamin 1977). By 1945, many of the studies concerned with racial differences were regrouped with those focusing on bilingualism and reviewed only from the point of view of bilingualism effects. The review by Arsenian (1945) shows a marked contrast in this regard with pre-war review articles. Vernon (1960) wrote of seeking a 'middle road' on the issue as to whether intelligence was inborn or not. Vernon also insisted on an open verdict concerning 'geographical differences' involving rural Wales (pp.173 ff.). The avoidance of connecting the differences with race or linguistic status as a bilingual is a move well away from the previous decades. Vernon allowed that differences might be the

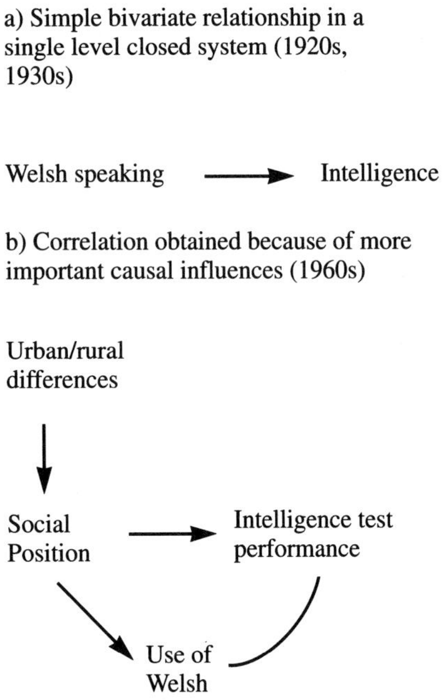

a) Simple bivariate relationship in a
single level closed system (1920s,
1930s)

Welsh speaking ⟶ Intelligence

b) Correlation obtained because of more
important causal influences (1960s)

Urban/rural
differences
↓
Social Position ⟶ Intelligence test performance
↘ Use of Welsh ↗

Figure 1: Relationships between bilingualism and intelligence as envisaged between the wars until the 1960s

result of intelligence tests favouring town children, or urban schools instilling greater 'test sophistication'. Nevertheless, he stopped short of acknowledging the influence of pedagogy. He was equivocal about attributing the results of pre-war studies to 'economic and social conditions and the best education'. Vernon preferred to insist that 'no tests can be devised which are "culturally neutral", that is equally fair to groups with very different upbringing' (p. 175). In the context of bilingualism research Skutnabb-Kangas (1984) was to develop the discussion as to whether test procedures can be 'culturally neutral'.

Units of analysis in bilingualism investigations

The discussion by Vernon (1960) in terms of 'geographical differences' highlights an aspect of investigations of bilingualism which could, in the case of Wales at least, have brought out the importance of school differences and shifted the emphasis to pedagogical practice. Most of the early studies treated individual children as the unit of analysis when working with the test results and results of questionnaires about the extent of the use of Welsh. So in spite of visiting many different schools in different areas, the location of the schools and the likely differences in pedagogic practice within those schools were not allowed for in the anlysis of results. Children were grouped solely on the basis of classification in terms of self reported use of Welsh.

In the terms of Goldstein (1987), the hierarchical nature of the data was being overlooked. The child was the lowest level unit, but then the next level up was the school class, and above that the school and finally the area or education authority. An analysis with current approaches would take account of the factors 'area', 'school within area', 'class within school' and finally 'child within class'. In the Welsh studies cited by Vygotsky (Saer, Smith and Hughes 1924), the urban monolingual children came from two towns − a university town and a highly prosperous magnet for rural/urban population shift (a town with a still successful tin-plate industry). Data analysis appropriate for the hierarchical nature of the data would not simply skip over the town differences within the uraban or rural classification. Contemporary methods would go on to show how much importance should be given to the factors 'class within school' and 'school within town'. The absence of such data analysis methods at the time masked the importance of the situation documented in a Board of Education report 'Welsh in Education and Life' published in 1927. The complaints about policy and practice in the report were very relevant for the overall aggregate difference between bilingual and monolingual children revealed by the mental tests. Only one education authority had any policy for classifying schools according to the linguistic status of the pupils (Denbighshire), and that was not an area included in the study. The rural schools in the study all came from authorities with no classification of schools. At the school level, there had been problems with recruiting Welsh-speaking head-teachers − many trainee teachers who spoke Welsh had taken positions in England. Policy for language use in the classroom was chaotic, even where teachers spoke Welsh.

Some later studies used aggregate figures per school as the unit of analysis (e.g. D. G. Lewis 1960). School means for intelligence test scores were related to school means of scores obtained by adding up instances of self-reported language usage. This showed the importance of individual schools, but did not allow for checking whether significant variation among classes within schools might be masked by relying on the aggregate figures. By the 1960s the computations needed were much in use in agricultural experimentations. However, there was a deeper reason why the importance of practice and policy were masked without concern for the way scores were aggregated. The deeper reason was the persisting influence of 'unjustified' pre-theoretical notions, as Vygotsky had labelled them. These were unjustified assumptions that dictated the whole direction of research in the correlational paradigm.

Bilingualism and educational capacity

One of the main sources of enthusiasm for the quest for a simple relationship between intelligence test performance and bilingualism concerned the equation of intelligence, as measured by mental tests, with educability or educational capacity. The assumption was so uncontroversial in the 1920s that a Board of Education report of 1924 was entitled 'Psychological Tests of Educational Capacity' (cited by Vernon 1960). If there is an amount of something to be measured, as in that way of thinking, it should be possible to see what factors may affect that amount. Given a basic presumption that mental tests measured educational capacity, researchers then had a tool to investigate assumptions like the one that bilingualism might lead to 'mental confusion'. During the 1920s this assumption had been most widespread in the English-speaking world but it spread from French-speaking to German-speaking Europe. In German-speaking Europe, there was more influence of the suspicion that speaking languages other than German might involve detrimental 'mental effort' (cf. the discussion of 'brain effort' and having slackness problems with two strings on a bow by Jesperson (1922, 148)). The flaws in such assumptions have been exposed by subsequent research, even though Vygotsky perceived their misleading nature well ahead of the rest of the discipline.

Capacity

A basic misunderstanding about how languages are learned and how other learning takes place lies behind the notion of 'educational capacity'. The idea is that of a 'container' and learning a language is like filling the container (Martin Jones and Romaine 1985; Romaine 1989). Baker (1993) compares this way of thinking to the idea of a balloon being filled and expanding to take up 'room' in the person's head. The worry was that having too many languages would somehow take up capacity or 'room' and leave less capacity for education generally (cf. Baker 1993, 108ff). The idea was given explicit formulation by Epstein (1916). Epstein believed that having two languages meant doubling the number of associative links between symbols and their referents, as compared with knowing one language. Epstein believed that it might help reduce the number of links if only a passive knowledge of extra languages was possessed, keeping just one language for both expression and comprehension. Vygotsky joined the German researcher on child language William Stern in dismissing Epstein's notions of 'simple mechanical crossing between...two language systems' out of hand.

Modularity in learning mechanisms

With advances in information technology, psychologists have had more powerful analogies than balloons in confined spaces or 'filling up room' with which to investigate human abilities. One of the features of language abilities is that they form an 'encapsulated' system unlike general problem-solving abilities. An important separation between two ways in which intellectual achievements can differ is emphasized by Fodor (see Fodor 1983). It is important to separate the distinction between an intellectual achievement that is computationally complex or otherwise, from the distinction between achievements which are 'encapsulated' or otherwise. An achievement like learning a language is undoubtedly computationally complex. The explicit statement of the rules of language, such as are mastered by young children, is a quest that exercises linguistic theoreticians and applied linguists continually. On the other hand, Fodor cites a wide range of evidence to show that language processing is 'modular'. That is, it takes place as if a separate special-purpose computer with its own database of background information was at work. Because of modularity, becoming multilingual, bilingual or monolingual is a complex process but one that is 'encapsulated'. That is to say, it takes place without crowding out other kinds of learning or intellectual achievements. Provided input conditions are suitable, it will start off and not encroach on other kinds of learning.

The way in which certain intellectual achievements can be 'encapsulated' is most dramatically demonstrated by cases of 'savants', or people who start with very low intelligence as measured by standardized tests, but nevertheless attain considerable intellectual accomplishments. If 'mental effort' was needed to become multilingual, and if intelligence tests measured how much could be expected from people, then cases of linguistic 'savants' could never be encountered. On the other hand, if becoming multilingual has little to do with whatever intelligence tests measure, then the 'encapsulated' language ability might well be exercised where other abilities are lacking. A striking case of a 'savant' – a man called 'Christopher' – has been discussed by Smith and Tsimpli (1991). The way in which Christopher could become multilingual without any influence in either direction on his 'general' intelligence shows how becoming multilingual is 'encapsulated'. Christopher was institutionalized because he was unable to look after himself. Doing up a button, cutting his finger nails or vacuuming the carpet were tasks of major difficulty. Nevertheless, he was able to become multilingual. Intelligence Quotients are scaled in such a way that two-thirds of people score between 90 and 110. On a well-known nonverbal test – the Ravens Matrices test – Christopher's IQ was 75. Probably the best-known test with a verbal component and less verbal components – the Wechsler Test – Christopher achieved a verbal IQ of 89 (just about average), but a performance IQ of only 42. On the Goodenough 'Draw a Man' test Christopher had an IQ of about 40. It is rare to have an average verbal IQ with a low performance IQ. What was even more remarkable was Christopher's ability to acquire foreign languages. To check his multilingualism he would be given a passage written in any of fifteen or sixteen languages. He could simply translate them into English at about the speed most English-speakers would read out an English passage of the same length. The existence of a case like 'Christopher' is enough to dispel old misconceptions about language abilities such as the worry that knowing too many would lead to too much 'mental effort'. It is also a misconception to think that 'mental confusion' might be a problem which arises from knowing too many languages.

Distributed memory

The worry about 'mental confusion' in multilingual people stems from 'capacity' or 'container' notions, and may be from seeing dictionaries occupy more and more space on bookshelves as more languages are catered for. The same misconceptions must be dispelled as for monolingual word storage.

Aitchinson (1987, chapter 1) discusses how monolingual people have stores for hundreds and thousands of words whether they know one language or more than one. Knowledge of language and memories generally are stored in the brain without taking up extra room, or requiring special effort. During the 1950s, people began to realize that neither monolinguals nor bilinguals keep a copy of memories in their brains with any kind of correspondence to the number of memories that can be evoked. Karl Lashley (1950) said 'It is not possible to demonstrate the isolated localization of a memory trace anywhere within the nervous system... Recall involves the synergic action or some sort of resonance among a very large number of neurons...' (pp.447–80). Lashley was thinking in physiological terms, but one field of research has explored the notion of distributed memory using machines – networks of units of computer memory. To get a machine to behave like a physiological or human system is the field of research known as 'artificial intelligence' (see Bellin 1991).

The 'synergic action' of memory units (whatever their actual physical nature) can be illustrated by thinking of a school which is constantly being written about in the local newspaper. In the kind of school which has so many activities that it is always in the local newspaper, there may be success stories for different sports events, dramatic productions, charity events and musical concerts. To the casual reader of the local paper, the impression given is that there is a separate group of people for each one of the separate activities. But to the careful reader, or insider at the school, an awareness would grow of the continued enthusiasm of a much smaller number of people than the number of separate activities. A small network of people who meet each other in different capacities during the day and maybe during evenings might well be responsible for considerable continued activity, and for activating major events like an eisteddfod. The secret is not in numbers but the connections between the enthusiasts and the different patterns of activity which can be excited by events. Different coalitions and groupings of basically the same total number of people form for separate activities. Each activity would appear from outside to be the result of a separate set of people but that need not be the case. It could be just another coalition working on a different enterprise in 'synergic action' – a different 'resonance' around basically the same network. In the same way, it is possible to show in artifical intelligence how a large amount of knowledge can be represented by the same network of units, each working in a different collective way to represent different items of knowledge.

The way in which language learning systems are 'encapsulated' and in which storage of linguistic knowledge is 'distributed' was discovered without specific consideration of bilingualism. Bilinguals learn their languages and store their vocabularies, just like monolinguals, with no prejudice to general intellectual achievement in other domains of knowledge. A major advance in psychology since Vygotsky's days and even more recent times has been appreciation of the fact that a bilingual person has just the same basic mechanisms as a monolingual, even though they may be put together in a unique and specific configuration (cf. Grosjean 1982, 1985, 1989; Romaine 1989).

Intelligence and educability

Research on bilingualism and intelligence was always uncritical about what intellectual operations lay behind the problem-solving that resulted in an intelligence test score. It was not thought crucial to define what intelligence meant, since the patterns of correlations between scores on different subtests within a test, and the correlations with plausible external criteria of 'brightness', were held up as an empirical alternative to clarity of definition. Vygotsky (1928/1929) complained about this 'radical empiricism'. It was out of character with most empirical approaches to psychology, since there is a jump from testing for intelligent behaviour to a belief in an underlying entity – intelligence. Doing well on an intelligence test is undoubtedly intelligent behaviour, but does that mean that the reason for doing well is possession of an unseen mysterious attribute – 'intelligence'? Howe (1988, 1989a, 1989b, 1990) makes much of this point in accepting 'intelligence' as a description of a kind of performance, but refusing to believe in an unseen possession to be labelled 'intelligence'. Howe follows many others who have called into question whether or not intelligence tests have anything to do with a general capacity for learning.

An article by David McClelland in 1973 entitled 'Testing for competence rather than "intelligence" ' released the grip of intelligence testing on a number of fields of psychology, especially training and vocational psychology. McClelland called into question the validity of intelligence tests in a new way. There had been developments in checks on 'internal validity' of tests by using statistical procedures to check that different test items measured more or less the same aspect of performance (see Vernon 1960, 46–8). But McClelland was concerned with 'external validity'. Intelligence tests by then were used for occupational selection as well as educational purposes, and McClelland could find only very poor indications that performance on the tests predicted occupational success. Only for high status occupations was there a strong correlation between intelligence test performance at school and later occupational success. Carroll (1993) has revived the debate about whether or not all intelligence tests tap a single general factor. McClelland did not question the existence of a single general factor, but he dismissed the idea of it being 'intelligence'. It was more likely to be possession of credentials for social advancement – a 'credentials factor'. McClelland denied that intelligence tests measured what had until then been assumed to be a general ability factor. Block and Dworkin (1974a, 1974b, 1977) discuss the procedures in test construction. Since there is an effort to have test items which discriminate between performance – having people who fit the criterion for intelligence score higher than others – Block and Dworkin conclude that evidence for a general factor is produced adventitiously. The use of tests goes in a kind of circle. Items which fit the statistical criteria for inclusion are those which separate groups used in external validation. The tests which include such items are then used extensively, and later intercorrelations with other tests indicate that validity assumptions match. Hence there is a build up in confidence in the further use of the interrelated tests. Later investigations report as a discovery the finding that the groups distinguished on social

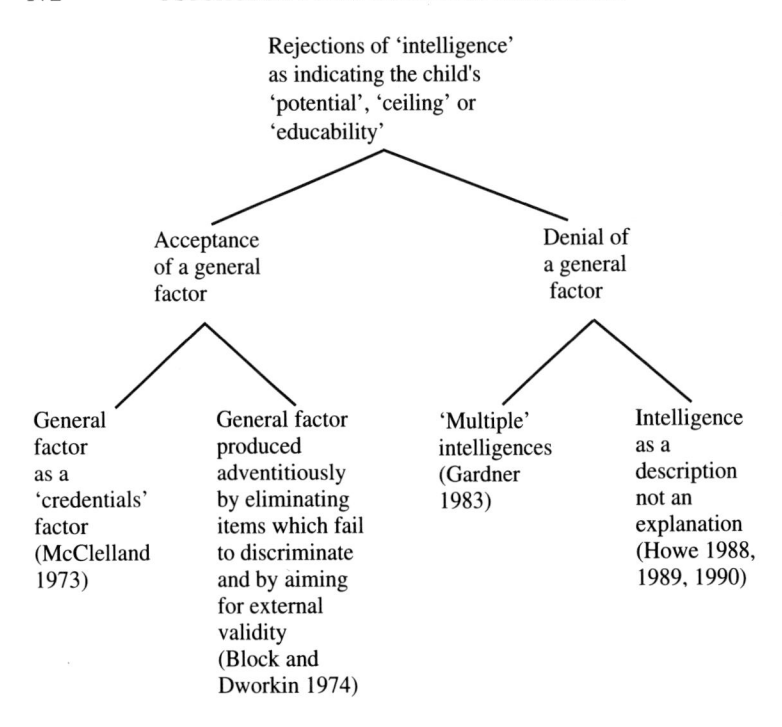

```
                Rejections of 'intelligence'
                as indicating the child's
                'potential', 'ceiling' or
                'educability'
               /                          \
    Acceptance                              Denial of
    of a general                            a general
    factor                                  factor
   /         \                             /         \
General    General factor        'Multiple'      Intelligence
factor     produced              intelligences   as a
as a       adventitiously        (Gardner        description
'credentials'  by eliminating    1983)           not an
factor     items which fail                      explanation
(McClelland  to discriminate                     (Howe 1988,
1973)      and by aiming                         1989, 1990)
           for external
           validity
           (Block and
           Dworkin 1974)
```

Note: The views of Sternberg (1985) can be seen as an attempt to reconcile disagreements about a general factor. But he would still reject crude notions of 'educability' in spite of accepting associations between test performance and certain kinds of reasoning and learning (cf. Sternberg 1988).

Figure 2: Views of 'Intelligence' which reject the equation with 'educability'

categories originally used in validation have different average scores. (See further in Block and Dworkin 1974a, 1977.) Block and Dworkin were therefore agreeing that a general factor might be measured by tests, but they insisted that it was not a general ability factor.

Figure 2 summarizes a range of views about what intelligence tests measure. Howe (1988, 1989a, 1989b, 1990) is adamant that all the results give is a description of a performance. There is no warrant for giving the tests and claiming an explanatory status for what has been measured. Gardner (1983) believes that seven distinct kinds of performance are measured by tests. Sternberg (1985, 1988) has a hierarchical theory of intelligence which can be thought of as reconciling the conflict about one or separate intelligences. Sternberg allows for subcomponents and some subcomponents are concerned with knowledge acquisition. The subcomponents concerned with knowledge acquisition are the basis for correlation between test performance and learning. Neither Sternberg's theory, nor any of those summarized in Figure 2 provide any basis for a notion of a general capacity which could be cramped by knowing too many languages. The core pre-theoretical notions which lay behind the quest for a simple relation between intelligence and bilingualism have been entirely superseded.

Intelligence and social position

The critique of the reliance on intelligence tests in psychology by McClelland (1973) is actually consistent with the evidence amassed by Carroll (1993) for a general factor measured by intelligence tests. Carroll wishes to take psychologists back to a belief in a general ability factor. But McClelland insisted that instead of measuring a capacity for learning, intelligence tests measure a class of achievements which can be correlated with credentials for social advancement. The general factor is a 'credentials factor'. The way reliance on the tests in education and occupational selection then produced a major industry feeding on itself is summarized in Figure 3. People already in a favourable social position are highly likely to have verbal and social skills which they can pass on to members of their family. These skills impress teachers and can lead to good performance in the kind of problem-solving required in intelligence tests.

McClelland described test results as measures of achievement, but the achievements are on tasks which are less content-specific than ordinary school attainment tests. Instead of the early claims that there is a wide gulf between intelligence tests and attainment tests (cf. Ballard 1920, 1923), McClelland argued that the real basis of the difference concerns the amount of material specific to syllabus content included in tests. The verbal puzzles, puzzles with analogies, puzzles with line drawings and problems with number series in tests can be valid for predicting school success, but not occupational success or coping in wider ranges of activities than those sampled in

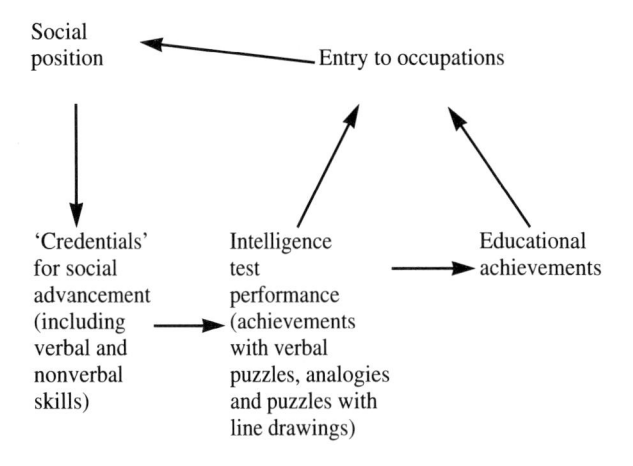

```
Social  ←――――――――  Entry to occupations
position
   │              ↗            ↖
   ↓             /               \
'Credentials'   Intelligence      Educational
for social      test          →   achievements
advancement     performance
(including   →  (achievements
verbal and      with verbal
nonverbal       puzzles, analogies
skills)         and puzzles with
                line drawings)
```

Note: See David McClelland (1973).
In the terminology of Burns, Baumgartner and DeVille (1985) McClelland has described a system having first-order causal linkages with feedback.

Figure 3: Relations between social position and intelligence test performance according to McClelland's 'competencies' point of view.

schools. Although not testing specific curriculum content, intelligence tests still test achievements that are too specialized to be relevant to general wisdom or general ability. Even so, achievements at the tests can indicate that a person is high in the credentials for acceptability in high status occupations, provided that the society in which they live has become ingrown and restricted the opportunities for different social groups to get ahead. Once intelligence tests became heavily relied upon for educational selection and occupational selection, over the history of testing, a circle of causal influences was formed which, as McClelland argued, actually explains the patchy evidence about the ties between test performance and various kinds of success in later life. A social system is set up with feedback, and, provided it can remain stable, confidence in the ingrown system can be maintained.

Processes behind obtaining test scores

The insistence that test performance is an achievement at a particular kind of problem-solving task has been borne out by a kind of investigation that Vygotsky wished to see. There have been investigations of the 'intellectual operations' in Vygotsky's terms, or the problem-solving strategies which lie behind attaining scores on intelligence tests. In order to answer test items successfully, it is important to have a set of skills which allows enough of a problem to be held in 'working memory' while the solution is being put together. Baddeley (1982) enlarges on the notion of 'working memory'. Any mental test involving number series and other arithmetic kinds of problem, needs a sub-skill of keeping a list of digits in 'working memory'. The Stanford-Binet intelligence test includes a direct test of how many digits can be kept in working memory – the digit span. Digit span is measured by giving a random list of digits, and the person tries to remember them. After each successful trial, the list is lengthened until two successive trials with mistakes. Most people have a span of between five and nine digits on such a test. Ellis and Hennelly (1980) demonstrated that digit span is affected by the language used for testing. The Ellis and Hennelly research was conducted with Welsh-speakers and provides an explanation for lower intelligence test scores obtained in many studies conducted in Wales. One way of sustaining digit span is to say over the list in the head – a rehearsal strategy. Rehearsal is a popular strategy on the way to a shop instead of writing down a shopping list. A factor in the ease of rehearsal is the length of the words. Rehearsing Welsh digits took Ellis and Henelly's volunteers a little longer than rehearsing English digits. The length difference in the words of the lists was responsible. So performance on a mental test administered in Welsh can be a different achievement from performance on the same test administered in English. The extent of the difference will depend on requirements for working memory as well as the relation of test items to problems encountered in school experience. Changing the language of the procedure will not necessarily improve performance, since the task requirements will be altered with the language change. A task effect will be confounded with a language effect.

Bilingual test results as an achievement measure

Applying the notion of test results as an achievement or performance changes completely the way of interpreting the studies of bilingualism and intelligence. During the 1920s, being a rural Welsh-speaker was regarded as costing about ten points in intelligence test scores. Since the test outcomes are an achievement, involving solving problems and building up skills with 'working memory' it is very simple to find the basis of the findings in actual pedagogic practice during the era when 'detrimental effects' (Baker 1993) kept being reported.

The Board of Education report of 1927 'Welsh in Education and Life' explains that in rural areas, teachers were allowed to use Welsh especially with younger children. However, apart from teacher supply problems and lack of policy at education authority level, what went on in classrooms allegedly using Welsh was very unlikely to build up useful problem-solving skills where any usage of 'working memory' might be involved. Since the target for any use of Welsh was eventual use of English, especially with numbers, teachers could be heard using language (paragraph 208) such as the following:

'*Darllenwch chi,* number one'   ('read number one')
'*Tynnwch* two *bant o* six'   ('take two away from six')
'*At* two *adwch* four   ('to two add four')

(In the first example, an instruction to read something out is given in Welsh, but what has to be read is given in English. The second example has English numerals, but the instruction to subtract the one from the other is in Welsh. The third example is similar but the instruction is for addition.)

During the 'period of neutral effects' (Baker 1993), when tests did not show significantly worse performance, Williams describes a much more consistent policy (Williams 1960). Up until seven years of age, using Welsh meant consistent pedagogic practice in rural Welsh-speaking areas. An important issue about using Welsh numerals in mental arithmetic was uniformly settled by that period. Earlier there was wavering between using the truly decimal type of numeral where forty is *pedwar deg* (literally 'four tens') rather than the older Celtic-style *deugain* (literally two twenties or 'two score').

(The practices followed for introducing arithmetic through the medium of Welsh in the 1960s are reviewed by Griffiths, 1968.) Many subparts of intelligence tests involve verbal skills. The 1920s was a period of inconsistent practice from the point of view of building up verbal skills in either Welsh or English. The 1927 report (paragraph 208) describes many schools starting to teach the reading of English before Welsh in order to speed children along. But that meant parotting things from a printed page that the child did not understand even in the English spoken by the teacher. Again, by the 'period of neutral effects' (Baker 1993), such pedagogic practices had been replaced by starting with reading Welsh in the early years where teaching through the medium of Welsh until the age of seven was taking place.

Dynamism in social systems

One of the aspirations of early psychologists was to find universal and ahistorical causal systems (cf. Danziger 1990). However, social systems tend to be unstable and show different patterns of relationship in different eras (see Baumgartner, Burns and Meeker 1977; Burns, Baumgartner and De Ville 1985). Depending on the cultural context, there can be an era where actors in a range of social positions can bring about instability in a system which will lead to change. The use of the law courts in the United States of America by groups suffering grievances from over-reliance on mental testing brought change. Legal challenges weakened reliance on mental testing. Psychologists in that culture and era nevertheless maintained an influential social position. McClelland's complaint that the situation depicted in Figure 3 ended up as a 'sentencing procedure' instead of an 'educational service' had considerable impact on vocational psychology, more so than the psychology of education. His call for attention to competencies and criterion sampling of behaviour were developments in occupational psychology and the psychology of training which would have a very wide influence (see Klemp 1978, 1980 and Boyatzis 1982).

The way Burns and others recommend thinking of such instability and dynamism in social systems is to distinguish single-level and multi-level systems. The causal linkages in Figure 1 and Figure 3 are all first-order linkages, even though the single-level systems differ from each other. To conceptualize change over time and multi-level

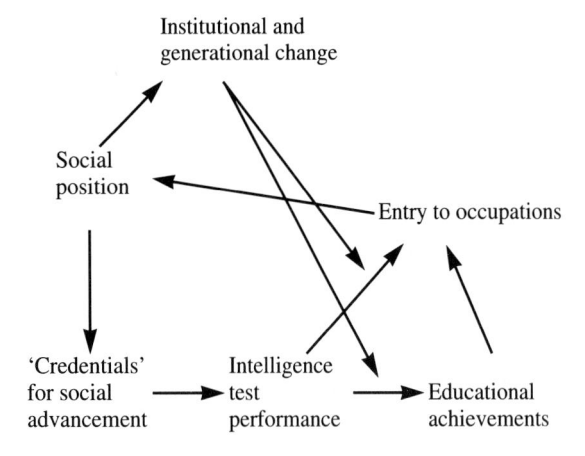

Note: See Burns, Baumgartner and De Ville (1985).

Figure 4: Modification to the McClelland system description (cf. Figure 3) to include higher-level factors with a second-order linkage as well as the first-order linkages with feedback

processes, causal linkages that operate on relationships can be included. These can be represented by arrows pointing to the middle of other arrows.

Figure 4 is like Figure 3, except that two arrows point at the middle of other arrows. Regulatory processes at a higher level than the system of Figure 3, along with generational changes, weakened two relationships. The relationship between intelligence test performance and occupational entry was made to change, and also the relationship between intelligence test performance and educational opportunity. Second-order linkages in the system must be regarded as a general feature of social systems, according to Burns and others, since stability is an exceptional condition of social systems.

The overall complex of social conditions

Thinking in terms of multi-level systems is a useful way of relating the history of intelligence testing and bilingualism to the 'overall complex of social conditions' in Vygotsky's terms. Thinking in such terms clarifies why, in the history of research with intelligence tests on bilingualism, a 'period of detrimental effects' could give way to a 'period of neutral effects' by the 1960s (see further in Baker 1993). Later decades are described by Baker as a 'period of additive effects'. Burns and others warn that changes over time in multi-level social systems can reverse the direction of influence as well as weakening influence. Because second-order influences can cause direction to reverse in first-order linkages, it is convenient to avoid indicating directions of influence in depictions of multi-level systems, like Figure 4. Figure 5 is an aid to understanding why, in the case of Welsh bilingual education, different directions of influence can occur at different periods.

The 1920s studies in Wales were among those which Vygotsky blamed for leading psychologists away from the central importance of the influence of pedagogy. The report literature for the period confirms the importance of the educational practices of the time for obtaining the test results. The intelligence test scores can readily be

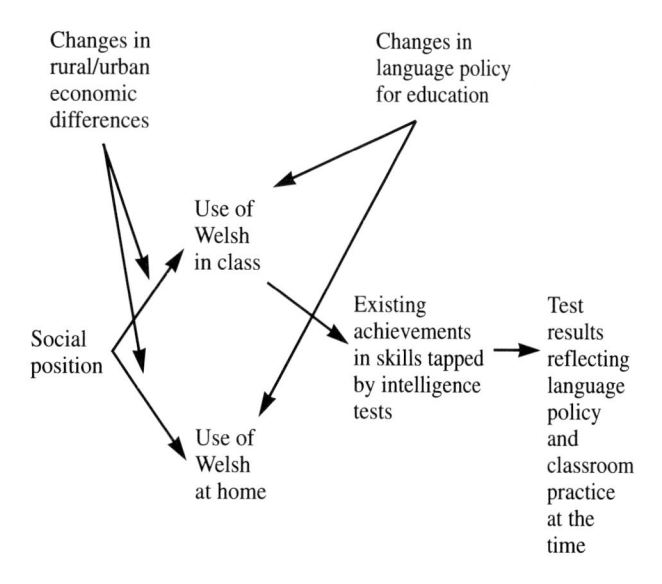

Figure 5: Changes in relations between bilingualism and intelligence test performance in Welsh studies

interpreted as representing limitations in the achievements of children when placed in a setting such as that described in the 1927 report for the Board of Education. The social position of rural populations was very far from the 'pull' in society or credentials for advancement traditionally associated with intelligence test results. Whether or not Welsh was used in class related to this unfavourable social position. By the 1930s, when the 1927 report had led to changes in practice, there were studies reporting lower achievements on verbal tests, but not on non-verbal tests (Barke 1933; Barke and Parry-Williams 1938). Changes in language policy allowed for classroom use of Welsh in a way more suited to building up skills called for in solving intelligence test problems.

After the 1939–45 war rural–urban differences were much changed. These changes were a second-order linkage allowing for more 'pull' in Welsh-speaking communities. Jac L. Williams emphasized the importance of a clause in the 1944 Education Act concerning parental wishes. Parents and local education authority leaders were able to use this clause to advance Welsh-medium education in the early school years (see Williams 1966, 86ff. and Jones 1963). The more consistent practices in Welsh-medium instruction referred to by Jac L. Williams (1960) began to spread. So by the 1960s intelligence test results showed only that children in certain rural schools fell short of norms based on monolingual (English-only) children. This is the alternative interpretation of the D. G. Lewis (1960) results. Jac L. Williams was interpreting the research results as an outcome of the actual practice in the schools. The linkages between social factors, policy and pedagogy depicted in Figure 5 could have been appreciated as early as the 1920s, if only Vygotsky's original call for attention to the importance of pedagogy had been heeded. In the case of Wales, Jac L. Williams's call for directing research efforts at the means of attaining community aspirations for bilingualism (Williams 1960) showed appreciation of the linkages. A period of 'additive effects' in the terms of Baker (1993) does not just happen. Additive effects have to be brought about. Allowing for prevailing social factors, policy has to favour pedagogic practices aimed at producing additive effects.

The overall complex of social conditions is important for explaining why Vygotsky seemed so far ahead of his contemporaries thirty years before the disagreements recorded in the 1960 volume of the *British Journal of Educational Psychology* and sixty years before publications like those of Grosjean (1982) and Romaine (1989). Under the Czarist regime and after the Bolshevik revolution, any developmental psychology would have to have relevance for, as Vygotsky put it, geographical 'areas where multilingualism forms a fundamental fact in the child's development'. Vygotsky's own multilingualism (five languages) had been part and parcel of overcoming residential and educational restrictions within the Pale (see Blanck 1990). Vygotsky's writing on multilingualism was in the context of the Leninist policy of promoting linguistic pluralism (see Rosa and Montero 1990 and Kreindler 1993). Kreindler (1993) explains that the linguistic pluralism when Lunacharsky was in charge of education was not a policy of making concessions to assertive peripheral nationalities, or some kind of divide and rule tactic. It was *korenizatsiia* – a 'nativization program'. Because the early Bolsheviks believed that literacy was a prerequisite to taking part in politics, minority nationalities were encouraged to standardize their own mother tongues and defeat illiteracy by promoting minority language use.

Multilingualism research focusing on educational practice, as advocated by Vygotsky, has a special place at the beginning of the twenty-first century. Globalism in economics and the internationalization of technology will mean that people will want to speak languages which will enable them to communicate well beyong their own frontiers. But David Laitin – a researcher into the spread of English (Laitin 1992) – refuses to believe that language competition will necessarily lead to language replacement. Laitin makes the prediction (Laitin 1993) that 'the maintenance of multilingual repertoires rather than the replacement of competing languages in all domains by English will be the mark of the emerging world language system'. There seems to be no reason why Wales, like some of the geographical areas which Laitin has studied, should not feature as a political and cultural unit in such a system. As such there would be importance for both indigenous langues (Welsh and English) and also further languages. In the context of maintaining such a repertoire, the exhortation to psychologists by Jac L. Williams to make a worthwhile contribution to the study of bilingualism can yet be heeded.

References

Aitchinson, J. (1987). *Words in the Mind: an Introduction to the Mental Lexicon* (Oxford, Blackwell).
Arsenian, S. (1945). 'Bilingualism in the post-war world', *Psychological Bulletin* 42, 65–86.
Baddeley, A. (1982). *Your Memory: A User's Guide* (London, Sidgwick & Jackson).
Baker, C. (1993). *Foundations of Bilingual Education and Bilingualism* (Clevedon, Avon, Multilingual Matters).
Ballard, P. B. (1920). *Mental Tests* (London, University of London Press).
Ballard, P. B. (1923). *The New Examiner* (London, University of London Press).
Barke, E. M. (1933). 'A study of the comparative intelligence of children in certain bilingual and monoglot schools in south Wales', *British Journal of Educational Psychology*, 3, 237–50.
Barke, E. M. and Parry Williams, D. E. (1938). 'A further study of comparative intelligence of children in certain bilingual and monoglot schools in south wales', *British Journal of Educational Psychology*, 8, 63–77.
Baumgartner, T., Burns, T. R. and Meeker, L. D. (1977). 'The description and analysis of system stability and change: multilevel concepts and methodology'. *Quality and Quantity*, 287–328.
Bellin, W. (1991). 'Psychological aspects of natural language', in Warwick, K. (ed.), *The Application of Artificial Intelligence* (Stevenage, Herts., Peter Peregrinus for the Institute of Electrical Engineers) 22–36.
Bellin, W. (1994). 'Caring professions and Welsh speakers: a perspective from language and social psychology/Proffesiynau gofal a siaradwyr Cymraeg: perspectif o safbwynt iaith a seicoleg gymdeithasol', in Huws Williams, Rh. Williams, H. and Davies, E. (eds.) *Social Work and the Welsh Language/Gwaith Cymdeithasol a'r Iaith Gymraeg*. (Cardiff/Caerdydd, University of Wales Press/Gwasg Prifysgol Cymru).
Bellin, W., Osmond, J. and Reynolds, D. (1994). *Towards an Educational Policy for Wales* (Cardiff, Institute of Welsh Affairs).
Blanck, G. (1990). 'Vygotsky: the man and his cause', in Moll, L. C. (ed.), *Vygotsky and Education: Instructional Implications and Applications of Sociohistorical Psychology* (Cambridge, Cambridge University Press).
Block, N. and Dworkin, G. (1974a). 'IQ, heritability and inequality, Part 1', *Philosophy and Public Affairs*, 3, 331–409.
Block, N and Dworkin, G. (1974b). 'IQ, heritability and inequality, Part 2', *Philosophy and Public Affairs*, 4, 40–99.
Block, N and Dworkin, G. (1977) (eds.). *The IQ Controversy* (London, Quartet Press).
Board of Education (1927). *Welsh in Education and Life* (London, HMSO).
Boyatzis, R. E. (1982). *The Competent Manager: a model for effective performance* (New York, Wiley).
Burns, T. R. Baumgartner, T. and De Ville, T. (1985). *Man, Decisions,*

Society: the Theory of Actor-System Dynamics for Social Scientists (New York, Gordon & Breach).

Carroll, J. B. (1993). *Human Cognitive Abilities: a Survey of Factor Analytic Studies* (Cambridge, Cambridge University Press).

Danziger, K. (1990). *Constructing the Subject: Historical Origins of Psychological Research* (Cambridge, Cambridge University Press).

Ellis, N. C. and Hennely, R. A. (1980). 'A bilingual word length effect: implications for intelligence testing and the relative ease of mental calculation in Welsh and English', *British Journal of Psychology*, 71, 43–52.

Epstein, I. (1916). *La Pensée et la Polyglossie: Essai psychologique et didactique* (Lausanne, Payot et cie).

Fodor, J. A. (1983). *The Modularity of Mind* (Cambridge, Mass, MIT Press).

Gardner, H. (1983). *Frames of Mind: the Theory of Multiple Intelligences.* (New York, Basic Books).

Goldstein, H. (1987). *Multilevel Models in Educational and Social Research* (London, Charles Griffin).

Griffiths, M. (1968). *Darganfod Rhif* (Caerdydd, Undeb Cenedlaethol Athrawon Cymru).

Grosjean, F. (1982). *Life with Two Languages* (Cambridge, Mass., Harvard University Press).

Grosjean, F. (1985). 'The Bilingual as a competent but specific speaker-hearer', *Journal of Multilingual and Multicultural Development*, 6, 467–77.

Grosjean, F. (1989). 'Neurolinguists beware! The bilingual is not two monolinguals in one person', *Brain and Language* 36, 3–15.

Howe, M. J. A. (1988). 'Intelligence as an explanation', *British Journal of Psychology* 79, 349–60.

Howe, M. J. A. (1989a). *Fragments of Genius: Idiots Savants and the Psychological Investigation of Remarkable Feats by Mentally Retarded Individuals,* (London, Routledge).

Howe, M. J. A. (1989b). 'Separate skills or general intelligence: the autonomy of human abilities', *British Journal of Educational Psychology*, 59, 351–60.

Howe, M. J. A. (1990). 'Does intelligence exist?' *The Psychologist* 3, 11, 490–3.

Jespersen, O. (1922). *Language* (London, George Allen & Unwin).

Jones, W. R. (1960a). 'A critical study of bilingualism and nonverbal intelligence', *British Journal of Educational Psychology*, 30, 71–7.

Jones, W. R. (1960b). 'Replies to comments by J. L. Williams', *British Journal of Educational Psychology*, 30, 272–3.

Jones, W. R. (1963).*Addysg Ddwyieithog yn Nghymru* (Caernarfon, Llyfraur Methodistiaid Calfinaidd).

Jones, W. R. (1966). *Bilingualism in Welsh Education* (Cardiff, University of Wales Press).

Kamin, L. (1977). *The Science and Politics of IQ* (Harmondsworth, Penguin).

Karier, C. J. (1972). 'Testing for order and control in the corporate liberal state', *Educational Theory,* 22, 154–80.
Klemp, G. O. Jr. (1978). *Job Competence Assessment* (Boston, McBer Co.).
Klemp, G. O. Jr. (ed.) (1980). *The Assessment of Occupational Competence* (Washington, DC, National Institute of Education).
Kreindler, I. T. (1993). 'Russian in retreat as a global language', *International Political Science Review,* 14, 257–74.
Laitin, D. D. (1992). *Language Repertoires and State Construction in Africa* (Cambridge, Cambridge University Press).
Laitin, D. D. (1993). 'The game theory of language régimes', *International Political Science Review,* 14, 227–39.
Lashley, K. (1950). 'In search of the engram', *Symposium of the Scoiety for Experimental Biology,* 4, 454–82.
Lewis, D. G. (1960). 'Differences in attainment between primary schools in mixed-language areas: their dependence on intelligence and linguistic background', *British Journal of Educational Psychology,* 30, 63–70.
Martin Jones, M. and Romaine, S. (1985). 'Semilingualism: a half-baked theory of communicative competence', *Applied Linguistics,* 6, 105–17.
McClelland, D. C. (1973). 'Testing for competence rather than intelligence', *American Psychologist,* 28, 1–14.
Romaine, S. (1989). *Bilingualism* (Oxford, Blackwell).
Rosa, A and Montero, A. (1990). 'The historical context of Vygotsky's work: a sociohistorical approach', in Moll, L. C. (ed.), *Vygotsky and Education: Instructional Implications and Applications of Sociohistorical Psychology* (Cambridge, Cambridge University Press).
Saer, D. J. (1992). 'An inquiry into the effect of bilingualism upon the intelligence of young children', *Journal of Experimental Pedagogy,* 6, 232–40 and 266–74.
Saer, D. J. (1923). 'The effects of bilingualism on intelligence', *British Journal of Psychology,* 14, 25–38.
Saer, D. J., Smith, F. and Hughes, J. (1924). *The Bilingual Problem: a Study based upon Experiments and Observations in Wales* (Wrexham, Hughes & Son).
Skutnabb-Kangas, T. (1984). *Bilingualism or Not: the Education of Minorities* (Clevedon, Avon, Multilingual Matters).
Smith, N and Tsimpli, I. M. (1991). 'Linguistic Modularity? A case study of a "savant" linguist', *Lingua,* 84, 315–51.
Sternberg, R. J. (1985). *Beyond IQ: a Triarchic Framework for Intelligence* (New York, Cambridge).
Sternberg, R. J. (1988). 'Explaining away intelligence; a reply to Howe', *British Journal of Psychology,* 79, 527–33.
Vernon, P. E. (1960). *Intelligence and Attainment Tests* (London, University of London Press).
Vygotsky, L. S. (1928/9). 'Multilingualism in Children', in Zankov, L. V., Shif, Zh. I. and Elkonin, D. B. (eds.) (1935). *Umstvennoe Razvitie Detei v Protsesse Obuchenniia (Mental Development of Children in the*

Process of Education: a Collection of Essays by L. S. Vygotsky) (Moscow and Leningrad, State Pedagogical Publishing House) 53–72, translated by M. Gulutsan and I. Arki (1980) in Polyglot, 2, 2.

Williams, J. L. (1960). 'Comments on articles by Mr D. G. Lewis and Mr W. R. Jones', *British Journal of Educational Psychology*, 30, 271.

Williams, J. L. (1966). 'Ein Canrif ni', in Williams, J. L. (ed.), *Addysg i Gymru: Ysgrifau Hanesyddol* (Cardiff, University of Wales Press).

III

Bilingualism in Other Countries

8
ASPECTS OF BILINGUAL EDUCATION IN AUSTRALIA
J. A. W. Caldwell and M. J. Berthold

Introduction

The growth of bilingual education programmes in Australia needs to be viewed in the light of the major contextual factors of Australian education and society. The most obvious of these is that education, on the one hand, is principally a states matter, even a 'states' rights' matter. Each of the eight states and territories legislates and funds its own educational policies and systems. In addition, around a quarter of the school population attends other non-government school systems, mainly Roman Catholic, which are strongly subsidized by state and federal governments. Their curriculum tends to follow patterns determined by state governments through their involvement in syllabuses and terminal examinations. On the other hand, the Commonwealth government has increasingly directed critical attention and funding towards elements of education which it has deemed crucial to social cohesion or national economic interest. The tensions and ambiguities of power and control created by this duality of purpose and execution were recently epitomized in an eleventh-hour abandonment of consultations over common National Curriculum guidelines, involving National Frameworks and National Profiles for the eight agreed Key Learning Areas. While the existence of negotiations indicates a desire for some commonality, states have traditionally pursued their own directions. In emergent areas of study and in areas of policy shift, the plurality provides interesting laboratories for the study of divergent strategies, though sensibly there tends to be transfer of the most successful developments between states. Such is the fact and potential of bilingual education strategies.

The second major factor relates to the nature of the Australian society itself, the historical process of its constitution and the resultant political demands and responses. Since Australia has only recently passed the bicentenary of European settlement, its societal composition has always involved immigration, though with differing periodic intensity. Sherington (1991) traces one main facet of this, namely the economic relationship between immigration, investment, trade and technology. Within this matrix, he registers the incidences of the dumping of unwanted population and the resistance to this in times of unemployment. He also notes the recognition of the need for population growth first for defence in an alien geographical environment and subsequently for sustained industrial growth in the post-1945 period. Others such as Birrell and Birrell (1981) have posited the more cynical concept of Australia's deliberate acceptance of immigration to maintain a reserve army of labour in order to keep the price of labour down. Certainly, conservative Liberal-National governments have favoured higher targets of immigration (Foster and Stockley 1988, 11).

Another salient facet of immigration relates to attitudes to ethnicity and racism. The White Australia Policy (1901) was a prime motive for the federation of the states. The post-1945 evolution of immigration policy moved through several phases. Firstly, it moved from rejection of non-British immigration to acceptance and assimilation of northern then southern Europeans. The official policy then shifted to one of integration (1964), followed by the abandonment of White Australia Policy (1967), and finally to the promotion of the multicultural concept which arose in the early 70s and was ultimately legitimized in the Galbally Report (1978). It is not surprising that these changes coincided in the early stages with a drying up of sources of immigration as European economies revived in the post-war years. Yet Foster and Stockley (1988, 2) posit that

> the Fraser government [from the mid-1970s] attempted to interpolate ethnicity as the prime determinant of experience and consciousness and hence to minimize people's consciousness of class. In turn, ethnicity was intended by the government to be interpreted in terms of surface features (dress etc.) and in terms of an 'ethnic aristocracy' (co-opted community leaders bought by offers of status) forming close and non-threatening links with the central government.

An underlying resentment based on these two motifs certainly was evident in multicultural conference participants in the early eighties. If this was indeed the plot, then it would appear that the momentum of multiculturalism, once engaged, has had unforeseen consequences which have favoured the advocates of bilingual education. Further elements sustaining Australia's earlier semi-official monolingualism were its isolation, which began to diminish with regular jet air travel, and the anti-intellectualism engendered by status differences in the early years of colonization.

This chapter takes five perspectives on bilingual education in Australia. Two of them are general: early manifestations of bilingual education; and policy developments and critiques that have impacted on bilingual education. The other three present several current case studies spawned by the diversity of educational systems and philosophies in different states and territories: bilingual education for immigrant communities; bilingual and bicultural education for aboriginal communities; and immersion programmes for foreign-language teaching.

Early manifestations of bilingual education

Early manifestations can have two quite distinct interpretations. The first involves the nineteenth-century ethnic schools, such as the Lutheran church schools set up in the 1870s by refugee German settlers in South Australia, though the earliest Lutheran school dates from 1842 (Moellner 1993, 1). Anti-ethnic hostility during the First World War led to the suppression of such programmes, which had grown in number to forty-nine in that state. The Anglo-Celtic monolingualism imposed at that time persisted far beyond the war period. In fact, it was not until 1986 that the Victoria government, for example, repealed a law prohibiting teaching through a language other than English. Nevertheless, Moellner (1993, 1) dates Aboriginal bilingual education in South Australia from the 1930s. *A National Language Policy* (PLANLangPol 1984, 86) indicates the oldest extant Aboriginal bilingual programme as the government school at Ernabella, South Australia, teaching bilingual English – Pitjantjatjara since 1940.

The salient interpretation is the one which refers to developments arising from the changes in attitude towards the ethnic composition of Australian society in the 1970s. Here one must distinguish clearly from the experience of traditional teaching of 'foreign' languages. It should also be pointed out that most of these second-phase manifestations have essentially been *transitional* bilingual programmes, that is programmes designed to begin schooling in the first language on the basis of perceived advantages to conceptual development, self-esteem and minimum disorientation. Subsequently, English assumes dominance as the use of the first language is reduced to a language maintenance programme or abandoned completely. Mills (1982) reports that the first Aboriginal bilingual programmes in the Northern Territory were begun in 1973 at Milingimbi, Yuendumu and Yayaya. That the intent of these programmes was primarily focused on the transition to English is suggested in the emphasis on the reporting of only the English-based achievements in the Gupapunygu–English programme at Milingimbi (Gale *et al.* 1981, 309). Similar programmes began in primary schools in Victoria and South Australia in 1976. Transitional programmes in languages of new arrivals such as Arabic, Vietnamese and Turkish featured noticeably from the early eighties in state education policies. Yet the Senate Standing Committee (PLANLangPol 1984, 57–8) remained wary of even transitional bilingual education, though it gave its fullest support to *maintenance* bilingual education for Aboriginals (p. 88).

Cahill (1984) gives a careful evaluation of an early instance of a transitional bilingual programme with language maintenance continuity established in the changing climate of multiculturalism. Prior to this period, Greek communities had striven to maintain bilingualism with some success through the establishment of part-time ethnic schools. In addition, the Italian community organization, Co.As.It., had for some time been exemplary in promoting bilingualism in several states by funding language insertion classes. While neither of these approaches constituted bilingual education programmes, they did support the aims of language maintenance and bilingualism. In 1979 the Greek community in Victoria asked the government to establish bilingual programmes in primary and secondary schools, despite mixed feelings from some who favoured the establishment of full-time ethnic schools to preserve biculturalism. The very nature of transitional bilingual education suggested to many that the Hellenization would be inevitably supplanted. It is evident from the Northern Territory case study which is discussed in a later section that Aboriginal communities have long had the same perceptions.

Four schools in the Richmond–Collingwood area were staffed to offer the programmes from 1981. Cahill paints a picture of a lack of real collaboration and consultation between the Department's Steering Committee, the Greek community and the schools. Little preparatory work was done to prepare schools for the concept of bilingual education, to prepare physical resources or to provide in-service training for the sometimes belatedly chosen staff. Nevertheless, the supernumerary provision of two Greek teachers and a Greek aide was generous, particularly as some of the schools attracted small and/or declining numbers of Greek children and children from non-Greek backgrounds were not admitted to the programme (though many teachers and school executives thought they should be). The first year involved Greek–English instruction ratios of between 2:1 and 4:1 with gradual reduction until the bilingual aspect ceased when the children were eight to nine years of age (at the end of Year 3 of the K-3 programme). The principle of *une personne, une langue* was adhered to and physical domains for the different languages were separated as much as possible. Assessment by teachers of the programme indicated higher levels of success in English than Greek children normally achieved through standard programmes, and greater degrees of confidence and feelings of success in the children. Staff felt cognitive development was being more beneficially sustained.

Three interesting observations emerged from this pioneering programme. Firstly, it evoked strong questioning as to why Greek or other Languages were not being taught to all primary pupils (Cahill 1984, 78). In other words, the value of bilingualism was being recognized more widely because of the programme. This reaction resulted, in 1985, in a Greek Community Language programme for all other children from Prep (Kindergarten) to Year 6 at Richmond Primary School (Lo Bianco 1989, 41). Secondly, the reasons given by the parents for their interest in the programme can be ranked as follows: its provision of both languages and cultures (36 per cent), as against facilitating social adjustment to the school (18 per cent), maintaining the Greek language and culture (16 per cent), promoting multiculturalism (10 per cent) and making access to English easier (the transitional goal, 10 per cent) (Cahill 1984, 86). The parents appeared to comprehend and favour the bilingual aspect quite markedly, despite the attested lack of specific communciation to them by the authorities prior to the introduction of the programme. Thirdly, the limitations of transitional bilingual education in both language domains were clearly recognized:

It is not an educational panacea that will of itself bring children from non-English-speaking backgrounds up to the level of their middle-class Anglo-Australian peers. But it does assist that process, as well as maintaining the home language to a far greater extent and avoiding the more serious effects of semilingualism. This was shown in the fact that on average the children performed somewhat better in Greek on the concept test. In other words, a firm grounding in language as such has been imparted. (Cahill 1984, 111)

There were also reservations expressed about the prospect of de-Hellenization (Cahill 1984, 113–14). The need for biculturalism, including knowledge of contemporary Greek society on the part of the Greek teachers was suggested (thus parallelling the Northern Territory developments). Furthermore, Greek families persevere strongly in language maintenance at home. While only 32 per cent of Italian families indicated using L1 at mealtimes, 88 per cent of Greek families did so (Cahill 1984, 83). Limited transitional bilingual education might not be sufficient for language maintenance where the home use of the ethnic language has declined significantly.

Bilingual education and state and national policies

In the past two decades, three phases of attitude to the promotion of bilingual education are revealed in policy documents and academic critiques. The first relates directly to pluralism expressed through the concept of multiculturalism and ethnic rights and specifically advocates a general right to the maintenance of first language and culture. The second emerges from the first as a reaction to the political nature of the linguistic/cultural maintenance debate. This reaction suggests that the social empowerment of ethnic minorities might not be best served by uncritical drives to maintain ethnic language and culture. Rather, LOTE (Language other than English) might best be supported for the intellectual and cognitive benefits it bestows *when brought to a high level of competence by extended years of serious commitment*, as would be the case in long-term language maintenance or bilingual education programmes. The third phase is an extension of the second. It sees this genuine depth of language study as being crucial to the nation's economic and trading interests.

The first phase of ethnic rights provision that was based around the concept of multiculturalism and language rights (cf. Di Biase and Dyson 1988) produced a number of Commonwealth-funded programmes, particularly those involving transitional bilingual education programmes. In New South Wales, for example, thirty specialist teachers were appointed in 1981 (with subsequent further increases) to provide transitional bilingual programmes (Foster and Stockley 1988, 63). The subsequent policy documents issued by the New South Wales Ministry provided for a number of ethnic studies and multicultural and language awareness approaches, but hedged noticeably about the issues of sustained community languages and language maintenance programmes of the bilingual type. These years were the hub of the activities of FECCA (the Federation of Ethnic Communty Councils of Australia) and their linguistic allies in the PLANLangPol Committee (1983) to secure a National Language Policy to promote language learning, including language maintenance and bilingualism.

The second phase, coinciding with harsher budget constraints, involved a strong critique of the intellectual 'softness' of the arguments mounted by the proponents of language preservation *per se*. This approach is clearly exemplified in the theoretical discussion by Kalantzis *et al.* (1986) which relates to a project commissioned by the Department of Immigration and Ethnic Affairs on the attitudes of German and Macedonian migrant parents and children in Shellharbour, New South Wales. The project itself revealed differential and ambivalent attitudes to language maintenance, the more recently settled and closely linked Macedonian community showing greater commitment, even to the point of feeling a need to defend Macedonian as a viable language in itself. Funding of language maintenance programmes was seen more as contributing to the prestige and valuing of the particular ethnic community. Kalantis *et al.* (1986, 5–6) saw no 'link between maintaining a first language, the learning of English and cognitive development', that is, the benefits of transitional bilingual education. Of greater significance to the children particularly were the school subjects which offered job opportunities and thereby access to economic benefits (p.155). This theme of social empowerment is taken up by the authors to question the previous uncritical advocacy of language and culture maintenance as valuable ends in themselves or for change to xenophobic attitudes. Based on immediate ethnic politics, such proposals often led to tokenistic smatterings of community languages being offered in schools. Cahill *et al.* (1984, 324), in reviewing the Commonwealth Multicultural Education Program found this 'minor language sensitization' approach to be the norm. Kalantzis *et al.* (1986, 88) contrast this with the more socially utilitarian aspects of transitional bilingual education: 'Presently, the two lines of action, the one towards social empowerment and the other towards cultural maintenance, sit together in tension in government policy.'

These authors claim that many agrarian-based ethnic languages have little functional purpose (that is, they are structurally unnecessary) in western industrial society and that, in any case, English provides the necessary general communication and economic benefits in this particular society. In such circumstances, language maintenance depends on a diglossic situation of home−work language separation (cf. Fishman 1976). They argue that because of the large number of ethnic-language groups in Australia, diglossia can only be sustained by the continued use of the ethnic language in the home (and extended family cf. Clyne 1991b, 113). For ethnic groups of high language shift, e.g. German, Dutch, Maltese (Clyne 1991b, 82−3), maintenance then becomes problematical. In passing, they sustain the case for *transitional* bilingual education (with the option of later language maintenance) for those with a non-English first language on the basis of Cummins's (1979) Developmental Independency and Threshold Hypotheses. They are wary of the effects of early compound bilingualism (where the second language is learnt through 'translation' from the first language) on the cognitive development of minority-language school beginners, citing especially the *semilingualism* revealed by Skutnabb-Kangas and Toukomaa (1976) among minority groups in Sweden. They too advocated transitional bilingual education as the remedy.

Beyond language as a basic cultural function and language as the source of social empowerment, both of which are seen as the province of English in Australian society, Kalantzis *et al.* (1986, 159) do support one of the purposes for language study stated in the Senate Standing Committee on Education and the Arts Report, *A National Language Policy* (PLANLangPol 1984): namely, that concerning the development of general cognitive and linguistic abilities. Here they are unequivocal in supporting transitional and maintenance bilingual programmes as well as general teaching of languages involving 'a standard and a degree of intellectual seriousness similar to that traditionally expected in foreign language teaching (without necessarily being traditional in terms of pedagogy), beginning as early as possible and sustained over a number of years'. This marks a strong shift towards sustained, serious bilingual education but away from sentimentalized and politicized multiculturalism. Similarly, Clyne (1991b, 124) signals that current Australian bilingual programmes 'generally combine the cognitive and identification functions of language'. He claims that the Richmond – Collingwood Greek and South Australian Italian programmes (cf. Rubichi 1983) 'have been transformed from transitional to maintenance programs as needs insights and ideologies have changed' (Clyne 1991b, 125).

The third phase is exemplified in a series of government-commissioned documents at the state and national level, including the *National Policy on Languages* (Lo Bianco 1987), *Victoria Languages Action Plan* (Lo Bianco, 1989) and *Languages at the Crossroads* (NLLIA, 1993). Building on the intellectual shift revealed in phase two, Lo Bianco (1989, 10) finds a political justification for the learning of other languages which fits times of economic rationalism, while also raising LOTE-learning to a level of national importance: 'An important change has occurred. Essentially this has been brought about by a realisation that language matters intersect with a wide array of national interest issues and are of concern, therefore, to areas of public interest not previously assumed to be involved in policy development for language education.' At the same time, ostensibly on pedagogical grounds, he urges bilingual education approaches, particularly at primary level, as a promising alternative to traditional language teaching methods which had resulted in a continuous decline in formal language learning from 1964 (cf. Lo Bianco 1989, 51):

> These arguments [for language maintenance] do not mean that bilingual programs aiming at bilingual proficiency should be restricted to children for whom English is the second language. On the contrary, school programs immersing English mother tongue children in another language are the best possible sorts of second language programs and can yield very high levels of mastery over both languages, if for no other reason than that these children have a longer more continuous access to a richer form of language input than would result from traditional second or foreign language teaching methods. (Lo Bianco 1989, 16)

In this way, three goals are simultaneously supported: the right of those of non-English-speaking background to language and culture maintenance through transitional bilingual education and subsequent maintenance programmes; the satisfaction of cognitive and linguistic development for the bulk of the populace through a wider range of available languages, including so-called community languages, languages of wide international use and geographically and economically utilitarian languages; and the satisfaction of the instrumental needs of economic rationalism, including trade, tourism and diplomacy (Lo Bianco 1989, 10–11, 17–19). In fact, evolution to this three-part policy is embraced politically by both the Victoria premier and the minister for education in their preamble to the *Victoria Languages Action Plan* (Lo Bianco 1989, 6): 'it is truly likely that we are witnessing a renaissance in the appreciation of both the *intellectual* and *cultural* worth of knowing more than one language on the one hand and also the *very substantial practical and economic benefits available to individuals, and to the whole society*, through such skills.' (our emphases). Lo Bianco's political acumen is further endorsed by the comprehensive implementation document, *Languages at the Crossroads* (NLLIA 1993). It is significant that this project was funded by the Commonwealth Department of Employment, Education and Training, commissioned by the Australian Advisory Council on Languages and Multicultural Education and the National Languages and Literacy Institute of Australia (NLLIA). It is known colloquially as the Nicholas report from the name of a Victorian colleague involved. The Report suggests a huge number of strategies (in 116 recommendations), ranging from telematics to teacher exchanges, to ensure quality provision of as many languages as possible to a wide population, thus supporting all three goals. Equally significantly the enquiry (NLLIA 1993, 216–17) 'endorses bilingual programs (full or partial) as an effective model of language teaching particularly in primary schools' and

> recommends that the NLLIA act to support education systems to achieve a steady and carefully monitored, long-term, State-wide increase in such programs. The NLLIA should disseminate information about the factors which support bilingual education and assist education systems to develop four-year programs for the development, establishment and evaluation of a balanced range of bilingual education for first language maintenance and second language introduction.

The director of NLLIA is in fact Lo Bianco. The significance of the bilingual education emphasis is increased by the recommendation for the extension of LOTE learning to all schoolchildren (cf. Recommendation 86, NLLIA 1993, 215), a policy first enunciated clearly in Victoria in 1984 (Victoria: Ministry of Education 1984, 17). Further, the strengths of bilingual education are seen to align closely with four of the eight factors predicting successful LOTE learning (cf. Scarino *et al.* 1988, 17–27).

Through these three phases, there is a manifest shift from personal/group rights claims (or a *personality* approach to language maintenance) to national responsibilities to preserve and promote bilingualism for instrumental purposes (seemingly a *territorial* incorporation of the fact of Australia's multilingualism), alongside selected promotion of further 'needs' languages such as those of the major Asian countries. It is probably imponderable as to whether this constitutes a clever turning of ethnic-rights claims to the purposes of the state or, conversely, the hitching of the ethnic-language preservation waggon to the powerful beast of economic rationalism. Certainly, the national economic benefit is now being widely touted. A recent article by the president of the AFMLTA (Australian Federation of Modern Language Teachers Associations), David Ingram, openly espouses the commercial value of quality language learning. Ingram (1993, 8) cites the significant series of reports that are indicative of this utilitarian interest, including those provided by the Asian Studies Council (1988), Ingleson (1989), Stanley *et al.* (1990), Valverde (1990) and Leal *et al.* (1991), as well as the impact of 1990 Language is Good Business conference on language planning. In any case, these developments involve an evident swing towards bilingual education, whether manifested through ethnic-language preservation programmes or through the concomitant extension of bilingual and immersion methodologies to the wider language-teaching field.

Bilingual programmes for immigrant communities

New South Wales: the null example

The most populous state of Australia represents, in terms of full bilingual education, the null example. The Ministerial Working Party on the State Language Policy (1988, 4) noted the following:

full bilingual programs are not available in New South Wales Schools, although language programs of a bilingual nature complement both the ESL and LOTE provision. The Working Party recognises the value of bilingual programs and has advanced recommendations which seek to increase the number of available teachers in the field of bilingual education and which propose initiatives for developing programs where the curriculum is taught in English and selected languages.

One explanation for this lack may reside in the traditional strength of the out-of-hours ethnic schools centred mainly in the three major urban agglomerations of Sydney, Newcastle and Wollongong (cf. Norst 1982). These might be posited to support bilingual education in two separate doses, especially through supplementation in the religious and cultural domains. Nevertheless, Kalantzis *et al.* (1986, 153) maintain that research evidence shows that their role is more 'to ensure the reproduction of the social group' than to promote bilingualism.

Victoria: bilingual education for all
By contrast, Victoria has had a strong involvement in bilingual education from its early manifestations. Eminent Victorian advocates of community languages provision such as Clyne (1982 1991b), Lo Bianco, Nicholas and Sussex (cf. PLANLangPol 1983) have helped place Victoria at the forefront of bilingual practice. Apart from the early transitional bilingual education programmes featured in the Cahill review, two further developments are worthy of attention. The first involves an experiment which sought to make English–German bilingual education accessible to all students of particular cohorts at Bayswater South Primary School. The project has been thoroughly evaluated since its commencement in 1981, the time of the expansion of the transitional programmes (cf. Clyne 1986, 1991a; Fernandez 1992). The programme stretched from six years of age in Grade 1 (second year of school) through to twelve years of age in Grade 6. Salient features include the application of the *une personne, une langue* or *functional separation* principle; accessibility for both non-German and German-background children, largely on the logistical grounds of the difficulty of catering for separate groupings; five to five-and-a-half hours per week of subject teaching through the medium of German, reducing to four-and-a-half in Grade 4 and three in Grades 5 and 6.

Simultaneously, a half hour of language arts in German was provided in Grade 2 and one hour beyond that grade.

The particular division of subjects between English and German suggests that the programme was designed primarily for those beginning the study of German. Science, Physical Education and Art were taught totally in German. Science involved discovery and classification, thus linking linguistic and cognitive development. Art centred on basic notions of colour and size, practice in requests, emotional expressions of preferences and opportunities for interaction among teachers and pupils. Physical Education promoted sharper listening skills under noisy conditions. Reading and Drama were added in the third year, the latter designed to provide role-play opportunities to promote communicative ability. Health was later introduced in the third and fourth years. Music and Social Studies were taught in both languages, as they 'play an important role in the language-cultural link' (Clyne 1986, 21). While obviously catering for the cultural associations with the long-term German Templar group of the neighbourhood, the programme draws heavily in its initial years on concepts similar to those of the Canadian immersion experience, though less boldly in terms of quantity of time devoted to the target language. Thus it seems to be derived from ethnic-language retrieval and maintenance motives but leans increasingly towards the promotion of universal language education from an early age and specifically towards bilingual education for all. In the light of the third phase of policy evolution described above, it is significant that 'Bilingual Education for All' is the short title of the later 1991 report by Clyne (1991a). Evaluations by the Monash University team (Clyne 1986) of both the levels of linguistic achievement and general cognitive development provide reassuring confirmation of its efficacy.

Another important approach to universal bilingualism has been implemented at Brunswick East High School (Lo Bianco 1989, 69–70). It comprises compulsory language learning through the Years 7 to 10 of two types. For those of non-English-speaking background (Arabic, Greek, Turkish or Italian), a two-language team (LOTE and English-speakers) applies both languages in the same content and conceptual areas, working with ministerial support towards the establishment of bilingual curricula for each LOTE-English combination. In parallel, all other students undertake a basic Italian course. The programme continues the thrust of multicultural policy, being motivated by the desire of the school 'to respect and foster the(se) cultural interests of the community' (Lo Bianco 1989, 70). Yet, by implementing a dual compulsory stranding, it supports in the first instance bilingual education and, by parallel extension of general language provision, bilingualism for all.

Bilingual and bicultural programmes for Aboriginal communities

The Northern Territory is a region in the central north of Australia covering an area six times that of Great Britain, but with a population of only 170,000 people, including a large Aboriginal population. The education system in the Territory is facing a dilemma with regards to Aboriginal education:

> The dilemma is that Aborigines in remote communities want their children to learn the three Rs and to grow up aboriginal. But if these children succeed in the Western school system, this is likely to be at serious cost to their Aboriginal culture under the present school structure. The vision is that schools can be structured so that the new skills learned from another culture can be added to a person's primary cultural makeup, rather than displacing it. (Harris 1990, 1)

The resolution of this dilemma for the Aborigines is far more complex than simply learning another language (English) or maintaining their mother tongue. There is the cultural abyss that exists between the traditional Aboriginal cultures and the mainstream Anglophone Australian culture. If bilingual programmes are instituted in Europe between speakers of different European tongues there is a far narrower gap existing between the cultures of the two ethnic groups. How can one compare French–English bilingualism with Nunggubuya–English or Pitjantjatjara–English bilingualism? The current response to this dilemma is to try to develop programmes which are much more than bilingual, but rather bicultural 'two-way' programmes. That is, education which comprises two ways of learning, rather than one way in two languages. There is the need to preserve the language of the community and educate the children according to the norms and culture of the Aboriginal community, yet at the same time to develop English literacy skills and knowledge to enable the children to operate as adults in both cultures and widen their opportunities.

The communities do not want their children to become clones of the dominant white culture, but rather to maintain their identity and be able to move with equal confidence in white society. *Bicultural* education is an extremely complex issue in Aboriginal education:

> a theory of biculturalism which would apply to representatives of two major world cultures in contact which have similar world views and economy, may not be an appropriate theory for two cultures in contact where the population size, world view, political systems and economic structure are highly divergent. (Harris 1990, xiii)

The early efforts in the Northern Territory were more in the realms of bilingual education with a strand of mother-tongue culture. The first government-supported efforts in this regard came as a result of an announcement by the then prime minister, E. Gough Whitlam, on 14 December 1972, in which he stated that the federal government would 'launch a campaign to have Aboriginal children living in distinctive Aboriginal communities given their primary education in Aboriginal languages. The Government will also supplement education for Aboriginal children with teaching of traditional Aboriginal arts, crafts and skills mostly by Aboriginals themselves'. This policy could have left itself open to charges of tokenism, yet it was a major step forward in Aboriginal education for traditional communities. From this initiative, models developed which were implemented in states and territories, in schools within dominantly Aboriginal communities.

The Northern Territory responded promptly and in 1973 the first edition of the *Handbook for Aboriginal Bilingual Education in the Northern Territory* was produced. This handbook has been rewritten several times since due to 'developments in the Department's commitment in the field of bilingual education, as well as in the areas of theory and practice, evaluation, staffing, administration and inservice training, all of which reflected the growing expertise of the Aboriginal and non-Aboriginal teachers and literature production workers ...' (Northern Territory Department of Education 1986). The Northern Territory Department of Education (1986) provides information on policy, programmes, staffing and curriculum development. The bilingual programme promoted in the handbook can be summarized as:

> *Preschool* and *Transition*: 10 per cent English oral programme.
> The programme allows for a 'planned informal approach to vernacular literacy'.

Oral English is introduced.
Year 1: 20 per cent English oral programme.
A more formal approach to reading and writing in the vernacular with Mathematics and some topics possibly being taught in both languages.
Year 2: 30 per cent formal English programme.
An extension of the subjects taught through two languages.
Year 3: 40 per cent of the school programme taught through English.
Year 4: 50 per cent of the school programme taught through English.
Years 5–7: 80 per cent of daily instruction through English.

This 80/20 balance is to be maintained through secondary education, where possible, to maintain the local language.

It can thus be seen that the emphasis at this stage of development of Aboriginal programmes (1986) was on bilingual education and language maintenance, rather than a bicultural approach. It was primarily 'an academic program in a Western structure' (Harris 1990, 50). Even though Aboriginal languages are used at various year levels for significant proportions of the school days, the concepts, ideas, attitudes and content tend to be non-Aboriginal. There is also the damage done by the 'hidden values' curriculum of schools on Aboriginal culture — western attitudes such as being on time, keeping to a rigid programme, teachers' use of language or classroom practices which do not respect Aboriginal culture (use of names of dead community members, organization of classroom seating which ignores traditional avoidance rules and preferred Aboriginal age and sex roles, etc.). If the school structure continually reinforces western cultural values then there is an implied rejection of the Aboriginal values and customs. 'The hidden curriculum includes what rubs off over time onto students during the school experience although it may not be deliberately taught. It includes such important elements as values, priorities, attitudes and what is viewed as normal.' (Harris 1990, 8)

In recent years there has been a movement towards what Aborigines term as 'two-way Aboriginal schooling'. The first 'two-way' schools were at Strelley, Western Australia, in 1976, Yipirinya, Northern Territory, in 1979 and Noonkanbah, Western Australia, also in 1979. The success of these programmes has inspired numerous other Aboriginal communities to develop programmes which stress Aboriginality with an overlay of necessary western knowledge. It is more than working towards additive bilingualism, but rather aiming for additive biculturalism. They are programmes which will not only prepare students to remain in Aboriginal communities but also to be able to deal with western culture and bureaucracy when and where necesary. It is interesting to note that the innovation of bilingual education in 1973 was 'out of date' within three years (in Western Australia) and six years (in Northern Territory), being progressively replaced by the two-way schooling concept. Different communities are developing models which they see as most appropriate to their situation. The underlying concept, however, is that the children are to be educated in two separate cultures in separate ways by different instructors (teachers, family members, tribal elders). It attempts to avoid one cultural version which is taught through two languages, preferring two cultures which are taught through their own distinctly appropriate learning styles in the language appropriate to that culture.

For a 'two-way' Aboriginal programme to function the power has to be, and be seen to be, in the hands of Aborigines themselves. There will need to be a clear compartmentalization of teaching and learning according to the two cultures — staffing, content, language of instruction, teaching styles, context and timing of teaching. Harris presents us with numerous models of how these programmes are being implemented in remote communities. To sum up in his words:

> Two-way schooling is not something well-meaning non-Aboriginal teachers or administrators from outside can implement, though they can assist in many ways. By definition two-way schooling is an internal Aboriginal initiative. The main difference when compared with bilingual education (the next most positive educational strategy to two-way schooling) as it now exists in some Aboriginal schools is that bilingual education can be implemented by non-Aboriginal educators working in tandem with Aboriginal staff; two-way schooling cannot be implemented in such a way. (Harris, 1990, 19)

A further promising development related closely to the concept of 'two-way education' is the very recent production of the Australian Indigenous Languages Framework. This is a national cutticulum project for Years 11–12 (senior secondary education). It identifies six distinct types of Australian languages study, namely second language, first language maintenance, language revitalization, language renewal, language reclamation and language awareness. These are suited individually to the various contextual variables of the different Aboriginal groups and languages. Students will be expected not only to learn or develop an Australian (Aboriginal) language, where available and appropriate, but also to 'investigate the surrounding languages of the region' and to 'look at such issues as the support systems and pressures facing a particular language, its prospects for long-term survival, directions of language shift and the nature of language change occurring'. (Amery 1994, 3) The potential impact of such socially and ecologically based programmes for maintaining and extending bilingualism, within and outside the school context, would appear to be obvious.

Immersion programmes

Queensland, a state which incorporates the north-east of Australia, covers an area seven and a half times that of Great Britain with some three million inhabitants. It was here that Australia's first late-immersion-style language-teaching programme began in 1985 at Benowa State High School, Gold Coast – a partial late-immersion programme in French. The introduction of the programme was inspired by a teacher who was disillusioned with the lack of success of traditional language-teaching programmes which were generally not producing high levels of language proficiency by the end of high school (Berthold 1992). The teacher proposed the introduction of a quite limited partial-immersion programme to teach not only French, but Mathematics and Science through the medium of French to one class of twenty-six volunteer Year 8 students (Year 8 being the first year of high school in Queensland with most children being twelve years old). The proposal was to offer a one-year bilingual programme as an enrichment for high achievement students looking for a challenge. The students entering the programme had no prior knowledge of French and were therefore required to learn the language at the same time as the content matter in the other disciplines.

The initial proposal encountered strong opposition from various sectors within the school, necessitating a compromise between the proponents for and against the proposal. The compromise was that the immersion students would sit for the same Mathematics exam as their peers in the English-speaking classes at the end of Term 1. If the students appeared to have been disadvantaged by studying through the medium of French then the experiment was to be terminated. This put a great deal of pressure on the teacher, but fortunately was seen as a challenge by the students. They revelled in the competitive atmosphere that this produced and confidently sat for their exams. When the results of the Mathematics tests were released it was seen that the immersion class was second out of fourteen classes with a mean class mark only 0.5 per cent lower than the leading class. This strong performance ensured that the programme would continue at least until the end of the year. During the remainder of the year the students performed well in their assessment items, in comparison to their peers, in both language arts and the various discipline areas. The students and their parents were so pleased with the programme that they requested it to be extended to Year 10. This was duly done with the employment of additional teachers and a consequent expansion in the range of subjects offered through the medium of French, namely, – Physical Education, Social Science and History – becoming a 60 per cent partial-immersion programe in Years 8 to 10.

There have been a number of indications of the success of the Benowa programme highlighting the students' linguistic competence and scholastic achievements. They have performed prominently in various competitions (such as a state-wide Mathematics competition in 1985, the inaugural Gold Coast Grammar Competition in 1989, and an Australia-wide competition run by the Alliance Française in 1989 and 1990). In 1989 when the first immersion group graduated, five out of the six students who achieved the maximum grade in the Tertiary Entrance Score were former immersion students. In 1987, Dr Peter Cryle, Head of the Department of French at the University of Queensland, having evaluated the students' linguistic progress, compared the linguistic skills of the immersion students favourably with third-year students at university. He added: 'It is my strong hope that Australia will see in the near future some attempts to generalise the Benowa model, as a way of producing genuinely bilingual students.' The students' standards made such an impression on the University of Queensland that in 1988 their staff agreed to teach certain modules of the university's French programme during the final two years of their high school education. Testing and evaluation carried out by the University revealed quite impressive results.

One essential feature of the Benowa programme is the exchange programme that exists with Collège Georges Baudoux, Nouméa, New Caledonia, which has been operating since 1986. Every second year, Years 9 and 10 of the French immersion programme go to New Caledonia for four weeks, where the students are billeted with French families and go to school with the families' children. Activities and excursions are organized to make the exchange both linguistic and cultural. In alternate years, approximately forty students from Collège Georges Baudoux are hosted at Benowa. This ensures that every year there is at least a four-week block of continuous contact with French-speaking families and children. The programme has had continued success with the addition of an extra class per year group since 1992. Therefore by 1994 there will be two classes at each year level from Years 8 to 10. The Queensland Minister for Education, Paul Braddy, in a ministerial statement in July 1991, wrote:

> One model of languages education with considerable potential is the immersion program. At Benowa State High School . . . immersion students have reached high levels of French after three years of immersion study and have shown strong performance in their other subjects as well.
> Such programs can serve as exemplars of excellence for Queensland, developing a critical mass of teaching and student talent...
> One of our major new initiatives will be to expand the immersion model to additional languages and to areas outside Brisbane metropolitan centres. (Braddy 1991, 6)

The minister's plans have begun to be implemented as a result of Benowa's sustained and proven success. The Queensland Department of Education began pilot programmes in Brisbane at Mansfield Senior High School in French in 1991; at Kenmore Senior High School in German in 1992; at Park Ridge Senior High School in Indonesian in 1993. The growth in immersion programmes has not been restricted to the state educational system. The first independent secondary school to trial immersion-style teaching, the Southport School, also situated on the Gold Coast, began a French programme based on the Benowa model in 1992.

A major contrast between the two Gold Coast programmes and the three pilot programmes in Brisbane is that the former two were staff-inspired and school-funded whereas the latter were government initiatives financed by the coffers of the state and federal governments. This has led to significant differences in the operation of the programmes although they follow the same basic model. The school-based programmes were inspired by the teachers and were expected to be run within the normal resources of the school. No extra funding or supernumerary staff were provided, which resulted in the immersion staff teaching full timetables similar to those of their peers in the all-English classes. Therefore all the extra work necessary to write, translate and produce all of their teaching material had to be done within their own time. Conversely, the three official pilot programmes have been highly subsidized. Extra staffing has been provided so that participating teachers only teach a half timetable (the remaining time being devoted to resource development). In fact, at Kenmore, two teachers were employed a year in advance without any classes to teach, so that they could prepare resources for the following year, yet when the programme began they still only had half teaching workloads. It is envisaged that these half-time approaches will only continue for the first three years of each pilot programme to enable teachers progressively to develop their resources and teaching materials for Years 8 to 10. Surprisingly the pilot schools do not seem to have developed programmes and materials superior to the non-official programmes. Student satisfaction actually seems to be greater in the non-official schools according to a survey carried out with the five schools (Berthold 1993).

The first Australian university to institute a three-year Bachelor of Teaching degree based on an immersion model is the University of Central Queensland (Rockhampton). This programme, begun in 1993, is designed to prepare teachers of Japanese. The course developers opted to teach 50 to 80 per cent of each semester's programme through the medium of Japanese – modules concerned with classroom teacher development, foundation subjects, curriculum subjects and language. According to Tony Erben, one of the people instrumental in establishing the programme, it is

> A flexible pre-service teacher education program ... which aims to multiskill teacher trainees simultaneously in three areas; generalist primary, LOTE (Japanese) and immersion education. It is hoped that this program may set a standard for the direction that tertiary teacher education could take in order to equip LOTE/Immersion teachers for the 21st century and provide a platform from which the tensions of change and resistance may be reconciled. (Erben 1993, 51)

The Queensland models, at both secondary and tertiary levels, are being looked at by other state educational authorities and universities, to gauge the feasibility of implementing similar programmes in their own institutions.

Summary and comments

National and state funding measures for bilingual education for community languages have existed for just over a decade. They initially offered transitional and sometimes subsequent maintenance provision. For some, submerged in a plethora of multicultural sensitization projects, they were seen as a manifestation of the 'ethnic placebo'. Taken seriously by others, they have provided valuable pilots leading towards a universal extension of language learning, which is favoured particularly by perceived methodological advantages. Extended more recently to partial-immersion programmes, these initiatives provide a valuable fillip to the 'languages for all' policy in a context of previous language learning decline. Aboriginal Bilingual Education began just over two decades ago (in 1973) as a transitional programme with (some) linguistic and cultural maintenance availability. Within a handful of years, Aboriginal community leaders were seeking 'two-way' bilingual/bicultural programmes, more favourable to both cultural maintenance and retrieval and equitable empowerment. Policy recognition was achieved by 1984.

References

Amery, R. (1994). 'AILF: Promoting linguistic diversity', *Australian Language Matters*, 2 No. 1, Jan–Mar, 3–4.
Asian Studies Council (1988). *National Strategy for the Study of Asia in Australia* (Canberra, AGPS).
Berthold, M. (1992). 'An Australian experiment in French immersion', *The Canadian Modern Language Review*, 49 No. 1, October, 112–26.
Berthold, M. (1993). 'Selected elements from surveys of Queensland immersion students 1985–1992', *Proceedings from the First Biennial Conference of the Australian Association of Language Immersion Teachers* (Newcastle, Australia, June), 22–37.
Birrell, R. and Birrell, T. (1981). *An Issue of People: Population and Australian Society* (Melbourne, Longman Cheshire).
Braddy, P. (1991). *Languages Other Than English [LOTE]*, A statement from the Minister for Education, July (Department of Education, Queensland).

Cahill, D. (1984). *A Greek–English Bilingual Education Program: Its Implementation in Four Melbourne Schools* (Melbourne, Language and Literacy Centre, Phillip Institute of Technology).
Cahill, D. et al. (1984). *Review of The Commonwealth Multicultural Education Program* (Canberra, Commonwealth Schools Commission).
Clyne, M. (1982). *Multilingual Australia* (Melbourne, River Seine).
Clyne, M. (ed.) (1986). *An Early Start: Second Language at Primary School* (Melbourne, River Seine).
Clyne, M. (1991a). 'Bilingual education for All: an Australian pilot study and its policy implications', in O. Garcia (ed.), *Bilingual Education: Focusschrift in Honour of Joshua Fishman on the Occasion of his 65th Birthday, Volume 1* (Amsterdam, John Benjamins), 253–70.
Clyne, M. (1991b). *Community Languages: The Australian Experience* (Cambridge, Cambridge University Press).
Cummins, J. (1979). 'Linguistic interdependence and the educational development of bilingual children', *Review of Educational Research* 49 No. 2, 223–51.
Di Biase, B. and Dyson, B. (1988). *Language Rights and the School: Community Language Programs in Primary Schools in Australia* (Sydney, Inner City Education Centre/FILEF Italo-Australian Publications).
Erben, A. (1993). 'Teacher training through immersion', Proceedings from the First Biennial Conference of the Australian Association of Language Immersion Teachers (Newcastle, Australia, June 1993), 51–62.
Fernandez, J. (1992). *Room for Two: A Study of Bilingual Education at Bayswater South Primary School* (Melbourne, NLLIA).
Fishman, J. (1976). *Bilingual Education: An International Sociological Perspective* (Stanford, Stanford University Press).
Foster, L. and Stockley, D. (1988). *Australian Multiculturalism: A Documentary History and Critique* (Clevedon, Multilingual Matters).
Galbally, F. (Chair) (1978). *Migrant Services and Programs*, Report of the Review of Post-Arrival Programs and Services for Migrants (Canberra, AGPS).
Gale, K., McClay, D., Christie, M., and Harris, S. (1981). 'Academic achievement in the Milingimbi bilingual education program', *TESOL Quarterly* 15 No. 3, 297–314.
Harris, S. (1990). *Two-Way Aboriginal Schooling* (Canberra, Aboriginal Studies Press).
Ingleson, J. (1989). *Asia in Australian Higher Education*, report of the Inquiry into the Teaching of Asian Studies and Languages in Higher Education (Canberra, AGPS).
Ingram, D. (1993). 'Developing Language Education for Australia's Economic Future', *Babel* 28 No. 1, 6–17.
Kalantzis, M., Cope, B. and Slade, D. (1986) (for the Department of Immigration and Ethnic Affairs). *The Language Question: The Maintenance of Languages other than English, Vol. 1: Research Findings* (Canberra, AGPS).

Leal, B., Bettoni, C. and Malcolm, I. (1991). *Widening our Horizons*, report of the Review of the Teaching of Modern Languages in Higher Education (Canberra, AGPS).
Lo Bianco, J. (1987). *National Policy on Languages* (Canberra, AGPS).
Lo Bianco, J. (1989). *Victoria Languages Action Plan* (Melbourne, Ministry of Education, Victoria).
Mills, J. (1982). *Bilingual Education in Australian Schools* (Melbourne, ACER).
Ministerial Working Party of the State Language Policy (1988). Report of the Ministerial Working Party on the State Language Policy (Sydney, Government Printer).
Moellner, B. (1993). 'The development and growth of bilingual education in South Australian Education Department Schools and Future Plans', Proceedings of the First Biennial Conference of the Australian Association of Language Immersion Teachers (Newcastle, Australia, June 1993).
NLLIA (1993). *Languages at the Crossroads*: The Report of the National Enquiry into the Employment and Supply of Teachers of Languages Other Than English. (Melbourne, NLLIA).
Norst, M. (1982). 'Ethnic Schools', Australian National Survey of Ethnic Schools, unpublished Report.
Northern Territory Department of Education (1986). *Handbook for Aboriginal Bilingual Education in the Northern Territory* (Darwin, Northern Territory Department of Education).
PLANLangPol Committee (1983). A National Language Policy for Australia.
Rubichi, R. (1983). 'Planning and implementation of a bilingual program: Italian in South Australia', *Journal of Intercultural Studies* 4 No. 2, 37–54.
Scarino, A., Vale, D., McKay, P. and Clark, J. (1984). *Australian Language Levels Guidelines: Book 1: Language Learning in Australia* (Canberra, Curriculum Development Centre).
Senate Standing Committee on Education and the Arts (1984). *A National Language Policy* (Canberra, AGPS).
Sherington, G. (1991). *Australia's Immigrants, 1788–1988* (Sydney, Allen and Unwin).
Skutnabb-Kangas, T. and Toukomaa, P. (1976). 'Teaching Migrant Children's Mother Tongue and the Language of the Host Country in the Context of the Socio-Cultural Situation of the Migrant Family', Tutkimsuksia Research Report 15 (Finland, University of Tampere).
Stanley, J., Ingram, D. and Chittick, J. (1990). *The Relationship between International Trade and Linguistic Competence* (Canberra, AGPS).
Valverde, E. (1990). *Languages for Export* (Canberra, Department of the Prime Minister and Cabinet, Office of Multicultural Affairs).
Victoria Ministry of Education (1984). *Curriculum Development and Planning in Victoria*, Ministerial Paper No. 6 (Melbourne, Government Printer).

9

Acculturation, Ethnic Identity and Community Languages: A Study of Indo-Canadian Adolescents

Paul A. Singh Ghuman

Introduction

'Who am I?' Most young people in Britain and North America, at some stage during their adolescence, probably ask themselves this question. Also, most of them question parental authority over a range of issues and some even rebel against the formal institutions of state to claim and assert their individual identity. For young people of Asian origin, the quest for personal identity can be even more fraught with difficulties because of widespread racism in British society (Brown 1984) and the fact that their home values are quite often radically different from that of the school.

There is a clear role differentiation of men and women and boys and girls in most Asian households. Boys, normally, get preferential treatment in all walks of life, but particularly in enjoying more freedom than girls and parental encouragement to aim high. This can, and often does, lead to anxiety, frustration and sometimes leads to open rebellion among girls (Shaw 1988). The other important difference relates to the precedence of the family's interests (sometimes those of the kinship group as well) over that of the individual. This dimension has a close affinity with the conceptual model of Triandis (1991) who argues that people from traditional societies are more likely to be collective in their orientation, that is, they are more conscious of the social norms, more attuned to the value judgements of 'significant' others, and are generally more socially driven. Rotheram and Phinney (1987, 22) also suggest 'an orientation toward group affiliation and interdependence versus an individual orientation emphasizing independence and competition' as one of the dimensions which may be used to differentiate cultural groups. The schools in western Europe and North America encourage the development of personal autonomy, critical thinking and a generally questioning attitude to things, whereas Asian parents harmonize the family's interests with that of its individual members. They are generally conscious of the family's *Izzat* (honour) and traditions. This radical difference in values can lead to serious inter-generational conflict over such matters as dating, curfew, choice of clothes, music and videos. For some girls, staying on at school beyond the compulsory age may be very difficult. Rex (1985, 10) summarized these difficulties succinctly: 'Sometimes schools may be unnecessarily provocative as when some of these require participation of girls in mixed swimming classes, but more generally the whole ethos of the school, based as it is on the encouragement of individual choice and free competition strikes at the root of any tight-knit marriage and family system.'

Another related difference is in the field of religion, especially for Muslim youngsters. Generally speaking, Asian parents are very religious-minded, though there are differences amongst ethnic groups on the strength of their feelings. Schools, on the other hand, are mostly secular in their ethos. Muslim parents (Ashraf 1988) do not approve of the rational/secular outlook that their young people acquire at school. They feel the school undermines their young peoples' faith in Islam and therefore their way of life. This leads to conflict in several educational matters. There can be serious difficulties over school uniform and mixed classes, particularly in drama, dance, sex education and swimming lessons. The young people can be caught in the tussle between the two well-intentioned opposing forces, suffer from anxiety and guilt, and therefore become confused and alienated both from home and school. A study by Ullah and Brotherton (1989) reports significantly higher levels of anxiety among Asian adolescents as compared with their Afro-Caribbean and white peers. However, it must be pointed out that there can be enormous regional, class and caste differences between the various Asian communities in these value orientations. Also, most Asian parents belong to the middle stratum of their respective societies and attach a very high value to educational attainment. The majority have positive attitudes towards schools and teachers (Taylor and Hegarty 1985).

Researchers (Drury 1991; Wade and Souter 1991; Shaikh and Kelly 1989) working in this field have highlighted some of the problems resulting from home/school differences in values and their effect on young Asian girls. Drury (1991, 398) worked with Sikh girls in Nottingham and came to the conclusion that whilst there is no overt inter-generational conflict on a range of religious and social issues, the girls would like more 'choice and freedom and fewer restrictions for females with regard to: clothing norms; recreational and social activities; boyfriends and marriage partners and domestic responsibilities'. Shaikh and Kelly (1989) interviewed fifty Muslim girls on a range of social and cultural matters and came to a similar conclusion. However, there was a difference of opinion as to whether girls should stay on at school for higher qualifications; some parents were not keen on the idea. Wade and Souter (1991) also report that more Asian girls would like the opportunity to stay on for further education and training than their fathers would allow. However, a large-scale study by the Commission for Racial Equality (Anwar 1978) found a chasm between the older and younger generation in matters such as arranged marriages, dating and dress. One of the salient findings was that the second generation was more willing to accept British customs and social practices, while not entirely rejecting their own way of life. They were seeking some form of synthesis of the two cultures.

Most of the studies done on this topic are based in Britain. There are very few studies carried out in Canada on the Asian young people (see Fisher and Echols 1989). This researcher felt that it would be instructive to compare the situation of Indo-Canadian young people with that of the British Asians for a variety of reasons. In the first place, Canadian society appeared to be more pluralistic than the British. Secondly, the federal policies of successive governments have encouraged cultural diversity in general and multicultural education in particular. Thirdly, the Canadian schools, unlike British schools, are genuinely secular in that there is no provision, at all, for the teaching of any religion.

The major concern of this chapter, however, is with the attitude of Indo-Canadian youngsters to acculturation and their views on their personal identity. There is a variety of definitions to be found in the literature on the nature of the acculturation process (see Padilla 1980). For the purpose of this chapter, however, acculturation is defined as 'the degree to which the migrant communities take up the norms, values, customs and social practices of the host society'. This concept is used as 'value neutral', and does not carry any affective meanings. It is used as a pragmatic concept to explore the attitudes of young people to their home culture and Canadian culture respectively. Whilst the notion of Canadian norms could arouse much debate and discussion, I have looked for the key organizing ideas. In my view, the major dimensions are the following: firstly, the centrality of the individual orientation of Canadian people versus the collective bearings of Asian communities; and secondly, the gender equality in Canadian society in contrast to the role differentiation of women, often inferior to men, in Asian communities. In 1974, the researcher (see Ghuman 1975) constructed a Likert-type acculturation scale to assess the attitude of British Asian youngsters (aged fourteen to sixteen years) to their home culture and to British culture. The students showed a balanced outlook on the two cultures: they favoured retaining their Asian names, their religion and their language. However, they believed in the equality of the sexes, rejected exclusive friendship with Asians and watching Asian videos. They were positive about English food, English friends and Christianity but were ambivalent about dating, mixed marriages and living in a nuclear family situation. This pattern was confirmed, even more strongly, with a large sample of 465 boys and girls in 1987 (Ghuman 1991). The present study was designed with the following issues in mind:

1. To find out the acculturation attitudes of Indo-Canadian young people through the use of an established attitude scale (Ghuman 1975) and informal semi-structured interviews;
2. To establish the reliability and validity of the scale in another cultural milieu;
3. To explore the validity of the scale with a sample of Indo-Canadian adolescents;
4. To discover the nature of social identities of young people through in-depth interviews.

Additionally, the following hypotheses were set up and tested using the null hypothesis technique: (a) girls are more acculturated than boys: (b) Indo-Canadian young people show more favourable attitudes to acculturation compared to British Asians.

Methodology

The Likert-type acculturation scale was designed by the researcher in 1974 and again validated with a large sample of Asian young people (see Ghuman 1991). Its reliability coefficient (Spearman-Brown split-half) was 0.82 on a sample of ninety-eight Asian adolescents in 1974 and 0.85 with a larger sample (465) in 1987. The original scale was slightly modified to accommodate the Canadian situation. For instance, the term 'Canadian' was substituted for 'English' and the item on school dinners was replaced by another item as there are no school meals in Canada. The modified scale consists of thirty items: fifteen sample opinions on Asian culture and fifteen related to Canadian culture (see appendix for the scale).

Scoring

The standard procedure for scoring was followed: a numerical mark of 1 was awarded to 'strongly disagree'; 2 to 'disagree' and so on. The last category of 'strongly agree' was scored 5. As the scale is meant to assess acculturation into Canadian culture, the scoring of the items expression sympathy with the Asian culture was reversed; this is shown by an asterisk (*) mark on the scale. Any item not answered by the respondent was scored as a missing item for computer analysis. In addition, subjects were asked to supply information on the following variables: parents' occupation, language(s) spoken at home; whether (a) born in Canada, and (b) attended primary school in Canada; and family religion.

Berry and associates (1989) have used attitude scales extensively to explore the acculturation attitudes of a variety of ethnic groups in Canada and Australia with adult populations. They report high reliability indices and good 'face validity' for their scales. Likewise Weinreich (1983) has succesfully devised and used a method of scaling for assessing personal and social identities.

Sample

The Vancouver Schools Board was requested to allow the researcher to carry out the planned fieldwork in three or four ethnically mixed schools. The education authorities approached four ethnically mixed schools on my behalf. Two of the schools agreed to provide facilities for research, provided I secured parental consent and followed it up only if students were willing to co-operate of their free will. In the event, I was only able to interest one hundred students of fourteen, fifteen and sixteen years of age. There were fifty-one boys and forty-nine girls. The reader's attention is drawn to the following features of the sample: 81 per cent were born in Canada, and 94 per cent attended a primary school in Canada; the majority (70 per cent) came from 'manual' backgrounds and 84 per cent were bilingual; the majority (77 per cent) came from Sikh homes and the rest from the Hindu background.

Analysis and discussion (attitude scale)
The data from the scale can be analysed quantitatively as well as qualitatively. The numerical scores can be used to carry out 'tests of significance' and to form the Principal Component Analysis to discover the underlying factor structure. On the other hand, the scores can be treated qualitatively and the Chi-squared test used to evaluate the research questions. Both methods were used in the analysis. The maximum score obtainable on the scale is 150 ($30 \times 5 = 150$) and the minimum is 30 ($30 \times 1 = 30$). At one level of analysis, it may be deduced that the higher scores represent a more acculturated outlook; and conversely, lower scores show traditional attitude. However, it may be argued that such an approach is oversimplified because the middle category 'unsure/don't know' is scored 3 and the cumulative score may not truly reflect the higher level of acculturation. To overcome this objection, an item by item analysis has also been carried out. The descriptive statistics are given in Table 1.

Table 1: Mean and S.D. of the sample's scores on the scale

	Boys	Girls
Indo-Canadians		
M	107.06	109.45
S.D.	10.98	16.96
N	51	49
*British Asians		
(Hindu and Sikh sub-sample)		
M	96.45	105.21
S.D.	11.37	12.17
N	92	131

*Note: the data on the British Hindu and Sikh young people was collected in 1987 and the findings were reported in Ghuman (1991).

The Indo-Canadian boys and girls score significantly higher than the British Hindu and British Sikh boys and girls respectively (p = 0.001 for boys and p = 0.01 for girls). This supports the second hypothesis of the research. However, there was no significant difference between the boys and girls: the 't' value was only 0.7, which is not significant at 0.05 level, though girls score higher than boys in both samples. This was further analysed by submitting the raw data (without inversion of the scores) of the Indo-Canadian boys and girls, separately, to the Principal Component Analysis with Varimax rotation (using the SPSS programme). The emerged factor structure is presented in Table 2.

Table 2: Factor structure with girls' sample (factor loadings in parentheses)

Factor 1 (Acculturation 1):	explains 30% of the total variance and loads on 14 items: 1(0.57), 2(−0.38), 4(0.48), 5(0.66), 8(0.8) 10(0.57), 18(0.58), 19(−0.40), 20(0.61), 24(0.65), 27(0.42), 28(0.85), 29(−0.77) and 30(0.62).
Factor 2 (Traditional):	explains 10% of the total variance and loads on 14 items: 2(.57), 3(0.65), 6(0.83), 8(0.30), 9(0.66), 17(0.30), 19(0.43), 21(0.76), 23(0.52), 24(−0.46), 25(0.25), 26(0.27), 27(−0.26), and 29(0.30).
Factor 3 (Ultra-conservative):	explains 7.3% of the total variance and loads on: 5(−0.39), 9(0.51), 10(0.38), 17(0.45), 19(0.47), 20(−0.39), and 26(0.75).
Factor 4 (Acculturation 2):	explains 6.6% of the total variance and loads on: 14(−0.82), 16(0.67), 19*60.35), and 22(0.59).

Notes: 1.*Odd man out item. 2. Four factors explain 54.6% of the variance.

The emerging factor structure is an elegant one in that the four factors explain over 50 per cent of the total variance and the major factor to materialize is that of acculturation. The analysis, in a way, supports the high validity of the scale. The first factor loads highly on items such as: 'we should visit English language films'; 'I would like inter-ethnic friendship'; 'celebrate Christmas'; 'visit our Canadian friends'. The second factor carries such items as: 'attend places of worship'; 'our films are more entertaining'; 'school should accept our traditional dress'. The third factor labelled as ultra-conservative loads highly on: 'better off living with our own community'; 'only make friends with my own countrymen' and rejecting even minor contact with the host community. The last factor, radical, has items like 'ignore our own language'; 'alter our names so that teachers can say them easily' − except item 19, which relates to living in our own community.

Table 3: Factor structure with boys' sample (factor loadings in parentheses)

Factor 1 (Acculturation 1):	explains 16.5% of the total variance and loads on 9 items: 5(0.65), 13(0.40), 15(0.58), 18(0.24), 22(0.24), 27(0.76), 28(0.76), 29(−0.24), and 30(0.53)
Factor 2 (Traditional):	explains 11.1% of the total variance and loads on 10 items: 2(0.24), 6(0.66), 10(0.27), 11(0.25), 13(0.34), 18(−0.69), 19(0.80), 20(−0.50), 23(0.40), and 27(0.29)
Factor 3 (Acculturation 2 − rejection of narrow traditional outlook):	explains 8.5% of the total variance and loads on 7 items: 3(−0.37), 4(0.56), 20(0.66), 21(−0.48), 23(−0.42), 24(0.78), and 26(−0.35)
Factor 4 (Ultra-conservative):	explains 7.1% of the total variance and loads on 8 items: 6(0.35), 11(0.78), 12(0.41), 1460.26), 21(0.25), 22*(0.26), 25(0.79), and 29(0.42)

Notes: 1.*Odd man out item. 2. Four factors explain 43.1% of the total variance.

The discovered factor pattern is very close to the factor structure found with the girls' sample, but with an important difference. The first factor, named acculturation, explains only 16.5 percent of the variance and is therefore less significant for boys. This confirms the consistency of the scale because boys hold slightly more traditional attitudes as compared to the girls. The result is in line with that of other researchers (Northover 1989).

Reliability of the scale
The reliability index of the scale with the British sample (Ghuman 1991) was very high indeed: the Spearman-Brown quotient was 0.83 and Cronbach l = 0.78. With the present sample the coefficients are 0.87 and 0.75 respectively. These split-half reliability coefficients, once again, provide us with strong evidence that the items were answered fairly consistently and that the boys and girls must have understood the meanings and implications of the statements.

Qualitative analysis
The young people showed their acculturation outlook by scoring highly on the following items: girls and boys should be treated the same; going out with Canadian boys and girls; celebrating Christmas; visiting Canadian friends at home; choice of clothes; visiting English-medium cinemas; and women should wear European-style clothing. Their traditional outlook was demonstrated by their scores on the items: attend our temples; learn our language; fulfil parents' wishes, and scoring low and changing names. Their scoring on the following items was almost equally distributed in the five categories: 2 – school should accept our traditional clothes; 4 – no wish to go back to the country of origin; 10 – parents and children should live on their own; 13 – learn something about Christianity; 24 – more inter-ethnic marriages; and 26 – our women behaving like Canadian women. This indicates their ambivalence to these areas of behaviour.

They rejected the following items expressing negative attitudes towards some elements of their home culture: 6 – eat own food all the time; 9 – living in one's own community; 11 – a woman's place in the home; 12 – only our own doctors can understand our illnesses; 17 – making friends with only my own countrymen; 19 – living in the same area as the community; 21 – our films are more entertaining than English; and 29 – marriages should be arranged by the family. As compared to the British sample, students in the present study showed more favourable responses on most items, except on 'we should learn something about Christianity' and 'our films are more entertaining than English films'. The present sample was more favourable to acculturation in intensity as well, that is, more students ticked the 'strongly agree' category on the scale.

Gender differences

Differences between boys and girls have emerged on the Principal Component Analysis and on their total scores; although these are not statistically significant, they are quite marked. It was thought appropriate to highlight those items on the scale on which differences were most marked. The Chi-squared test of significance was used to evaluate each item of the scale. The results are reported in Table 4.

Table 4: Items on which differences appeared between the boys and girls(%)

		Strongly Agree + Agree	*Undecided*	*Strongly disagree + Disagree*
1. Girls and boys should be treated the same	G	96	4	0
	B	92	8	0
9. We are better off with people from our community	G	26	12	62
	B	10	22	68
11. Woman's place is in the home	G	12	4	84
	B	12	16	72
21. Our films are more entertaining	G	22	21	57
	B	16	20	64
22. We should ignore our language	G	2	2	96
	B	7	12	81
25. Men should make decisions	G	2	8	90
	B	18	19	63

Note: all differences are significant beyond $p = 0.05$; the Chi-squared was calculated with full five point scale, on the raw data, with four degrees of freedom. G = girls; B = boys.

The inference that can be safely drawn from the table is that girls, as expected, score highly on the items relating to gender equality. Also, they are more in favour of retaining their community language and find Asian films more entertaining than the boys do. It appears from the research that girls are striking a better balance than the boys –

they are trying to achieve the 'best of both worlds'. Northover (1989) also found Gujarati girls to be more in favour of mixing with the indigenous whites as compared to boys. The explanation for this difference is mainly due to the position of women in Asian communities. Women are often thought to be 'different' from men. The traditional role of women was/is confined to the household activities of child care, housekeeping and being a good hostess. This notion is not very unlike the one held by British men before the First World War, and some feminists would argue it is even cherished now by the majority (Greer 1984). Through contact with the schools and other aspects of British lifestyles, girls know that they have most to gain in the domain of personal autonomy, choice of clothes and friends and equality with boys. In my 'qualitative' study of Indo-Canadian young people (Ghuman 1993), girls gave vivid descriptions of perceived injustices they met in their family and expressed their strong desire to modify and change their traditional way of life.

Discussion
The findings of this enquiry can be interpreted within a framework of a conceptual model that suggests that acculturation may be mapped on a bipolar dimension. On one end of this continuum can be placed the concept of 'assimilation' (complete absorption) and on the polar end the notion of accommodation. The concept of accommodation is well defined by Rose *et al.* (1969, 25):

> it implies that the immigrant has taken the first steps towards fitting in but may wish to remain encapsulated within his own group; he may be said to be seeking accommodation through self-segregation; or he may seek to adapt himself more fully to the ways of the receiving society but may experience rejection.

Integration lies somewhat in the middle of the acculturation continuum and may be defined as

> a process whereby a minority group, while retaining its own culture and religion, adapts itself or is accepted as a permanent member of the majority society in all the external aspects of association (Rose *et al.* 1969, 25).

The young people in this study appear to be aiming, at this stage, in their adaptation strategy, for integration. They reject the inward-looking attitudes of their parents (not mixing with the whites, sticking to their food, living in the areas where the community has settled, adherence to traditional arranged marriages), but are positive about the home language, going to places of worship and retaining their religious names. While they would like to adopt the values of Canadian society and mix with Canadians freely, they are trying to synthesize and create new idioms of expression in the field of music, dress, art and cuisine (see Ghuman 1993). This process is also under way in Britain, where Asian young people are learning to cope with two cultures. Drury (1991, 388) summarizes her research findings succinctly:

> I found that my respondents were neither fully culturally assimilated into white culture, nor entirely encapsulated within their parental culture ... my study indicated that respondents were relatively conversant and comfortable with both socio-cultures...

Shaikh and Kelly (1989, 18) arrive at a similar conclusion:

> The picture that emerges from this research as that from Miles (1984), is of British girls from Pakistani families who are successfully mixing the two traditions and creating their own way of living ... the task is to mix and match cultures to create their own design.

The fact that the Canadian young people show more favourable attitudes to their host culture as compared to the British sample needs an explanation. In Canada, politicians of all persuasions since the seventies have encouraged cultural pluralism. A Dutch sociologist, Campfens (1980) describes the situation as follows:

> Canadian policy introduced in 1971 is an explicit commitment to multiculturalism within the framework of Canada's bilingualism and biculturalism, and has permitted many immigrant groups and their descendants to maintain a high degree of cultural and institutional pluralism.

The situation in Britain, on the other hand, has shifted from downright hostility to a vague notion of assimilation as judged from the informal remarks of previous government ministers. Comments such as 'we don't want to be swamped by the immigrants' or 'the second generation should pass a simple Cricket test' and 'the education system does not recognise the skin colour of its pupils', do not inspire confidence in ethnic communities. Multicultural initiatives have virtually ceased since the passing of the Education

Act of 1988. Then, in 1988, there was the Rushdie affair which somewhat frightened the Asian community in Britain. The Muslims, in particular, were the target of the tabloid press's ridicule and cynicism on their archaic and narrow world view. During the Gulf War there were many attacks on mosques and Muslim properties. In my opinion, the combination of these factors created a climate of insecurity and anxiety in the Asian communities; in the eighties and nineties the situation has been aggravated by a long and deep economic recession. In these situations, the migrant communities tend to draw inwards to seek psychological security from within their roots. It is not surprising, therefore, that British Muslim boys and girls in my previous research scored the lowest points on the acculturation scale (Ghuman 1991).

The acculturation process is much affected by the degree of discrimination meted out to the migrants by the host communities. In particular, the role of the educational institutions is very important in this respect. Canadian schools have a clear policy on multicultural education and it is fully supported by the local boards of education and by the federal government (see Fisher and Echols 1989). A well-known researcher and established author, Bagely (1989, 103), who has worked both in Britain and Canada, summarizes the differences as follows:

> Education for all can be meaningless unless it is linked to an obvious career strategy, and self-sufficient economic roles. There is little evidence that the curriculum of the average secondary school in Britain has achieved this. The result, especially for black students in Britain, is a degree of profound alienation that negates any concept of universality in education (Bagely 1982). No systematic evidence exists of such profound alienation amongst the children of black and Asian immigrants to Canada... Though discrimination against minorities does persist in Canada, its nature and extent appear to be considerably less than discrimination in the United Kingdom.

Analysis and discussion of interview data

Twenty-five young people were interviewed individually on a range of social and personal issues in order to understand the nature of their cultural identity. The interviews were transcribed in full by the researcher to discover patterns of adaptation to the Canadian way of life and to compare the responses with the data obtained from the scale. There is a large element of subjectivity in the interpretation of such data, but the author attempted to present the full range of opinions expressed by the young people and their teachers. An attempt was made to give the strength of feelings of the respondents on various issues by extensive quotes from the interview schedule.

Community languages (mother-tongue teaching)
Most young people (80 per cent) were in favour of their home language at the spoken level – which is in agreement with the responses obtained from the acculturation scale. A Sikh boy's reply is typical: 'We should learn Punjabi – (where?) – anywhere, in schools or Gurudwara. It comes back from our ancestors. I felt weird when I could not speak it when I was in Punjab.' The majority (80 per cent) of students speak a mixture of English/Punjabi (English/Hindi) at home; my impression is that Hindi/Punjabi is spoken with parents and English with siblings and friends. Almost all are bilingual at a spoken level, anyway.

All the teachers and counsellors interviewed for the study supported bilingualism (English/French) and the teaching of community languages. A TESL teacher enthused: 'It would be fantastic if schools could teach the community languages ... I would like to see more heritage language taught in the school system. We are just beginning to ... second language in a university does not have to be French, it could be any other community language.' This school started to teach Mandarin as part of the school activities and was fully supported by the Vancouver Schools Board, although the teachers were also aware of the practical problems of including, say, three or four community languages in the school syllabus. Some of the difficulties mentioned were: financial resources; recruitment of qualified staff; and the lack of teaching material. In this context, the reader might find it interesting to note that the Indo-Canadian community does provide weekend facility for the teaching of Punjabi and Hindi, but the attendance at these classes is very poor. There are several reasons to account for this stage of affairs: poorly trained and badly paid teachers, outmoded books, large classes and often uninteresting and dogmatic methods of teaching; all are regrettably features of these schools.

My researches with Punjabi parents in the West Midlands (England) and Vancouver (Ghuman 1980, Ghuman 1993), with Bengali parents in Cardiff, Wales (Ghuman and Gallop 1981), and with Chinese parents in Manchester, England (Ghuman and Wong 1989), have found an overwhelming support for the teaching of community languages within the school curriculum. Most parents believe their language provides an important link with their cultural and social heritage. It was considered to be the core element of their culture. For the majority of parents in the studies, language is also an important part of their ethnic and religious identity.

Attendance at Gurudwara/Mandir

Most students (72 per cent) attend their family's place of worship. Nine, out of twenty-five, go regularly and the rest on special occasions, such as weddings or religious ceremonies. However, their knowledge of their religion is very rudimentary. Most of them have picked it up from their parents' informal chats and casual conversations and not from the places of worship. Few students could answer more than one or two questions on matters relating to religion. A Sikh girl summed up the situation very intelligently: 'I know the MOOL MANTIR, but I don't understand what's going on in the Gurudwara ... I tried hard, but I don't understand their old Punjabi. Now I have quit going now.' My impression after reading the interview transcripts was that these Indo-Canadian youngsters were keen to know about their religion, but the priests (Bhai and Brahmin) in the Gurudwaras and Mandirs could neither speak English fluently nor could they express religious beliefs and doctrines in a relevant idiom, for example, stories and anecdotes which could interest and motivate the young people. The parents have not got the time nor the deep knowledge of their respective religions to help their children. The students showed a very superficial knowledge of their religion, and most of them did not show the same degree of respect and reverence as their parents. A Hindu parent sounded a warning:

> Parents do not have the background and knowledge to explain to their children the basics of their religions. For instance, parents say: 'Hanuman had a tail.' Kids say 'why?' They have no answer to such questions ... Next generation will carry only 25–30 per cent of our religious knowledge and influence, then it will go down. Mandirs and Gurudwaras will be empty ... owls would howl in these places. Brahmins and Bhais can't speak English. Tell me how can young people learn? Muslims are full of zeal, they are doing better. Mosques are full.

Equality of treatment of boys and girls at home
The practice of favouring boys over girls is well-established in the Indian subcontinent (Wilson 1978). It was interesting to find out whether this custom has changed at all. The responses are tabulated in Table 5.

Table 5: Reponse pattern on equality of treatment

	Equal	Not equal	Not sure	Total
Boys	7	4	2	13
Girls	6	6	–	12
Total	13	10	2	25

There is no significant difference between the boys and girls. The responses of the young people are interesting; one said:

> Yes, my Mum says we should be treated the same. But in our community boys get better treatment. [in what way?] This girl was kidnapped – the first thing my Dad asked was whether it is a boy or a girl. My Mum says there are three sisters. He said it is OK then. That enraged my mother ... boys turn out worse. Girls are always trying to impress their parents, whereas boys couldn't care less.

> No, I live under curfew – I have to be in by six – boys are allowed to stay out.... Well the main thing is not able to go out with your friends, which I like to do. My parents think in early teens daughters should be protected.

The other source of resentment is that parents often turn a blind eye if boys go out with white girls, whereas girls are not allowed out after school. The school counsellors often hear this complaint from their girl students. A woman counsellor elaborated:

> Most of the problems I have dealt with are the girls' – some girls tend to skip school, they are expected to be home after school. They get very disenchanted that they are not allowed to 'date' – whereas Canadian students can. In some cases they sneak off and have boyfriends. Some of them are very afraid of their families, especially fathers ... Boys have privileges; there doesn't seem to be any problem with them dating white girls; they are certainly allowed.

A home–school worker provides another perspective:

It is a problem – the moment they come to school they go to the washrooms, put make-up on, untie their hair. When they go home, they braid it back. I have seen it many times. I don't blame them ... they like to be like everybody else. At home parents are too strict – there should be a medium way. Teachers encourage them to be independent, whereas parents want to keep them under their wings.

This, in a way, crystallizes the dilemma: the individual orientation of the Canadian society as represented by the school versus the collective approach of the Punjabi way of life. The best hope is some form of compromise on a range of issues between the parents and their young people.

Cultural activities – Asian music and videos

Table 6: Cultural activities – Asian music and videos

	Yes	No	Total
Asian music	16	9	25
Asian videos	16	9	25
Total	32	18	**50**

Here we have clear-cut evidence that the majority still likes to listen to Asian music and watch Indian films in the company of their parents. But all the respondents who say 'yes' to Asian music also affirmed that they listen to 'Rock' or 'Funk' music. A significant number (10/25) also watch Asian programmes on the TV. This pattern suggests a considerable attachment to the traditional forms of entertainment. This, however, does not mean they do not enjoy English-medium films and music. This is a good example of emerging bicultural tastes amongst the young people in the study.

Family type, food and friends
Eighteen boys and girls live in a nuclear family and seven in an extended family type. This shows a clear trend towards the Canadian norm of nuclear family structure and away from the traditional custom of having uncles and aunties living in the same household. As regards the food habits of the families the majority (15 out of 25) cook traditional food, for example, chappatis, a variety of curries, yoghurt and rice. However, a significant number (10 out of 25) have changed their traditional cooking to a mixed

variety: Italian pizzas are popular, so are the Chinese dishes. Among the interesting replies were: 'It is a mixture of both — something like pasta or pizza.' 'Chappatis are OK but not every day.' 'Italian is my favourite.' All the students preferred to have sandwiches or another Canadian-style food for lunch during the school terms. A Sikh girl commented: 'Curried vegetables would smell so much, so I don't bother.'

As regards friendship patterns, it was interesting to observe a fair degree of cross-ethnic friendship, though not cross-gender in the case of Indo-Canadians. This was confirmed during the interview sessions. The friendship choices were wide and varied. None of the students admitted to having friends exclusively from their own ethnic group, but on further probing two of them admitted to having intimate friends within their own community. Typical responses were: 'My friends are from all groups — white, Chinese and Filipinos. I enjoy their company.' 'I have mixed friends — East Indians, white and Chinese.' The teachers endorsed the views of students on inter-ethnic friendship.

Asian teachers
It is generally considered desirable to have ethnic teachers on the school staff to provide good role models for young people (Swann 1985). Students' responses endorse this view: thirteen say 'yes' and twelve say that it does not matter. The reasons given for having more teachers are interesting: 'It's a good idea, just like other teachers — it gives our people a chance.' 'Yes, I love it — you feel proud.' Reasons given for 'doesn't matter' responses were: 'All that matters is how the teacher teaches,' or 'Teachers are teachers, it doesn't matter who they are'.

Equality of opportunity
The majority (23 out of 25) think they would be equally treated in the job market. This is a surprising finding. In the UK it was quite the reverse — the majority thought they would be discriminated against. Their answers are revealing. A Sikh girl replied: 'Yes, I think so. In a job all they want is education, if you have it — you be OK.' A Hindu boy was a bit more cautious: 'I hope so. [You are not sure?] Some people think different, they don't like East Indians. Some are racist. Maybe one out of ten would be of this type. But I haven't met any racism ... my uncle is owner of a dentist shop. He started from the bottom and made it.'

The teachers were ambivalent about the equality of opportunity issue. I had a range of opinions: 'I would love to say yes, but I don't think it is going to happen. [Majority of students think they will?] ... it is good that they do, but one has to be honest.' Another teacher responded: 'Now there are − but in my generation, no. The new generation believes in equality.' A perceptive teacher remarked: 'There is racism against Indian people in Vancouver. East Indians are doing low grade jobs. Sikh extremists blew up a plane; this has affected the situation. There is prejudice against recently arrived Hong Kong Chinese ... it is acceptable to have immigrants without money, but it is not acceptable that they have more money than we do!' It seems to me that although most of the teachers and others are optimistic, there is still discrimination in desirable jobs against the so called 'visible minorities'. In Britain, there is clear-cut evidence for the fact that second-generation blacks and Asians are in no better a position than the first (see Brown 1984). However, my impression after the interviews was that the young people shared the North American dream of their parents: 'To get to the top all you need is hard work and the right qualifications.' This is in sharp contrast to the perceptions of young British Asians, who believe one ought to have at least 'twice' the qualifications of whites to compete with them.

Identity
To the question, 'Do you feel Canadian or East Indian, or Indo-Canadian?', the majority (20/25) of young people replied: 'Indo-Canadian'. The rest believed that they are just Canadian. No one said that it was tied to their religion or parents' country of origin, that is Hindu, Sikh or East Indian. I was surprised by their self-confidence and positive self-image; again the reversal of the picture I gained from the young people in Britain (Ghuman 1993), where the majority described their identity in terms of their religion or nationality of the country of origin. A Hindu/Christian girl's response shows desire to change and adapt: 'I follow other religions − I go to Church, I try to fit. I do my best − I still believe in my religion − Hindu religion. But I can fit in both religions ... [pause] You have to. I do. I was raised here. My parents tried to make me Hindi [*sic*], but I mixed with East Indians and white people ... now they have accepted my biculturalism.'

Teachers' comments were sought on this important issue. The

answers, once again, reflected a diversity of opinions: 'I got my multicultural background but I wouldn't say I am French/Polish-Canadian background. I never use it. East Indians? To my mind, they are Canadians. I don't think that they are Indo-Canadian, but probably a lot of people do.' 'We are all immigrants here, in England white English have been there all the time. So I feel Indo-Canadian have a firmer and securer identity here.' 'They are Canadians all right; Sikh population has achieved power in Alberta. In the Liberal party, they are determining who is going to run as a candidate for the leadership of the party.' 'I have seen and heard both; it is difficult. You are Canadian, Yet you bring into the mainstream your home culture. In Vancouver there is so much diversity. Identity is not a issue ... multiple-identity is or I say nested identities.'

Conclusions

The acculturation scale measures culture change as expressed by students in response to a range of verbal stimuli. Opinions held by an individual do influence his/her behaviour, but do not necessarily determine it. But through my long interviews with the young people, I was able to assess their behaviour as well as their opinions on important personal, social and cultural aspects of living. The response patterns elicited by both the assessment techniques converged to a remarkable degree. There are four main inferences which can be drawn from the quantitative and qualitative data.

First, the young people wish to retain the core values of their home culture, namely: language, Asian names, aspects of religion and family cohesion. Stopes-Roe and Cochrane (1990) also report similar findings. Drury (1991), in her study with a sample of Sikh girls in Nottingham, found that a large majority wants the teaching of Punjabi to be a part of the primary school curriculum. How far the language of an ethnic minority community is an essential part of its identity is a contentious issue (see Ross 1979, 3). There are two main schools of thought: objectivist and subjectivist. Objectivists posit that 'ethnic boundaries can be drawn through the identification of discrete cultural institutions and processes. Chief among those that may serve as a daily language in use, or, alternatively, serve as a language of ritual ... it is the vehicle for a world view that makes the group different from all others'. But the other school of thought argues that 'language, as an issue, is important, not in itself, but as a symbol of an underlying image of group purpose and identity'. Whether language is a cause or effect of 'ethnicity' is difficult to resolve as the comparative and historical analysis points to a very complex picture (see Ross 1979). For instance, for the Welsh, the true ethnic identity and national aspiration seems to lie in their language, whereas for the Scots it is the social and political institutions which are important for distinctive ethnic identity and act as a clear marker of national boundary. But it is important to appreciate the deep concerns of ethnic communities over the lack of recognition of their language. The older generation migrants have expressed their frustration and anxiety over their young people's inability to communicate in their mother tongue (see Joly 1987). Most Asian names are derived from the holy religious texts and have significant symbolic and emotional meanings for the individuals. Some teachers, by constant mispronunciation of Asian names, put unintentional pressure on students to Anglicize their names or to adopt a British/Canadian name. This can lower children's and young people's self esteem.

Secondly, most youngsters support the idea of mixing with indigenous whites. They reject the 'ghetto mentality' of living in their own community. However, if the majority opinions are racist and these are expressed both covertly and overtly, then it is likely that the minority groups will seek refuge within their enclaves. Witness the case of Muslim communities in the UK in the wake of the Rushdie affair. The Muslim young people shunned the popular pastimes of 'coke/beer and snooker' and returned to their religion to show their solidarity and loyalty to their community. Thirdly, the students reject, or are ambivalent about, some of the customs of their families, the most troublesome being the tradition of arranged marriages. However, most parents are making changes, but they are probably not radical enough for some young people. Finally, it became clear that the students are very positively inclined to accept the norms and values of the Canadian society. The strength of their feelings and empathy towards the host society is shown through their self-identity: most of them consider themselves to be Indo-Canadian.

References

Anwar, M. (1978). *Between Two Cultures: A Study of Relationships between Generations in Asian Community in Britain*. (London, Commission for Racial Equality).

Ashraf, A. S. (1988). 'A View of Education – an Islamic perspective', in B. O'Keefe (ed.), *Schools For Tomorrow* (London, The Falmer Press), 69–80.

Bagely, C. (1989). 'Education For All: A Canadian perspective', in K.G. Verma (ed.), *Education For All: A Landmark in Pluralism* (London, The Falmer Press), 98–117.

Berry, J. W., Kim, V., Power, S., Young, M. and Bujaki, M. (1989). 'Acculturation attitudes in plural societies', *Applied Psychology: An International Review*, 2, 185–206.

Brown, C. (1984). *Black and White Britain: The third PSI Survey*. (London, Gower).

Campfens, H. (1980). *The Integration of Ethno-Cultural Minorities in the Netherlands and Canada* (The Hague, Ministry of Cultural Affairs).

Drury, B. (1991). 'Sikh girls and the maintenance of an ethnic culture', *New Community* 17, 3, 387–400.

Fisher, D. and Echols, F. (1989). *Evaluation Report on the Vancouver School Board's Race Relations Policy* (Vancouver, Vancouver School Board).

Ghuman, P. A. S. (1975). *The Cutural Context of Thinking* (Slough, National Foundation of Educational Research).

Ghuman, P. A. S. (1980). 'Punjabi parents and English education', *Educational Research* 22, 2, 121–30.

Ghuman, P. A. S. and Gallop, R. (1981). 'Educational attitudes of Bengali families in Cardiff', *Journal of Multilingual and Multicultural Development* 2, 2, 127–44.

Ghuman, P. A. S. and Wong, R. (1989). 'Chinese parents and education', *Educational Research* 31, 2, 134–40.

Ghuman, P. A. S. (1991). 'Best or worst of two worlds: A study of Asian adolescents', *Educational Research* 33, 2, 121–32.

Ghuman, P. A. S. (1993). *Coping With Two Cultures: A Study of British Asian and Indo-Canadian Adolescents* (Clevedon, Multilingual Matters).

Greer, G. (1984). *Sex and Destiny: Politics of Human Fertility* (London, Picador Books).

Joly, D. (1987). 'Making a place for Islam in British society: Muslims in Birmingham', *Research Papers in Ethnic Relations*, No. 4, Economic and Social Research Council (Warwick, Centre for Research in Ethnic Relations).

Northover, M. (1989). 'Ethnic identity in Gujrati/English bilingual language and social context', paper presented at Second Regional Conference of International Association of Cross-Cultural Psychology, Amsterdam, The Netherlands, 27 July–1 August, 1989.

Padilla, M. A. (1980). 'The role of cultural awareness and ethnic loyalty in acculturation', in M. Padilla (ed.), *Acculturation: Theory, Models and*

Some New Findings (Colorado, Active Press), 48–84.
Rex, J. (1985). 'The concept of a multicultural society', *Occasional Papers in Ethnic Relations*, No. 3 (Coventry, Centre for Research in Ethnic Relations, University of Warwick, Coventry).
Rose, E. J. B. *et al.* (1969). *Colour and Citizenship: A Report on British Race Relations* (London, Oxford University Press).
Ross, A. J. (1979). 'Language and the mobilisation of ethnic identity', in H. Giles and B. Saint Jaques (eds.), *Language and Ethnic Relations* (London, Pergamon Press).
Rotheram, J. R. and Phinney, S. J. (1987). 'Introduction: definitions and perspectives in the study of children's ethnic socialization', in S. J. Phinney and J. M. Rotheram (eds.), *Children's Ethnic Socialization: Pluralism and development* (London, Sage Publications).
Shaikh, S. and Kelly, A. (1989). 'To mix or not to mix: Pakistani girls in British schools', *Educational Research* 31, 1, 10–19.
Shaw, A. (1988). *A Pakistani Community in Britain* (London, Basil Blackwell).
Stopes-Roe, M. and Cochrane, R. (1990). *Citizens of This Country: The Asian-British* (Clevedon, Multilingual Matters).
Swann, M. (1985). *Education for All* (London, HMSO).
Taylor, M. H. and Hegarty, S. (1985). *The Best of Both Worlds...?* (Windsor, National Foundation for Educational Research and Nelson).
Triandis, C. H. (1991). 'Individualism and Collectivism', invited address to the IACCP Conference, Debrecan, Hungary, 4–7 July 1991.
Ullah, P. and Brotherton, C. (1989). 'Sex, social class and ethnic differences in the expectations of unemployment and psychological wellbeing of secondary school pupils in England', *British Journal of Educational Psychology*, 59, 1, 49–59.
Wade, B. and Souter, P. (1991). *Continuing to Think: The British Asian Girls* (Clevedon, Multilingual Matters).
Weinreich, P. (1983). 'A conceptual framework for exploring identity development, Identity Structure Analysis and IDEX', A paper given at the tenth International Congress of the International Association for Child and Adolescent Psychiatry and Allied Professions (Dublin, Trinity College, Dublin).
Wilson, A. (1978). *Finding a Voice: Asian Women in Britain* (London, Virago).

Appendix: Acculturation scale used with Vancouver sample (* indicates reverse scoring)

1. Girls and boys should be treated the same .... SA A U D SD
*2. Schools should accept our traditional clothes .... SA A U D SD
*3. We should attend our places of worship (e.g. Gurudwara, temple) .... SA A U D SD
4. I have no wish to go back to live in the country my parents came from .... SA A U D SD

5. I would like to see boys and girls from our community going out with white Canadian boys and girls ..... SA A U D SD
*6. I would rather eat our own food all the time .... SA A U D SD
*7. We should always try to fulfil our parents' wishes.. SA A U D SD
8. We shold celebrate Christmas as we celebrate our own religious festivals .... SA A U D SD
*9. We are better off living with people from our own countries .... SA A U D SD
10. Parents and children should live on their own and not with grandparents and uncles .... SA A U D SD
*11. A woman's place is in the house .... SA A U D SD
*12. Only our own doctors can understand our illnesses . SA A U D SD
13. We should learn something about Christianity ..... SA A U D SD
*14. We should learn to speak and write our own language SA A U D SD
15. Sometimes we should cook Canadian food in our own homes .... SA A U D SD
16. We should alter our names so that our teachers can say them easily .... SA A U D SD
*17. I would only like to make friends with my countrymen SA A U D SD
18. Boys and girls should be allowed to meet each other in youth clubs .... SA A U D SD
*19. I would prefer to live in an area where there are families from our own community................ SA A U D SD
20. We should visit the homes of our white Canadian friends .... SA A U D SD
*21. Our films are more entertaining than English-language films .... SA A U D SD
22. We should ignore our own language if we want to get on in this country .... SA A U D SD
*23. I feel very uneasy with white Canadians .... SA A U D SD
24. There should be more marriages between our people and white Canadians .... SA A U D SD
*25. Men should make all the decisions about the affairs of the family..................................... SA A U D SD
*26. I would not like our women to behave like white Canadian women .... SA A U D SD
27. We should be allowed to choose our own clothes ... SA A U D SD
28. We should visit English-language cinemas and playhouses .... SA A U D SD
*29. Marriages should be arranged by the family .... SA A U D SD
30. Our women should wear Canadian (European-style) clothes .... SA A U D SD

10

ASPECTS OF BILINGUAL EDUCATION IN NIGERIA

Adebisi Afolayan

Introduction

Four goals are set for this chapter. Firstly, an attempt is made to show that in spite of the fact that Nigeria is a country with numerous languages, formal education there has been primarily bilingual rather than multilingual. Secondly, a picture of the current Nigerian educational programme in language will be given. Thirdly, an analysis of the bilingual educational goals inherent in the current Nigerian educational programme is to be presented. Finally, the discussion will recommend steps to promote bilingualism and multilingualism.

Bilingual education in multilingual Nigeria

Bilingual education in Nigeria is a paradox. Nigeria is a multilingual country; although the exact number of languages in use in the country has not been fully identified, reliable studies such as that of Bendor-Samuel and Stanford (1976) have firmly established that the languages number several hundreds. It is, therefore, natural and more practicable to link the country with multilingual education. Yet, bilingual, rather than multilingual, education is what can be and is being effectively pressed into the service of Nigeria. This is because Nigeria is not simply a multilingual country where hundreds of languages are being used, it is more importantly a multi-nationality polity. Each language is generally the instrument of a nationality, pejoratively called a tribe. Consequently, before the British colonial amalgamation of the various nationalities into a political unit in 1914, the basic interaction — generally trading — was always between any two different nationalities. Even after the amalgamation, the basic pattern of interactions continued.

Naturally, therefore, the instruments of such interactions have always been the two languages of the nationalities involved, freely borrowing from each other as needs arise, as studies such as Ajolore (1982) have shown. This means, of course, that members of the two nationalities involved in such interactions, usually traders, have always had to be bilingual.

The type of picture just painted antedated the coming of Europeans, continued during days of Nigerian colonization and has generally prevailed until today. This means that the coming of the Europeans did not radically change the basic bilingual nature of inter-nationality interactions. Transactions were simply conceived as operations between a European nationality and a Nigerian nationality. This was the reason why, for example, it has been the policy for new European missionaries to spend their first few months or even a year or more in the country learning relevant Nigerian languages before embarking on any missionary activities. It also explained why British administrators in colonial northern Nigeria, for example, learnt Hausa. It also contributed substantially to a situation in which, as was reported in Umo (1989, 84 citing Adesina 1982), Sir Hugh Clifford, the Colonial Governor of Nigeria, was led to lament, as late as 1939, that

> After two decades of British occupation the Northern provinces have not yet produced a single native of these provices who is sufficiently educated to enable him to fill *the most minor clerical post* [Umo's emphasis] in the office of any government department.

This means that generally, to be effective, interactions between Europeans and Nigerians were expected to take place in situations similar to those which prevailed between any two Nigerian nationalities. For this reason, for example, the British Colonial Government tried to court the lasting friendship of the Sultan of Sokoto and the Emirs of Gwandu and Kano, and invited the three northern Nigerian rulers to London in June 1934. During this visit, according to Omolewa (1989, 11), Lt. Colonel Beddington 'appealed to their sensibilities' in these words:

> We feel that the Fulani and the English races have much in common. Both have had a long experience and special aptitude for administering their own and other people's affairs. Ancestors of both races share that enterprise of outlook which in the old days sent them over the face of the earth to strange countries, among foreign

peoples, and today has inspired you to come to London. (Reported in *West Africa*, 30 June 1934)

In effect, the instruments of transactions betwen people of any European nationality and those of any Nigerian nationality were the European language (for example, English) and the Nigerian language. As in the case of two Nigerian languages, the English language, for example, and the Nigerian languages freely borrowed from each other as studies such as Rowland's (1963) aptly entitled 'Yoruba and English — a problem of co-existence' clearly shows. That was also why the need arose for interpreters as assistants to the colonial administrators or the Christian missionaries in order to facilitate the effectiveness of what were essentially bilingual transactions.

It seems clear that the atmosphere that encouraged the perception of inter-nationality transactions in terms of that type of bilingual interactions must have been one that had regarded the various languages, whether indigenous or foreign, as independent and equal. With the coming of colonial administration, however, this atmosphere of mutual respect and equality existing between any two languages began to change. The idea that British culture together with its linguistic tool was superior to each native Nigerian culture together with its linguistic tool began to take root until it seemed to be firmly established before the expiration of the British colonial administration. Of great importance is the fact that the superiority complex that was introduced by the impact of the British colonial administration had the radical official backing of the formal system of education imposed on the country. According to studies such as Ologunde (1982), Fajana (1979) and Afolayan (1989a), the history of language in Nigerian education can be divided into three periods: the period of missionary control; the period of government participation; and the period of government control.

The first period covered the time between the arrival of the Christian missionaries in 1842 and the amalgamation of northern and southern Nigeria into a political unit in 1914. This period was characterized by primary Christian activities of propagating the gospel of Jesus Christ. Consequently, at this stage the educational programme aimed at the production of converts literate in the local Nigerian languages and the production of pastors and catechists who might, in addition, be literate in English (Ajayi 1965, Ayandele

1966 and Fajana 1979). Understandably, such new local church leaders were expected to communicate with the missionaries, present the new religion to the local people, and also represent whatever the missionaries wanted to say to their local people.

The second period, covering the time from 1914 to 1960, the last portion of British colonial administration, was characterized by collaboration between the government and various voluntary agencies. It was a period that witnessed increasing participation of the government until it culminated in government control of the system after independence. The period was marked by the founding of more Christian mission schools, of Islamic mission schools, of native administration schools, and of direct government schools. Apart from the very few direct government schools, which were fully financed by the government, the others were voluntary agency schools which were financed by their sponsors, aided by grants from government. To emphasize the change in the primary objective of the educational system from that of producing catechists and pastors to that of producing clerks and interpreters, the ordinance on government grants provided that grants would be paid for English only, and not for the vernacular. Thus the increasing participation of colonial administration in the formal education of Nigerians had significant effects on Nigerians and the Nigerian educational system, three of which deserve mentioning here. Firstly, it firmly established in Nigerians the unfortunate impression that the English language together with the culture it expresses is superior to any indigenous Nigerian language and its culture. Secondly, the products of the education progressively became less balanced bilinguals. Thirdly, it gave rise to the exaggeratedly important, often negatively domineering, role assigned to the English language in the process of educating Nigerians. For example, this exaggerated importance has been reflected in the undue role played by translation into and from the English language in school, college, and even university *courses and examinations in Nigerian languages*!

The third historical period of government control of the Nigerian educational system corresponds to the post-colonial phase of Nigerian history. It has witnessed the persistence of non-balanced bilingualism, significantly because the inferiority complex which the colonial educational system has firmly established in Nigerians has persistently resisted any positive change. Thus, although the current educational system apparently aims at achieving balanced bilingual education, as can be seen in the discussion that immediately follows, the political will that lies behind the pursuit and implementation of the policy is characteristically half-hearted and not goal-directed.

Language in the current Nigerian educational programme

For the documentary source of the data on current Nigerian practice in bilingualism we have to turn to the current *National Policy on Education of the Federal Republic of Nigeria* (1977, 1981), henceforth abbreviated to *NPE*. To start with, two relevant preliminary points about the *NPE* are worth noting: firstly, it is a document on the formal educational system; and secondly, there is no expressed explicit provision for bilingual education in the document and one has to infer an adopted policy of bilingual education from the overall statements on language and languages found it in. Therefore, what I shall attempt to do here is to reproduce its various provisions in respect of language education for the various levels of formal education: *pre-primary, primary, secondary* and *tertiary*.

Besides the specific provisions in respect of the various levels of education, there is a preliminary important statement made in the first section, entitled 'Philosophy of Nigerian Education'. It is found in the last paragraph of the section and it is subtitled, 'The Importance of Language'. Because of its significance I shall quote it in full as follows:

> In addition to appreciating the importance of language in the educational process, and as a means of preserving the people's culture, the Government considers it to be in the interest of national unity that each child should be encouraged to learn one of the three major languages other than his own mother tongue. In this connection, the Government considers the three major languages in Nigeria to be Hausa, Ibo and Yoruba. (*NPE*, 9)

Pre-primary education is provided for in Section 2 of the *NPE*. After defining pre-primary education and stating its purpose, the document proposes that in order to 'achieve the above objectives Government will'

> ensure that the medium of instruction will be principally the mother-tongue or the language of the immediate community ... (*NPE*, 10)

Next, in respect of primary education, again after defining primary education and stating its objectives, the *NPE* has this relevant provision in paragraph 15(4) of its Section 3:

> Government will see to it that the medium of instruction in the primary school is initially the mother-tongue or the language of the immediate community and, at a later stage, English. (*NPE*, 12–13)

Secion 4 provides for two parts of secondary education: the junior secondary and the senior secondary. In each case, the provision is in respect of the specified contents of the curriculum as follows. After defining secondary education and stating its aims and objectives, it proposes that, 'to achieve the stated objectives'

> The junior secondary school will be both pre-vocational and academic; it will be free as soon as possible and will teach all the basic subjects which will enable pupils to acquire further knowledge and develop skills. The curriculum should be structured as follows:

Core Subjects	*Pre-Vocational Subjects*	*Non-Vocational Subjects*
Mathematics	Woodwork...	Arabic Studies
English		French
Nigerian Languages (2)		
Science...		

> In selecting two Nigerian languages students should study the language of their own area in addition to any of the three main Nigerian languages, Hausa, Ibo and Yoruba, subject to availability of teachers...

> The senior secondary school will be for those able and willing to have a complete six-year secondary education. It will be comprehensive but will have a core-curriculum designed to broaden pupils' knowledge and out-look. The core-curriculum is the group of subjects which every pupil must take in addition to his or her specialities.
>
> A. *Core Subjects*
> 1. English Language ...
> 2. One Nigerian Language ...
> B. *Electives*
> Every student will be expected to select 3 of those subjects depending on the choice of career up to the end of the second year and may drop one of the non-compulsory subjects out of the 9 subjects in the last

year of the Senior High School course: Biology ... Arabic studies ... French ... (*NPE*: 16-18).

(It should be noted that, in all, twenty-eight subjects are here in an in-exhaustive list of electives).

From a critical examination of the provisions of the *NPE* in respect of primary and secondary education just effected, it can be concluded that the policy says nothing about which languages to teach as subjects at the primary school and which language(s) to use as the medium(s) of secondary education. Logical inferences can only be made from the quoted provisions. In respect of primary education, it can be inferred that, since the child's mother tongue (or its functional substitute) and the English language are expected to be used as the media of instruction they must also be learnt as subjects appropriately. Also, in respect of secondary education, it can be assumed that the English language that has been prescribed as the medium of the later stage of primary education will continue to be the medium. Understandably, the two languages cannot effectively serve as media of primary education without teaching them formally as primary school subjects. Similarly, a return to the adoption of the mother tongue or 'the language of the immediate community', the initial medium of primary education, is illogical. Indeed, in both cases the implementation of the policy has been in full accordance with those logical inferences. Finally, although the *NPE* provides for various forms of tertiary education, its new revised 1981 edition does not explicitly say anything about the type of language education that is expected to take place at this level. However, it is pertinent to note that, in practice, in addition to using English as the medium of instruction, following a provision in the initial 1977 edition, there is a compulsory use of an English course, a sort of English for academic purposes programme, for all students at each university or polytechnic or college of education.

Bilingual educational goals inherent in the current Nigerian education programme

As has been noted, the *NPE* does not explicitly specify bilingual education as the goal of Nigerian education. Nevertheless, I would like to suggest strongly that indisputable bilingual educational goals are inherent in its provisions as reproduced above. The aim of this section is, therefore, to draw attention to such possible inferences and to examine critically how far these inferred bilingual goals are currently achieved.

The first provision is found in the concluding paragraph of the first section of the *NPE* on the importance of language. Certainly, the provision has a clearly stated bilingual goal of encouraging each Nigerian child to master his or her mother tongue 'and one of the three major languages other than his own mother-tongue'. This means that even if the child has one of the three major languages as his or her mother tongue he or she must also master one of the other two. Thus each Nigerian child is to be encouraged to be bilingual in two Nigerian languages.

However, there are three snags in this provision. The first is that the provision does not state at which level of formal education the child is expected to pursue this bilingual objective. Secondly, the provision fails to show how the inferred bilingual objective is to be pursued or achieved. No indication is given on how the educational process is to reflect generally the importance of language; and neither is any specification of the manner of preserving the Nigerian people's culture, or of promoting national unity, made here or anywhere else in the *NPE*. Thirdly, the provision fails to take cognizance of the importance of the English language in the country. Despite this oversight, English looms large in the specific provisions for primary and secondary levels of education. What is more, recognizing the need to accommodate the English language within this general provision will at once turn the bilingual policy into a multilingual one. In view of the various shortcomings of this provision, it is therefore not surprising to find that the provision has not so far achieved its stated bilingual objective.

As can be seen from the specifications, the provision in respect of pre-primary education is generally monolingual rather than bilingual. the only possible exceptions to this overall monolingual picture can be found in the pockets of multilingual communities within the country. There, those children, who are native speakers of any language other than 'the language of the immediate community' which is to be adopted as the medium of instruction, will have to be bilingual. But this situation may not be a serious handicap to the attainment of the primary bilingual objective of the overall educational programme, particularly as pre-primary education can be perceived as the first stage, the monolingual stage, of a sequential bilingual educational process.

Pertinently, to start with, the *NPE* leaves the establishment of pre-primary schools to private rather than government efforts (paragraph 11 (1)). This has two anticipated consequences: firstly, clients of such private schools will be the children of sophisticated and rich parents, dwelling mostly in urban centres of the country; and secondly, the primary school is expected to be the first contact with formal education by most Nigerian children. In effect, children with the privileged experience of pre-primary schools are too few (definitely less than 5 per cent of all children) to affect significantly the type of overall bilingual education envisaged for the country. More significantly, the implementation of the *NPE*'s provisions in respect of pre-primary education is not intended to affect adversely the *NPE*'s overall bilingual objective. Rather, the implementation is meant to contribute positively to the achievement of the objective. This is because the policy envisages that all Nigerian children will have pre-school education either non-formally at home and/or formally at school. Whether at home or at school, children are expected not only to learn their mother tongues but also to undergo their entire pre-school educational process through the same mother tongues. The only exception is for children who attend pre-schools in multilingual centres and whose mother tongues are minority languages in the centres. For such schools, the policy prescribes 'the language of the immediate community', which is generally the majority language of the community, as the medium of instruction of such nursery education. But that exceptional situation that imposes bilingualism in two Nigerian languages (their mother tongue and 'the language of the immediate community') on such children only anticipates what will happen in the primary schools. After all, the same provision obtains for primary schools in such communities.

It is in actual practice that the privately sponsored pre-schools have generally disrupted the bilingual objective set by the *NPE*. Although it is permissible to consider English as 'the language of the immediate community' in certain multilingual centres of the country, both before and after the formulation of the *NPE* in 1977, the medium of Nigerian pre-schools was and is still generally English. Consequently, the products of pre-schools constitute an anomaly in the anticipated national balanced bilingualism. Thus, Nigerian pre-schools have always been an agent for the implementation of the 'straight-for-English' alternative policy, inappropriately seeking to make Nigerian children effectively monolingual in English!

Next comes the provision in respect of primary education. Certainly, as can be seen in its specifications, the provision demands a bilingual educational process. Unfortunately, however, the possibility of attaining a national bilingual objective through the provision remains generally theoretical rather than real, although in practice both specified languages are taught as subjects and used as media of instruction. To begin with, the *NPE* fails to relate the primary school bilingual requirements to the stated objectives of bilingual education that it has earlier attached to the general importance of language. The bilingual goal that it sets does not demand the mastery of two Nigerian languages, the child's own mother tongue and one of the main Nigerian language of Hausa, Ibo and Yoruba. Rather, the provision is for a bilingual educational process in a Nigerian language (the 'child's own mother tongue or the language of the community') and the English language. Besides, more importantly, when seen against the background of the stated objectives of primary education *per se*, the *NPE*'s provision cannot lead to the attainment of any meaningful bilingual objective. The objectives the *NPE* prescribes for primary education are:

(a) the inculcation of permanent literacy and numeracy, and the ability to communicate effectively;
(b) the laying of a sound basis for scientific and reflexive thinking;
(c) citizenship education as a basis for effective participation in and contribution to the life of the society;
(d) character and moral training and the development of sound attitudes;
(e) developing in the child the ability to adapt to his changing environment;
(f) giving the child opportunities for developing manipulative skills that will enable him to function effectively in the society within the limit of his capacity;
(g) providing basic tools for further educational advancement, including preparation for trades and crafts of the locality. (*NPE*, 12)

Certainly, the use of the child's mother tongue ('or the language of the immediate community') as the medium of instruction for the first three years and of the subsequent use of the English language as the medium of instruction in the last three years of primary education cannot result in functional bilingualism that will achieve any of those seven objectives set for primary education. The crucial yardstick that has been used in passing judgement on the adequacy of the *NPE*'s provision is the requirement that the bilingualism to be achieved by Nigerians should be functional. What does this requirement mean? It demands that the type of bilingualism should be diglossic (Fishman 1971, 560). In effect, the learning and use of the two languages involved must be in a complementary manner. This means that, although the bilinguals are capable of using one language more in certain domains and the other language in other domains, they are capable of covering all domains effectively by one or the other of the two languages mastered. In respect of primary education, it means that the stated objectives must be effectively achieved through one of the two languages, the Nigerian child's mother tongue or the English language.

Now, consider the first of the seven objectives stated above, for example. How far can the use of the child's mother tongue or its functional substitute as the medium of instruction for the first three years of primary education guarantee the attainment of 'permanent literacy and numeracy' in the language? Will the child have been given the opportunity to learn all necessary literacy skills or all numbers in the first three years of going to school? Is it also possible for the child to have mastered during that period all oracy, let alone literacy, skills of English, a complete new language, entirely foreign to his or her cultural background and living within three years? More importantly, could the mastery be in such a way that would have enabled the child to use the language effectively as the medium of learning new concepts, skills and information, beginning with the fourth year? It is, therefore, not surprising to find that several studies such as Banjo *et al.* (1961), Taiwo *et al.* (1968), Fafunwa (1982) and Afolayan (1976, 1989a) have clearly shown, for example, that the products of Nigerian primary schools are unfortunately not permanently literate in either their mother tongue or the English language. More unfortunately, the other six objectives do not fare better in their ultimate realization!

From the provisions for secondary education two types of bilingual education may be inferred: one based on two Nigerian languages, and the other based on a Nigerian language and the English language. If the first is pursued, it wil be in keeping with the provision relating to the *NPE*'s statement on the general importance of language; and, if the second is pursued, it will be a continuation of the implementation of the *NPE*'s provisions in respect of primary education. It is true that bilingualism in two Nigerian languages may be seen as one of the goals of Nigerian junior secondary education. But unfortunately, the caveat 'subject to availability of teachers' attached to the specification renders the objective of bilingualism entirely provisional. Indeed, since the implementation of the policy began over ten years ago, teachers have never been available to make the policy effective! It is also true that generally Nigerian secondary education involves the learning of a Nigerian language and the English language. The teaching or learning of the languages is however not carried out within any expressly stated or well-articulated bilingual objective. Not many of the hundreds of Nigerian languages are ever taught; and those that are taught are not functionally or contextually related to the English language.

Of course, we might reasonably expect that senior secondary and/or tertiary education would produce bilingualism in Nigerians from the continued pursuit of the learning/teaching of English and a Nigerian language. Again, that expectation is either idealistic or patently theoretical. Any resultant bilingualism cannot be expected to be the direct product of the provision of the *NPE*. All that we can expect is at best incidental bilingualism based on two assumptions. Firstly, it could be assumed that the secondary school children would have gained a mastery of their respective mother tongues by the end of their course. Secondly, since the English language is the medium of secondary and tertiary levels of education, the mastery of the language could be set up as one of the major goals of Nigerian senior secondary and/or tertiary education. But, even if it is assumed that bilingualism arises from that situation, it will not be according to any of the goals set for Nigerian secondary and/or tertiary education by the *NPE*. More importantly, such incidental bilingualism cannot be a general characteristic end-product of the Nigerian educational system. Rather it will be that type of incidental bilingualism found in selected individual Nigerians, particularly those who are native speakers of the few Nigerian languages adopted for learning or teaching in an *ad hoc* manner within the current implementation of the educational system prescribed by the *NPE*.

Recommendations and conclusion

From the analysis so far, it is clear that current Nigerian educational programmes have not been achieving the objective of turning Nigerian children into adult bilinguals. This closing section will propose steps to promote greater bilingualism and multilingualism.

The first step is a clear declaration that the overall educational programmes are meant to achieve greater bilingualism and multilingualism. This will have to be supported by political will which will establish bilingual and multilingual education as a national ideology (Afolayan 1978, 1984, 1989b). The spirit of subjecting local or zonal interests to the overall national good will have to be cultivated (Emenanjo 1985). Efforts must be made to gain the support of parents in particular and the public in general. There should therefore be a campaign to inform parents of the nature and advantages of bilingual and multilingual education. In order to counteract feelings that local languages are being neglected, the adoption of each Nigerian child's mother tongue as an instrument of the child's education must be pursued singlemindedly. It is by so doing that no minority language or community will feel neglected or cheated and that negative linguistic politics will be avoided (Williamson 1983).

The new provisions should clearly state the languages which are to be involved in education, namely the community (or local) language, the major Nigerian languages – Hausa, Ibo and Yoruba – and English. The place and use of these languages in the schools must also be specified. The community language should be used in all the years of the primary school as the medium of instruction and also taught as a subject. At this level, English should be taught as a second language. The basic defects at this level, which have been previously identified in this chapter, are the inadequate duration of using the child's mother tongue as the medium of instruction at the early stage and the ineffective introduction of English as the medium of instruction at the later stage. This recommendation clearly specifies the roles of both the community language and English.

At post-primary levels, a major Nigerian language should be taught as a subject and used partially, as appropriate, as the medium of instruction. At these levels, too, English should continue to be taught as a second language but also used as a medium of instruction, supplemented appropriately with a Nigerian language. It has previously been shown that there are two basic defects in respect of the junior secondary school: the failure to specify English as a medium of instruction and the inclusion of the caveat 'subject to the availability of teachers' in respect of the use of Nigerian languages. In these recommendations, English is expressly specified as a medium of instruction, and the inhibiting caveat is removed. At the level of the secondary school, English is recommended as a medium of instruction and it is recognized that students have an option of being bilingual either in two Nigerian languages or in one Nigerian language and English. These proposals must also be accompanied by recommendations on teacher training to ensure a supply of teachers who are linguistically competent in community languages, major Nigerian languages and English. The training must also equip teachers with a sound knowledge of the principles of bilingual education and effective methods of language teaching, and the importance of liaising with parents so that they are kept adequately informed about school policy.

These recommendations propose a bilingual and multilingual approach instead of the exclusive reliance on the English language. In acknowledging community languages, these recommendations accept second-language status for English and the three major Nigerian languages where they are different to the community language (Afolayan 1987, in press). It cannot at any stage be appropriate to treat Nigerians as if they were native speakers of English. Neither is it profitable to expect junior secondary school pupils whose community language is not a major Nigerian language to be able to operate in any one of Hausa, Ibo and Yoruba as if it were a mother tongue. Hence, these languages are gradually taught at various levels as described above as second languages and introduced as media of instruction. The most significant consequence of this approach is a reappraisal of the belief that Mathematics, Science and Technology can be effectively taught, even to beginners, only through the medium of English. As a result, these recommendations implicitly question the view that Nigerians' forebears were entirely ignorant of Mathematics, Science and Technology. Thus a stop would be put to the current situation whereby most of the Nigerian past and even current native scientific and technological achievements still remain unrecognized.

There are many countries which are multilingual like Nigeria, and this discussion will hopefully provide points of comparison and contrast, both in terms of the descriptive details and also in terms of the recommendations. If this chapter can provoke further discussion, I feel that that would be a fitting way to honour Professor Jac L. Williams.

References

Adesina, Segun (1982). *Planning and Educational Development in Nigeria* (Lagos Board Publications Ltd.).

Afolayan, Adebisi (1976). 'The six year primary project (Nigeria)', in A. Bamgbose (ed.), *Mother Tongue Education: The West African Experience* (London, Hodder and Stoughton, and Paris, the UNESCO Press).

Afolayan, Adebisi (1978). 'Towards an adequate theory of bilingual education for Africa', in J. E. Alatis (ed.), *International Dimensions of Bilingualism* (Washington D.C.: Georgetown University Round Table on Language and Linguistics), 330–90.

Afolayan, Adebisi (1984). 'The English language in Nigerian education as an agent of proper multilingual and multicultural development', *Journal of Multilingual and Multicultural Development*, Vol. 5, No. 1, 1–22.

Afolayan, Adebisi (1987). 'English as a second language: a variety or a myth', *Journal of English as a Second Language (JESEL)* No. 1, 4–16.

Afolayan, Adebisi (in press). *The African Mother Tongue: Its Teaching and Significance for Development* (Lagos, Longman, New African Library of Studies in English as a second language).

Afolayan, Adebisi (1989a). 'Language and education: policies, programmes, problems and prospects', in Tekena N. Tamuno and J. A. Atanda (eds.), *Nigeria Since Independence: The First 25 Years, Volume III: Education* (Heinemann Educational Books (Nigeria)).

Afolayan, Adebisi (1989b). 'The concept of English as a second language (ESL) as an applied linguistic policy for development', *Journal of English as a Second Language (JESEL)*, No. 3, 6–21.

Ajayi, J. F. Ade (1965). *Christian Missions in Nigeria 1841–1891*, (London, Longman, Ibadan History series).

Ajolore, Olusola (1982). 'Lexical borrowing in Yoruba', in A. Afolayan (ed.), *Yoruba Language and Literature*, (Ibadan, University of Ife Press and UPL), 145–64.

Ayandele, E. A. (1966). *The Missionary Impact on Modern Nigeria, 1842–1914* (London, Longman, Ibadan History Series).

Banjo, S. A. *et al.* (1961). Report of the Commission Appointed to Review the Primary Education System of Western Nigeria (Ibadan, Government Printer).

Bendor-Samuel, K. J. and Standford J., (1976). *An Index of Nigerian Languages: Studies in Nigerian Languages 5* (London, Summer Institute of Linguistics).

Emenanjo, E. N. (1985). 'Nigerian language policy: perspective and prospective', *JOLAN* No. 3.
Fafunwa, A. Babs (1982). 'Yoruba in education – an integrated primary school curriculum in Nigeria: A six-year project', in A. Afolayan (ed.), *Yoruba Language and Literature*, (Ibadan, University of Ife Press and UPL), 291–9.
Fajana, A. (1979). *Education in Nigeria 1842–1939: An Historical Analysis* (Ikeja, Longman Nigeria).
Federal Ministry of Information (1977, revised 1981). *Federal Republic of Nigeria National Policy on Education* (Lagos).
Federal Ministry of Information (1989). *The Constitution of The Federal Republic of Nigeria* (Lagos).
Fishman, Joshua A. (1971). 'Sociolinguistic perspective on the study of bilingualism', in J. A. Fishman, R. L. Cooper, R. Macdonald, *et al.* (eds.), *Bilingualism in Barrio*, 557–82, Indiana University publications, Linguistic Science Monograph H7, The Hague, Mouton.
Ologunde, Agboola, (1982). 'The Yoruba Language in Education,' in A. Afolayan (ed.), *Yoruba Language and Literature*, 145–64 (Ibadan, University of Ife Press and UPL).
Omolewa, Michael, (1989). 'Myth and Reality of the Colonial Legacy in Nigerian Education, 1951–84,' in Tekena N. Tamuno and J. A. Atanda (eds.) *Nigeria Since Independence: The First 25 Years, Volume III: Education* (Heinemann Educational Books (Nigeria)).
Rowlands, E. C. (1963). 'Yoruba and English – a problem of co-existence' *African Language Studies* (SOAS, London).
Taiwo, C. O., *et al* (1968). Report of the Committee on the Review of the Primary Education System in the Western State of Nigeria, Ibadan.
Umo, Joe U., (1989). 'Political Economy of Nigerian Education, 1960–1985,' in Tekena N. Tamuno and J. A. Atanda (eds.), *Nigeria Since Independence: The First 25 Years, Volume III: Education* (Heinemann Educational Books (Nigeria)).
Williamson, J. (1983). 'Development of minority languages: Publishing problems and prospects,' paper presented at the national symposium on culture and the book industry in Nigeria, Maiduguri.

JAC L. WILLIAMS: A SELECTED BIBLIOGRAPHY

Elgan Davies

Editors' note: The following titles are a selection from a much fuller bibliography compiled by Mr Elgan Davies, Librarian, Old College Library, University of Wales, Aberystwyth. The editors are very grateful to Mr Davies for allowing them full use of his material, but they are wholly responsible for the presentation below. This selection concentrates upon Professor Williams's academic output which is relevant to this volume, and gives no account of his prolific and varied writings in many other fields including politics, union matters, religion, literature and the eisteddfodic tradition in Welsh culture.

1946	'Y Gymraeg yn yr ysgolion: rhai awgrymiadau', *Y Faner*, 17 April.
1947a	*Straeon y Meirw* (Llandybie, Llyfrau'r Dryw).
b	'Hyfforddi athrawon', *Undeb/Unity*, 4 November, 7−9.
1948a	'Hyfforddi athrawon II', *Undeb/Unity*, 2 February, 6−8.
b	Review of *How To Learn A Language* by Charles Duff, *Undeb/Unity*, 4 April, 15−6.
1948−50	'Rhai o eiriau'r clos a'r buarth', *Bulletin of the Board of Celtic Studies*, Vol. XIII Part III, 138−41.
1953	*A Sociological Study of Llanddewi-Aberarth, A Welsh Rural Parish*, Ph.D. thesis, University of London.
1955a	Review of *Llyfrau Darllen Enid Blyton 6*, translated by Myrddin and Irene Davies, *Yr Athro* Vol. IV No. 6, 171−2.
b	'Un iaith neu ddwy?', *Welsh Anvil/Yr Einion*, Vol. 7, 73−81.
1956	Review of *Crwydro Sir Gâr* by Aneirin Talfan Davies, *Llafar*, Vol. V No. 2, 95−8.

1957 a	'Iaith a chymdeithas', *Y Traethodydd*, 25, July, 122–8.
b	'Y ddwy iaith yn yr ysgol', *Y Faner*, 24 October, 6.
c	'Y ddwy iaith yn yr ysgol', *Yr Athro*, Vol. VIII No. 4, 109–12.
1958 a	'Rhai o oblygiadau'r adroddiad ar gyraeddiadau addysgol plant dwyieithog', *Yr Athro*, Vol. VIII No. 6, 162–5.
b	'Cwrs ar ddysgu rhifyddeg', *Yr Athro*, Vol. VIII No. 7, 214–15.
c	'Cynadleddau ar ddysgu iaith', *Yr Athro*, Vol. VIII No. 10, 291–3.
d	'The national language in the social pattern in Wales, *Studies*, Vol. 47, Autumn, 247–58.
e	'This bilingual game', *Welsh Anvil/Yr Einion*, Vol. VIII, 32–40.
1959 a	'Llyfrau "dysgwyr"', *Noddwyr Llyfrau Cymraeg*, No. 2, 1–4.
b	'Hyfforddi athrawon yng Nghymru', *Y Faner*, 16 April, 3.
c	'Some social consequences of grammar school education in a rural area in Wales', *British Journal Of Sociology*, Vol. 10, 125–8.
d	'Hyfforddi athrawon yng Nghymru', *Yr Athro*, Vol. IX No. 10, 318.
1960 a	'Y ddwy iaith yn Arfon', *Y Faner*, 20 April, 6.
b	'Ymchwil addysgol yng Nghymru', *Y Faner*, 26 May, 6.
c	'Replies to comments by D. G. Lewis and W. R. Jones on bilingualism', *British Journal Of Educational Psychology*, Vol. 30, 271.
d	*Llyfryddiaeth dwyieitheg/Bilingualism: a bibliography with special reference to Wales*, Aberystwyth: Cyfadran Addysg Coleg Prifysgol Cymru (Faculty of Education, University College of Wales), (Pamphlet No. 7).
1961 a	'Cysylltiad cymdeithasol y plentyn', in Jac L. Williams (ed.), *Y Plentyn Ysgol* (Cardiff, University of Wales Press), 57–80.
b	'Geirfa fer', in Jac L. Williams (ed.), *Y Plentyn Ysgol* (Cardiff, University of Wales Press), 110–13.
c	Review of *Ieithyddiaeth* by T. Arwyn Watkins, *Yr Athro*, Vol. XII No. 3, 90–6.

1962 a	'The place of the second language', in *Bilingualism in the Schools of Wales* (Cardiff, Ministry of Education), 17–27.
b	'Methiant y polisi iaith; mor wir â'r pader; mor amlwg â'r dydd', *Y Cymro*, 25 January, 7.
c	'Welsh can help in teaching the child how to read', *The Teacher in Wales*, Vol. 2 No. 6, 4–5.
d	'Dwyieithrwydd ar gynnydd', *Lleufer* 18, 70–2.
e	'Arolwg iaith 1961', *Bwletin UCAC*, No. 8, 7–10.
f	'Cyfrifiad 1961', *Bwletin UCAC*, No. 9, 6–8.
g	'Dadl y ddwy iaith', *Barn* 1, 5–6.
h	'Dadl y ddwy iaith' (continuation), *Barn* 2, 26–7.
1963 a	'Bilingualism', in *Encyclopedia Americana*, Vol. 3 (New York, Americana Corporation), 703–5.
b	'The turn of the tide: some thoughts on the Welsh language in education', *Transactions of the Honourable Society of Cymmrodorion*, Part I, 48–69.
c	'Dadl y ddwy iaith', *Barn* 3, 82–3.
d	'Bilingual Wales: lessons for the language teacher', *Times Educational Supplement*, No. 2491, 15 February, 299.
1964 a	'Yr iaith Gymraeg heddiw', *Bwletin UCAC*, No. 14, 8–9.
b	Review of 'Dau lyfr i blant': *Profion Cymraeg* by D. G. Walters, *Y Ddraig Goch*, Vol. 33 No. 12, 5.
1965 a	'Educational and social aspects of the teaching of a second language', in *Report of the Conference on Second Language Teaching*, The St Patrick's Training College, Dublin, on 5–9 July, 32–5.
b	'Y Gymraeg all achub Cymru', *Y Ddraig Goch*, Vol. 35 No. 8, 8.
c	'Preserving the Welsh language', *Welsh Nation*, 7.
d	'Compulsory Welsh in the 11-plus examination', *The Teacher In Wales*, Vol. 6 No. 3, 1–3.
1966 a	'Ein canrif ni', in Jac L. Williams (ed.), *Addysg i Gymru* (Cardiff, University of Wales Press), 76–125.
b	'Consequences of bilingualism', *Undeb/Unity*, Easter, 8–12.
c	'Addysg ddwyieithog yn Iwerddon', review of *Bilingualism and Primary Education: A Study of Irish Experience* by John Macnamara, *Undeb/Unity*, August, 10–12.

1967 a	*Bilingualism Today* (Baile Atha Cliath, Comhdail Naisiunta na Gaeilge).
b	'Bilingualism today', in Nollaig O Gadhra (ed.), *Celtic Advance in Atomic Age* (annual volume of the Celtic League), 4–16.
c	'Education as an undergraduate subject at Aberystwyth', *Education For Teaching*, Vol. 72, 48–50.
d	'Plowden is sound – but not for Wales', *The Teacher in Wales*, Vol. 7 No. 14, 1–2.
e	'Pont i ddysgwyr ond wfft i "Gymraeg Byw"', *Barn* 55, 174, 182.
f	'The B.Ed. dilemma', *The Teacher in Wales*, Vol. 8 No. 8, 1–3.
1968 a	'Sociology and education in contemporary Wales', in Schools Council Welsh Committee, *Educational Research In Wales* (London, HMSO), 35–65.
b	'Addysg', in Dyfnallt Morgan (ed.), *Gwŷr Llên Y Bedwaredd Ganrif Ar Bymtheg* (Llandybïe, Llyfrau'r Dryw), 107–18.
c	'Addysg', in R. Gerallt Jones (ed.), *Arolwg* (Liverpool, Cyhoeddiadau Modern Cymreig), 5–9.
d	'Education: unwillingly to school', *The Spectator*, 19 January, 65–6.
1970 a	'Addysg', in Ednyfed Hudson Davies (ed.), *Arolwg* 5, (Liverpool, Cyhoeddiadau Modern Cymreig), 7–11.
b	'Y Brifysgol yng Nghymru', *Efrydiau Athronyddol*, Vol. XXXIII, 16–25.
c	'Deddf Addysg 1870', *Gwrandawr* [*Barn* 92], 2.
d	'Dyfodol y colegau addysg', *Barn* 96, 320–1, 327.
1971 a	'Reviving a language', in *Celtic Unity – Ten Years On* (Baile Atha Cliath, Celtic League), 130–3.
b	'Tbilisi 1970: addysg mewn gwlad Sofietaidd', *Barn* 100, 108–9.
c	'Dyfodol addysg brifysgol', *Barn* 107, 312–13.
d	'The future pattern of teacher training', *The Teacher in Wales*, Vol. 11 No. 8, 1–2.
e	*Bilingualism/Dwyieitheg: a bibliography of 1000 references with special reference to Wales*, Cardiff: University of Wales Press, (Welsh Studies in Education, vol. 3).

JAC L. WILLIAMS: A SELECTED BIBLIOGRAPHY

1972 a 'An expression of opinion on the nature of government in Britain with special reference to Wales', in *Commission on the Constitution, Written Evidence, Vol. 7, Wales* (London, HMSO), 151.
b 'Angen mwy ar unwaith', *Meithrin*, No. 1, 1.
c 'Her adroddiad James i'r colegau addysg', *Barn* 114, 154–5.
d 'Nid damwain i gyd', a review of *A Chapter of Accidents* by Goronwy Rees, *Barn* 115, 173–5.
e 'We need more nursery schools now', *Meithrin*, No. 2, 6.
f 'Prifysgol ddwyieithog', *Barn* 116, 207–8.
g 'Prifysgol sy'n cefnogi iaith genedlaethol', *Barn* 117, 236.
h 'Y dull dwyieithog yn ddeg oed', *Yr Athro*, Vol. XXIV, 3–6.
i 'Prif ddinas Cymru a'r Gymraeg', *Yr Athro*, Vol. XXIV, 82–3.
j 'Y Coleg Cenedlaethol', *Barn* 121, 12–14.
k 'Dwyieithrwydd ar gynnydd a chymeradwyo dull yr Ysgol Feithrin', *Meithrin*, No. 3, 3.

1973 a 'The Welsh Language in Education', in Meic Stephens (ed.), *The Welsh Language Today* (Llandysul, Gomer Press), 92–109.
b 'Bilingual education marches on', *Meithrin*, No. 4, 5.
c 'Bilingual education', *Times Educational Supplement*, 27 April, 18.
d 'Yr encilwyr a'r meddianwyr: crynodeb o anerchiad i athrawon Cymraeg fel ail iaith', *Barn* 128, 339–42.
e 'Cymraeg ar bob sianel', *Y Faner*, 3 August, 1.
f 'Fy ateb i'r unsianelwyr', *Y Faner*, 14 September, 1.
g 'Fy ateb i'r unsianelwyr II', *Y Faner*, 21 September, 2.
h 'Atal y llithriad', *Barn* 132, 531–2.
i 'Education for immigrants', *Times Educational Supplement*, 23 November, 19.
j 'Dadysgolia' *Barn* 123, 112–14.

1974 a 'Bilingualism in Wales', *System* (University of Linkoping), 2/3, 60–6.
b Review of *Multilingualism in the Soviet Union* by Glyn Lewis, *Planet*, 21 January, 94–6.
c 'Bilingual education comes of age', *Meithrin*, No. 7, 3.
d 'Welsh language survival', *The Times*, 15 August, 3.

258 JAC L. WILLIAMS: A SELECTED BIBLIOGRAPHY

- e 'Welsh teacher training', *Times Higher Educational Supplement*, 13 September, 13.
- f 'Bro'r Wyddeleg', *Barn* 143, 483 – 5.
- g 'Mae'r byd yn ymddiddori', *Barn* 142, 432 – 3.

1975
- a Review of *Language in Bilingual Communities* by Derrick Sharp, and *Some Aspects of Welsh and English – Rhai Agweddau ar Gymraeg a Saesneg: Arolwg yn Ysgolion Cymru* by Derrick Sharp *et al.*, *Trivium* 10, 175 – 7.
- b 'Bilingual schooling in Wales', *Times Educational Supplement*, 28 February, 18.
- c 'Bilingual education', *Times Educational Supplement*, 24 October, 19.
- d 'Geni iaith', *Barn* 154, 867 – 70.
- e Review of *Languages of the British Isles Past and Present* by W. B. Lockwood, *Y Faner*, 26 December, 4.

1976
- a 'Language restoration in Wales', *An Baher Kernewek – The Cornish Banner*, Vol. 1 No. 6, 33 – 5.
- b Review (continuation) of *Languages of the British Isles Past and Present* by W. B. Lockwood, *Y Faner*, 2 January, 5.
- c Review of *Geiriadur y Gwerinwr* by D. Moelwyn Williams, *Y Traethodydd* 131, 177 – 80.
- d 'Tafodiaith newydd i'r Gymraeg', *Barn* 160, 151 – 3.
- e 'Mature students', *Times Educational Supplement*, 6 August, 11.
- f 'Y Gymraeg ar y teledu', *Y Faner*, 1 October, 1.
- g 'Adult education', *Times Educational Supplement*, 19 November, 18.

1977
- a 'Camp Meic Stephens I', review of *Linguistic Minorities in Western Europe* by Meic Stephens, *Y Faner*, 28 January, 2.
- b 'Ystadegau Addysg yng Nghymru', *Barn* 169, 42 – 5.
- c 'Cyfle i wella cynllun y Cyngor Ysgolion ac arfer y Gymraeg', *Yr Athro*, Vol. XXXVIII, 173 – 5.
- d 'Camp Meic Stephens II', review of *Linguistic Minorities in Western Europe* by Meic Stephens, *Y Faner*, 4 February, 2.
- e 'Comprehensive education', *Sunday Times*, 27 March, 19.
- f 'Lladd neu adfer yr iaith', *Y Traethodydd*, Vol. CXXXII No. 563, 66 – 75.

g 'Y sianel Gymraeg' (part of a discussion on HTV's programme *Yr Wythnos* between Jac L. Williams and Dafydd Iwan), *Barn* 174/5, 215-18.

Professor Jac L. Williams also edited the following:

Undeb/Unity. Joint editor from August 1947 until Summer 1950.

Y Plentyn Ysgol. Published by the University of Wales Press, Cardiff, 1961.

Adran Ysgolion A Cholegau (Schools And Colleges Section), *Barn*, from No. 27, January 1965, until No. 32, June 1965.

Cyfres Pamffledi Llenyddol Cyfadran Addysg, Coleg Prifysgol Cymru, Aberystwyth ('The Literary Pamphlets Series of the Faculty Of Education, University College of Wales, Aberystwyth'). Fourteen pamphlets by different authors published by Llyfrau'r Dryw, Llandybïe, between 1963 and 1968.

Cyfres y Dysgwyr ('Learners' Series'). Seven pamphlets by different authors published by Llyfrau'r Dryw, Llandybïe, between 1968 and 1972.

Cyfres yr Ysgol a'r Aelwyd ('The School and Home Series'). A selection of poems published by Christopher Davies, Llandybïe, and 16 recordings of the poets reading their works made by Recordiau'r Dryw, Llandybïe, between 1967 and the early 1970s.

Cyfres Pamffledi Cyfadran Addysg Coleg Prifysgol Cymru, Aberystwyth ('Series of Pamphlets of the Faculty of Education, University College of Wales, Aberystwyth'). Fourteen of a series of twenty pamphlets by different authors published by the Faculty between 1960 and 1977.

Welsh Studies in Education. Four works by different authors published by the University of Wales Press, Cardiff, between 1968 and 1974.

Ysgrifau ar Addysg ('Writings on Education'). Six works by different authors published by the University of Wales Press, Cardiff, between 1963 and 1976.

Geiriadur Termau/Dictionary of Terms. Published by the University of Wales Press, Cardiff, 1973.

History of Education in Wales, Vol. 1. Published by Christopher Davies, Swansea, 1978.

Index

Aborigines 191, 192, 202–6
accommodation 223
acculturation 213–36
  scale, Likert-type 216, 217
  acquisition, *see* first-language
    acquisition, second-language
    acquisition
Adesina 238
Afolayan 239, 247, 249, 250
Aitchison 169
Ajayi 239
Ajolore 238
Amery 206
Anglicization 63, 67
Anwar 215
Arabic 31, 192, 201, 243
Arsenian 163
Ashraf 214
Asians 213–36
assessment 6, 130–58
  criterion-referenced 132, 133–4
  language 134, 140
  norm-based tests 133
  purposes 134–5, 137–41
  validity 135–7
assimilation 223
attainment targets, language 132, 135–6
attitudes 2, 213–36
Australia 5, 8–9, 74, 154, 189–212
authority and language 69
Awbery 96
Ayandele 239

Baddeley 175
Baetens Beardsmore 114
Bagely 225
Baker 82, 105, 106, 136, 141, 151, 152, 153, 154, 167, 176, 179, 180
Ball 96

Ballard 160, 163, 173
Banjo *et al.* 247
Barke 180
Barke and Parry-Williams 180
Basque 32, 153
Baumgarter, Burns and De Ville 177
Baumgarter, Burns and Meeker 177
Bayly, Bishop Lewis 37
Beale 37
Beddington, Lt. Colonel 238
Bekos 82
Bellin 160, 169
Bendor-Samuel and Stanford 237
Bengali 226
Bennet 74, 75
Berry *et al.* 217
Berthold 209
bicultural education 202–6
bilingual method, *see* language teaching
bilingualism *passim*
  detrimental effects 6, 30, 161, 166, 176, 179
  incipient 4, 120
  institutional 3, 64–7
  maintenance 192, 196, 198
  neutral effects 176, 177, 179
  societal 2, 4
  transitional 191–4, 195, 196, 198, 200
  see also intelligence, mental confusion, school performance, social background
Binet 160
Birrell and Birrell 190
Blanck 181
Blenkin and Kelly 133
Block and Dworkin 163, 171, 172
Bloomfield 26

262 INDEX

Bolsheviks 181
Boyatzis 177
Braddy 208
Bradley 35
Breton 32, 63
Brown, C. 213, 231
Brown, S. 133
Bruner 118
Buisseret 33
Burling 120
Burns 177, 178, 179
Butler 130
Butzkamm 119, 126

CADW 72
Cahill 192, 193, 194, 200
Cahill et al. 196
Campfens 224
Canada 8, 33, 74, 75, 122, 153, 213–33
Carey 114
Carroll 171, 173
Castilian 32
Catalan 153
Catalonian 32
causal linkages (*see also* correlation) 177–8, 179
census data 49–56
Chamberlain 74
Chinese 33, 35, 277
classroom discourse 95–103, 111
Clifford 238
Clyne 154, 196, 197, 200, 201
collectivism 213–14, 216, 229
colonialism 68
Committee for the Development of Welsh Education (*see also* PDAG) 67
community languages (*see also* domains, ethnicity) 82–92, 222, 226–7
correction 121, 123, 125
correlation 171
  causal influences (*see also* causal linkages) 163–4
  correlational analysis 160
Corsican 32
credentials factor, *see* intelligence
criterion-referenced tests, *see* assessment
Crystal 30, 33
culture 85, 97, 103, 229
Cummins 196

Cummins and Genesee 114, 122
curriculum (*see also* Welsh-medium education) 4, 5, 92–103, 130–33, 191–210, 241–52
customs 229
CYD 105
Cymdeithas yr Iaith Gymraeg 30, 104
Cymraeg y pulpud 29

Danziger 160, 177
Davies, Dr John 37
Davies, J. 67
Davies, J. H. 37
Davies, W. 74
Dearing 133
deference 70
demographic changes 3
Denmark 75
designated bilingual schools, *see* Welsh-medium education
Di Biase and Dyson 195
diaspora 73–5
dictionaries 37
digit span and language 175
diglossia 196, 247
discourse acts 100–3
Dodson 110, 115, 116, 119, 122
Dodson and Thomas 111
domains 4, 5, 79, 82–6
  the community 82–92, 103–6
Drury 214, 224, 232
Dutch 195

Edmund Prys 37
educability 166
  intelligence 170–3
Education Act (1944) 130, 180
Education Reform Act (1988) 81, 130, 224–5
educational standards 130
Ellis and Hennelly 175
Emenanjo 249
empiricism 162, 170
employment 230–31
empowerment 195, 196
English *passim*
Epstein 167
Erben 209
errors in language (*see also* fossilized interlanguage) 5
Eskimo 31
ethnicity 71
  ethnic communities 9

INDEX 263

ethnic identity 4, 231–3
ethnic minorities 5
ethnic revival 62
ethnic rights (*see also* language) 193
ethnic schools 191, 200
ethnic teachers 230
Etiemble 33
Euskadi 62, 75
Evans, Revd D. Silvan 38–9, 43
Evans, E. 126
Evans, W.R. 47, 77
extension, *see* first-language acquisition, language teaching

Fafunwa 247
Fajana 239, 240
family 88
  structure 229
  extended 86, 94
  immediate 83–5, 94
Fantini 120
Ferguson 110
Fernandez 200
first language 83
  development 4, 112, 123
first-language acquisition (*see also* second-language acquisition) 117–18
  extension 118
  imitation 118
  substitution 118
Fisher and Echols 215, 225
Fishman 196, 247
Flemish 32
Fodor 167
fossilized interlanguage (*see also* errors in language) 5, 109
Foster and Stockley 190, 195
France 32, 32
French 5, 32, 33, 35, 42, 115, 201, 206–10, 226, 243
  Canadian 113–14, 122, 124
Friesland 75
Friuli 62, 75
functions of language 98

Galbally Report (1978) 190
Gale *et al.* 192
García 154
Gardner 172
gender 53, 213, 215, 216, 220, 222–3, 228–9
generation gap 213–14, 215

geography 3, 26, 60–64, 163, 164, 165, 176, 180
German 32, 33, 35, 42, 109, 110, 111, 166, 191, 195, 200–1
Ghuman 216, 217, 221, 223, 224, 225, 226, 231
Ghuman and Gallop 226
Ghuman and Wong 227
Gipps 134
gist understanding (*see also* school performance) 110–11, 115, 121
Gittins 113
Gittins Report 113
globalization 62
Goethe 32
Goldsmith 73
Goldstein 162, 165
Greek 33, 41, 82, 193–4, 201
Greer 223
Gregoire, l'Abbé 32
Griffiths 177
Grosjean 170, 181
Gruffudd, Pyrs 72
Gupapunygu 192

Halliday 98
Hammerly 114, 115, 124
Harris 203, 204, 205
Hausa 237–51 (*passim*)
heartland (*see also, Y Fro Gymraeg*) 47, 60–64, 71
Hindi 226
Hoffmann 109
Holt 119
Howe 171, 172
Howell 72
humanism 36–7

Ibo 237–51 (*passim*)
identity (*see also* ethnicity) *passim*
imitation, *see* first-language acquisition
immersion 4, 95, 109–17, 121, 122, 153, 201
individualism 216, 213–14, 229
Indo-Canadians 8, 213–36 (*passim*)
industrialization 67
Ingleson 199
Ingram 199
institutions 104
integration 223–4
intelligence (*see also* educability) 7
  artificial 169

INDEX

bilingualism 159–85
　credentials factor 171, 173–4
　IQ 168
　performance 171, 172
　social background 173–4
　tests 7
　tests and numerals 176
　tests and pedagogy 179, 180
　tests, Stanford-Binet 175
　tests, validity 171
interference 109
interlocutors 82–92
International Schools 110
internationalism 75–6
internationalization of English 3, 62–3
IQ, *see* intelligence
Israel 24
Italian 36, 197, 201
Italy 32
izzat 214

James 110
Japanese 209
Jespersen 34, 166
Johnston 74
Joly 233
Jones and Romaine 167
Jones, B. M. 82, 95, 96, 97, 103
Jones, Daniel Isaac 29–30
Jones, G. R. 62
Jones, H. 77
Jones, J. R. 67
Jones, R. M. 28, 126
Jones, R. O. 74
Jones, W. R. 159, 160, 162, 163, 180
Jones, William 74

Kalantzis *et al.* 195, 196, 200
Kamin 163
Karier 163
Kielhöfer and Jonekeit 126
Klemp 177
Krashen 111
Kreindler 181
Kyffin, Morris 36

Laitin 181
language
　acquisition (*see* first- and second-language acquisition)
　backgrounds 152–3
　choices 70–71, 82–106
　contact 1, 2, 34–6
　decline 50–51
　development 79, 81
　form 96
　maintenance 79, 82
　mixing 176
　planning 65
　reproduction 60, 64
　restoration (*see also* ethnicity) 79, 82
　rights (*see also* ethnicity) 65
　shift 63
language teaching 4, 5
　bilingual method 121–3
　extension (*see also* first-language acquisition) 116, 123
　substitution (*see also* first-language acquisition) 116, 123
Lashley 169
Latin 35, 36, 41
Leal *et al.* 199
learning 111
Leech 98
Leopold 120, 126
Lewis, D.G. 159, 160, 166, 180
Lewis, J.D. 77
Lewis, Saunders 73
Lindner 119
linguistic equality 2, 31, 239, 240
literacy 53
Lloyd 74
Lo Bianco 193, 197, 199, 200, 201, 202
Lunacharsky 181
Luther 32
Lutheran church schools 191
Lyons 98

Macedonian 195
Mackey 28, 62
majority language 3, 5, 151
Maltese 195
Martinet 29
mass media 64
McClelland 171, 173, 177
medium of teaching (*see also* curriculum, Welsh-medium education) 4, 241–51
medium-orientated language activities 117–18
memory 169–70
　working memory 175, 176
mental
　capacity 167, 169
　confusion 166–7, 169
　confusion and bilingualism 161, 162

mentrau 4, 104–5
Menter Taf Eláí 104–5
message-orientated language activities 117–18
migration 72
  immigrants 2, 8, 109
  immigration 49, 190
  in-migration 3, 63, 85
  out-migration 3
Miller 119
Mills 192
minority (*see also* ethnicity) 71
  indigenous 2, 9, 108
  language 2, 3, 5, 79, 108, 151–2
Mistral 32
mixed languages 34–5
mixed marriages 63
modularity in learning mechanisms 167–9
Moellner 191
monolingualism 51, 60, 85, 118, 244
Morgan, G. 73
Morgan, K. O. 73
Morgan, P. 72
Morris, L. 37
Morris-Jones, John 97
multiculturalism 8, 190, 191, 194, 224–5
multilingualism 9, 181, 237–52

National Curriculum, Welsh 130–33
nationalism 3, 40, 67, 76
NFER 142, 147, 149, 150
Nicholas and Sussex 200
Nigeria 9, 237–51
Ninnau 74, 75
non-census data 56–60
non-designated bilingual schools, *see* Welsh-medium education
norm-based tests, *see* assessment
normative data 162
Norst 200
North America 154
Northover 220, 223
Norway 75
numbers of Welsh-speakers 49–60
Nunggubuya 202

O'Hear and White 134
Ologunde 239
Omolewa 238
Owen-Pughe, Dr William 39

Padilla 215

Parry, Thomas 37
Patagonia 74
PDAG – *see* Pwyllgor Datblygu Addysg Gymraeg
Peate, Iorwerth 72
pedagogy 164, 176
  bilingualism 161
peers 86–7, 88, 229–30
Pellerin and Hammerly 124
periphery 47
Pilch 119
Pitjantjatjara 191, 202
Pobol y Cwm 75
Pont 105
Porsché 126
Price *et al.* 96, 98
Prosser 104
Provençal 32
Pryce and Williams 63
Pryce, Revd Shadrach 30
public sector 69–71
  bilingual forms 70
Punjabi 226
Pwyllgor Datblygu Addysg Gymraeg (*see also* Committee for the Development of Welsh Education) 65

racism 213, 230–31
Ramge 119
Ramirez *et al.* 154
reading 90–92
Rehbein 110
rehearsal strategy 175
Reich 109
religion 3, 26, 68–9, 85, 97, 131, 214, 227, 231, 239–40
Rex 214
Robert, Gruffydd 36
Romaine 167, 170, 181
Ronjat 126
Rosa and Montero 181
Ross 232
Rotheram and Phinney 213
Rowland 239
Rowntree 133
Rubichi 197
Rushdie 225
Russian 35

S4C 75
Saer 163
Saer, Smith and Hughes 163, 165

Salesbury, William 36
Saunders 126
savants 168
school performance and bilingualism (*see also* gist understanding) 141–53
schools, *see* curriculum, ethnicity, International Schools, Lutheran Church schools, Welsh-medium education
Schumann 109
second language 102, 108–26, 131, 142
 Welsh 96
second language acquisition 4 (*see also* first-language acquisition)
 bilingual strategies 120–24
Selinker 109
semilingualism 196
Shaikh and Kelly 214, 215, 224
Sharp *et al.* 82
Shaw 213
Shepard 133
Sherington 190
Shorrocks 148
Sierra and Olaziregi 153
Sinclair and Brazil 99
Sinclair and Coulthard 99, 100
Skutnabb-Kangas 164
Skutnabb-Kangas and Toukomaa 196
Smith and Tsimpli 168
social background 177–81
 bilingualism 161, 162
social class 71
Sopher 50
Southall 60
Spain 32, 153
Spanish 36
Spolsky 109
Stanley *et al.* 199
stereotypes 71–2
Stern 167
Sternberg 173
Stopes-Roe and Cochrane 232
style
 literary Welsh 97
 vernacular Welsh 97
submersion 153
substitution, *see* first-language acquisition, language teaching
Swain 126
Swann 230
Sweden 153, 196
synergic action 169

Taeschner 126
Taiwo *et al.* 247
Taylor and Hegarty 214
technological communication 63
television 90–92
Thomas and Thomas 96
Thomas, A. R. 85
Thomas, B. 96
Thomas, P. 74
Thomas, P. W. 96
transfer from mother tongue 109
Triandis 213
Turkish 109, 110, 111, 192, 201

Ullah and Bratherton 214
Umo 238
urbanization 67
Urdd 103
USA 74, 153, 154

Valverde 199
Verhoevan and de Jong 140
Vernon 163, 164, 166, 171
Vietnamese 192
vocabulary 2, 31–43
 borrowing 34–6
Vygotsky 7, 159–81 (*passim*)

Wade and Souter 214, 215
Walters, Revd John 38, 39, 43
Watkins 96
Weinreich 217
Weir 118
Weisgerber 27
Wells 118
Welsh (*see also* style) *passim*
Welsh Development Agency 72
Welsh Historic Monuments 72
Welsh Language Act (1993) 65
Welsh Language Board 60, 65, 66, 71, 76
Welsh Rugby Union 72
Welsh-medium education 40, 47, 79–106, 112–13, 142, 180
 designated bilingual schools 81
 non-designated bilingual schools 81
Welsh-speaking schools 81
Welsh-speaking schools, *see* Welsh-medium education
Welsh Tourist Board 72
White Australia Policy (1901, 1967) 190
Whitlam 203

INDEX

Whitney 26
Wilhelm von Humboldt 27
Wiliam Cynwal 37
Williams, C. H. 48, 50, 51, 62, 66, 106
Williams, G. 74, 85
Williams, Harri 73
Williams, Jac L. 95, 159, 160, 176, 180, 181
Williams, R. Bryn 74
Williams, Sian Rhiannon 67
Williams, T. 111, 127
Williamson 249
Wilson 228

Windisch 34
Wolf 134
Wood 134

Y Cymmrodorion 73
Y Drych 74, 75
Y Fro Gymraeg (*see also* heartland) 3, 71
Y Llyfrau Gleision 30
Yoruba 237–51 (*passim*)
Yr Enfys 74, 75

Zierer 126